AFTERNOON TEA

1 Centerpiece

Instructions on page 36.

2 *Centerpiece*

Instructions on page 38.

3 Cushion

Instructions on page 40.

4 Centerpiece *5 Centerpiece*

Instructions on page 42.

Instructions on page 44.

6 Tablecloth

Instructions on page 49.

7 Centerpiece & Chair back

Instructions on page 46.

8 Cushion

Instructions on page 48.

PIECES, Worked from Its Center Point

9 CENTERPIECE

Instructions on page 52.

10 CENTERPIECE

Instructions on page 54.

11 TABLECLOTH

Instructions on page 56.

12 TABLECLOTH

Instructions on page 59.

13 CUSHION

Instructions on page 58.

14 TABLECLOTH

Instructions on page 62.

15 CUSHION

Instructions on page 64.

16 CENTERPIECE

Instructions on page 65.

17 DOILY

Instructions
on page 68.

18 DRESSER MAT

Instructions
on page 53.

THE MOTIF HARMONY

Instructions on page 67.

19 tablecloth

Instructions on page 70.

20 cushion

Instructions on page 71.

21 centerpiece

22
uncheon mat

Instructions on page 75.

23
cushion

Instructions on page 78.

24 chair back

Instructions on page 92.

25 runner

Instructions on page 76.

26 centerpiece

Instructions on page 89.

SOMETHING NICE FOR THE FURNITURE

27 BEDSPREAD

Instructions on page 90.

28 BEDSPREAD

Instructions on page 96.

29 LUNCHEON MAT
Instructions on page 95.

30 COASTER
Instructions on page 97.

31 TRAY MAT
Instructions on pages 113 · 98.

32 DRESSER MAT

Instructions on page 114.

33 DRESSER MAT

Instructions on page 115.

34 DRESSER MAT

Instructions on page 80.

35 PIANO COVER

Instructions on page 33.

36 PIANO COVER

Instructions on page 34.

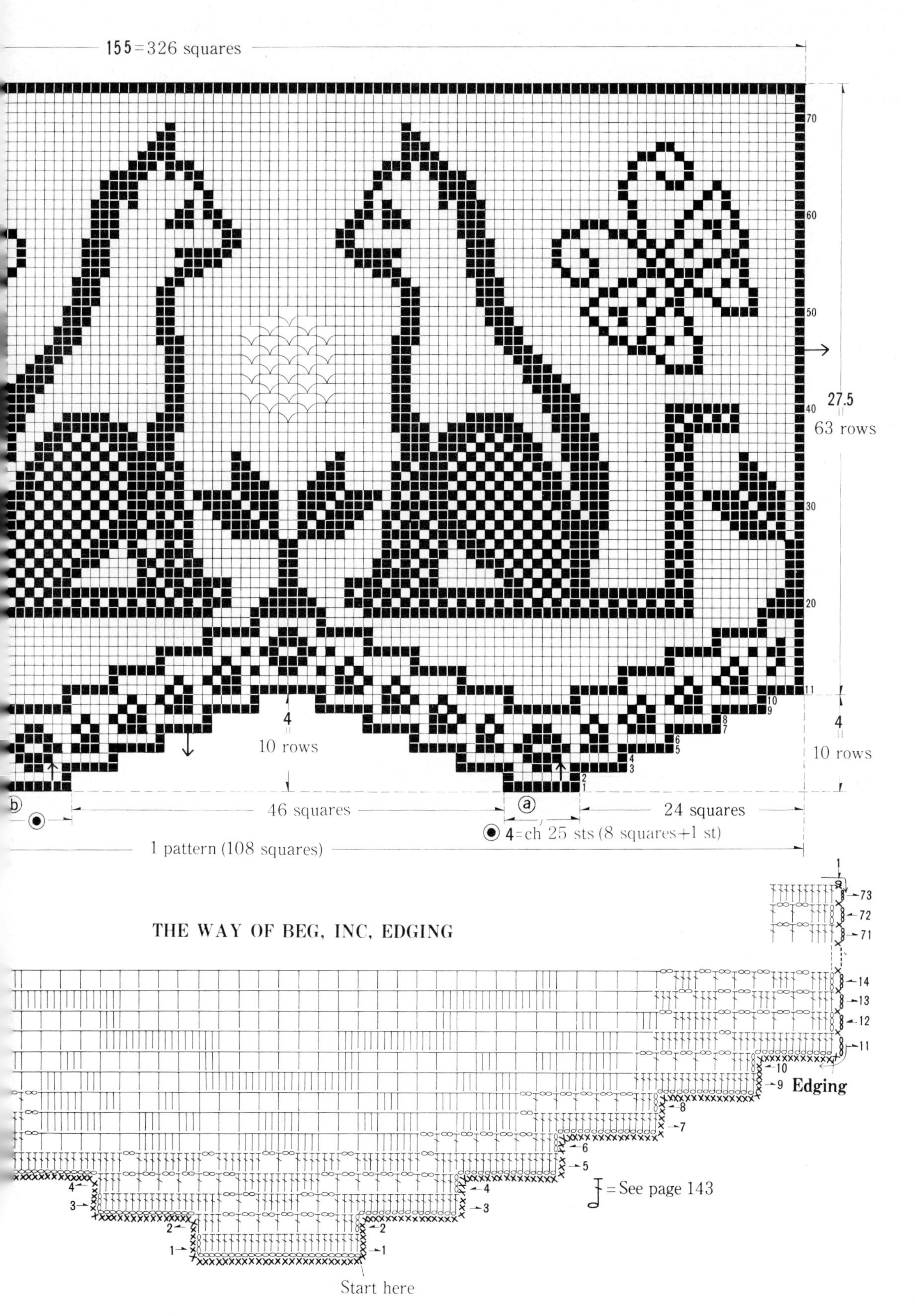
155=326 squares
27.5
63 rows
4
10 rows
4
10 rows
46 squares
24 squares
4=ch 25 sts (8 squares+1 st)
1 pattern (108 squares)
THE WAY OF BEG, INC, EDGING
Edging
= See page 143
Start here

Row 11: Ch 3 following last 12 sts of ⓐ, dc in 5th st from hook, 14 dc. Ch 2, sk 2 ch, dc in dc, (2 dc in 2 ch, dc in dc) 3 times, (ch 2, sk 2 ch, dc in dc) 2 times. Continue in same manner across, inc 12 sts in the manner of dc.
Rows 12–73: Work in same manner as for rows previous. Begin to work the pattern between cats on 39th row.
Row 39: Having worked 10 sps from the breast of cat, ch 3, sk 2 sts, sc in dc, ch 3, sk 2 ch, dc in dc.
Row 40: Work 8 sps from breast of cat, ch 3, sk 2 ch, sc in dc, ch 3, sk 2 ch, dc in dc. Ch 5, sk 2 3-ch lps, dc in dc. Ch 3, sk 2 ch, sc in dc. Ch 3, sk 2 ch, dc in dc.
Rows 41–50: Work as for rows 39–40.
EDGING: Work from the end of row 73. Ch 1, sc in edge st, ch 3, sc in between rows next. Ch 3, sc in between rows next. Repeat along length side. Work 2 sc at corner, sc in each st increased, sc 5 in 2 rows next, 2 sc at next corner. Work edging in same manner along 3 sides of the work.
FINISHING: Sew on lining referring to chart.

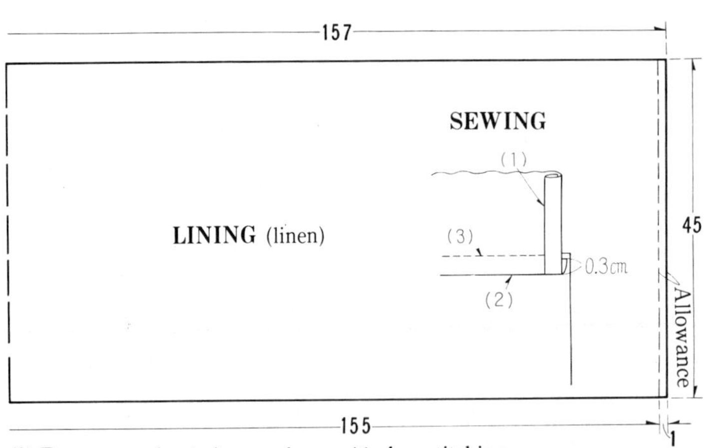

(1) Turn raw edge twice, work one-side hemstitching.
(2) Turn raw edge to right side, put over the crochet 1 row below the edge as shown, steady with slip stitch.
(3) Sew crochet on fabric steady.

ONE-SIDE HEMSTITCHING

①Pick up fabric threads from right to left as shown.

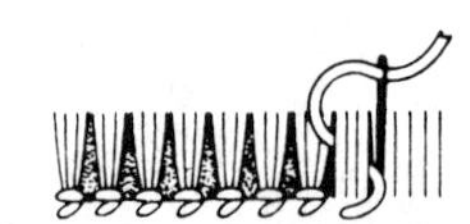

②Bring needle out right at the base of next st, draw thread through.

1 CENTERPIECE

YOU'LL NEED: Crochet cotton No. 20 7 20-gram balls White. Steel crochet hook size 0.90.
FINISHED SIZE: 76 cm by 44 cm
GAUGE: 10 cm of filet crochet=20.5 squares; 10 cm=20.5 rows.
MAKING INSTRUCTIONS:
Ch 262. **Row 1:** Ch 5, dc in 9th ch from hook, (ch 2, sk 2 ch, dc in next ch) 86 times.
Row 2: Ch 5, sk 2 ch, dc in dc. Dc in each st across to 1 sp this side of edge, ch 2, sk 2 ch, dc in next ch.
Row 3: Ch 5, sk 2 ch, dc in dc, 3 dc, (ch 2, sk 2 dc, dc in next dc) 83 times, 3 dc, ch 2, 1 dc.
Rows 4–153: Work straight referring to chart (1 sp =ch 2, 1 dc; 1 bl=3 dc). The pattern crochet in the middle is started on 28th row.
Row 29: Having worked 3 dc in 41 st square, (ch 5, sk 5 dc, dc in next dc), (ch 2, sk 2 dc, dc in next dc), (ch 5, sk 5 dc, dc in next dc), 3 dc in 47th square.
Row 30: Work squares 39th–41st with dc. Ch 3, sc in the middle of 5 ch, ch 3, dc in dc. Ch 3, sc in the middle of 5 ch, ch 3, 1 dc. Work squares 47th–49th with dc. Crochet middle patterns in same manner.

Edging: Row 1: 2 sc in 2 ch, ch 1, 2 sc in 2 ch, ch 1 repeat across. Work 3 sc, ch 1, 3 sc at every corner 2 sc in 1 row of dc length side. **Row 2:** Sc in ch, ch 3, sc in ch. Repeat, working sc in corner ch, ch 3, sc in same ch at every corner. **Row 3:** Sc in the middle of 3-ch lp. In next lp, work 2 dc, ch 2, 2 dc. Sc in next lp, 3 dc in corner lp, ch 3, 3 dc in same lp. Work so that sc comes in the lp next to corner lp.

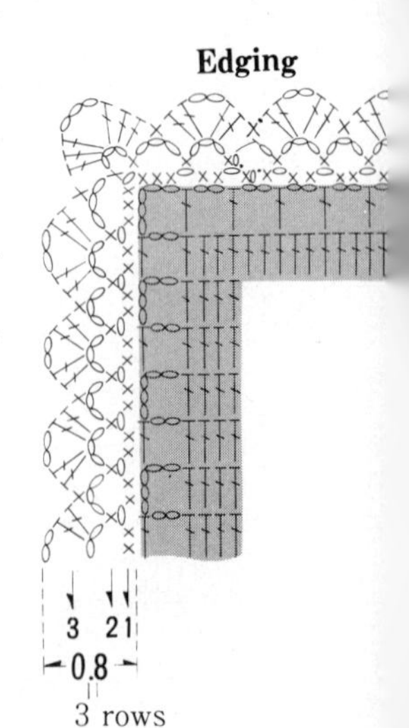

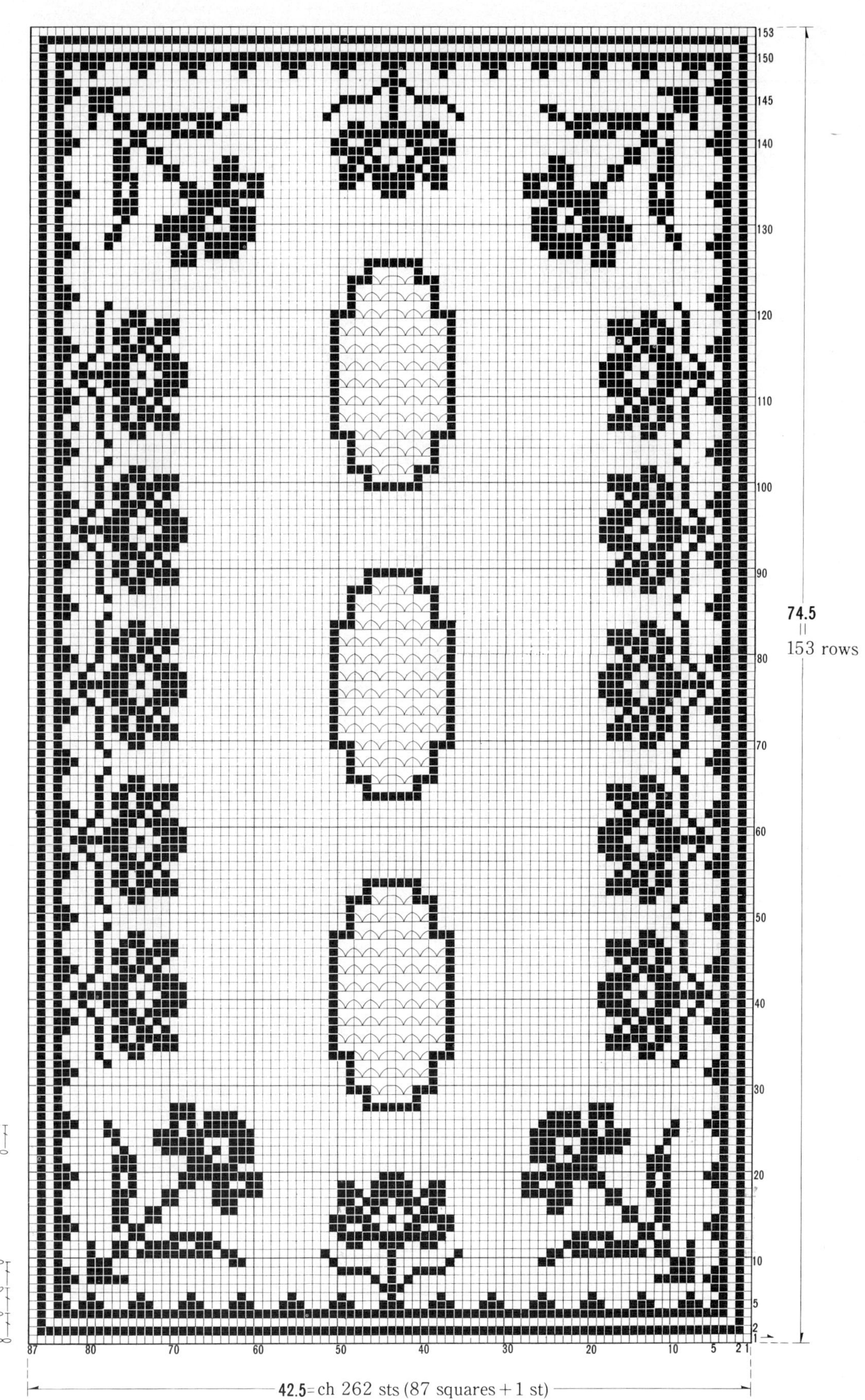
153
150
145
140
130
120
110
100
90
80
70
60
50
40
30
20
10
5
2
1
87
80
70
60
50
40
30
20
10
5
2 1
74.5
=
153 rows
42.5=ch 262 sts (87 squares + 1 st)

2 CENTERPIECE

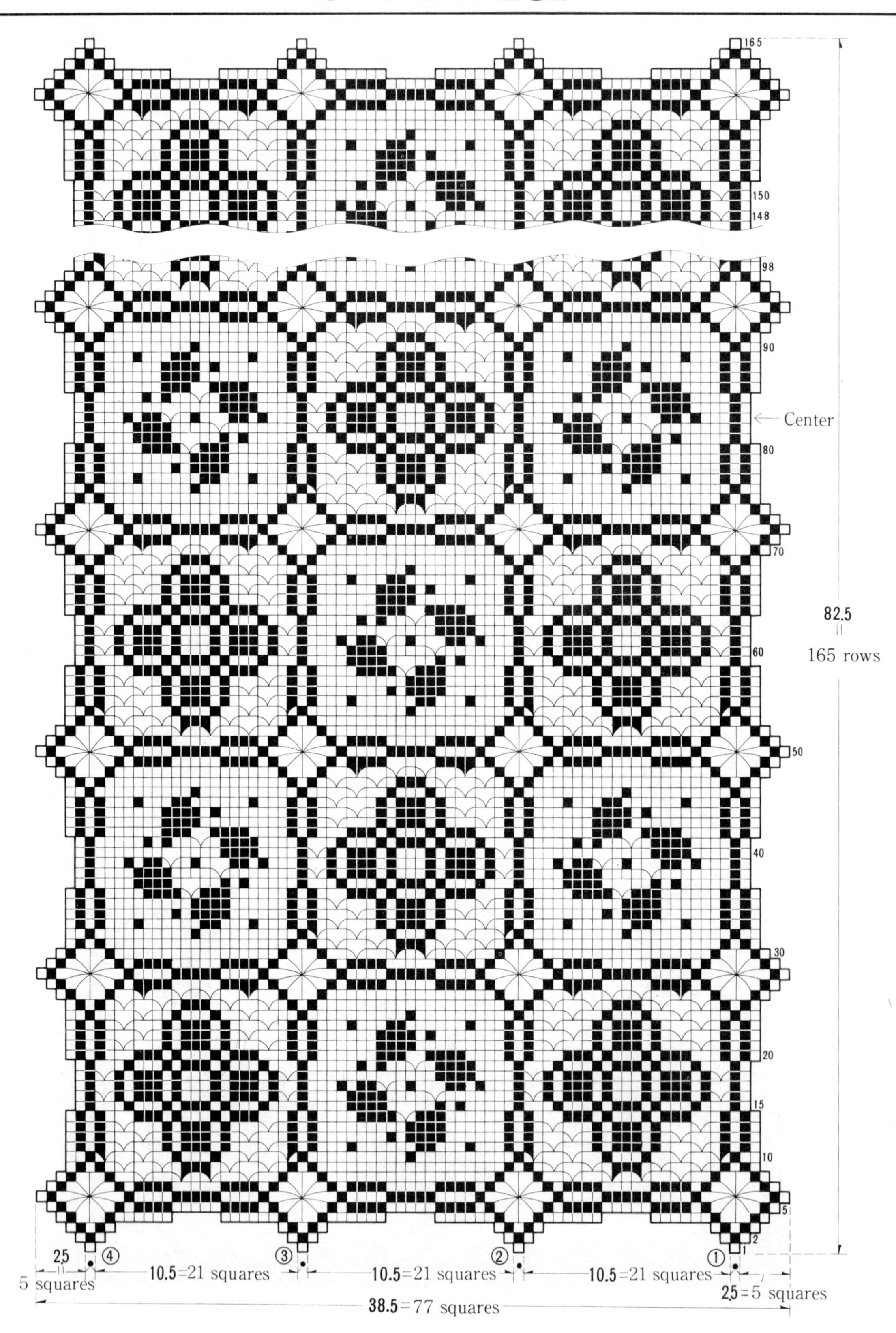

● = ch 4 sts (1 square +1 st)

YOU'LL NEED: Crochet cotton No. 20 6 20-gram balls White. Steel crochet hook size 0.90.
FINISHED SIZE: 83.5 cm by 39.5 cm
GAUGE: 10 cm of filet crochet=20 squares; 10 cm =20 rows.
MAKING INSTRUCTIONS:
①: Ch 4. **Row 1:** Ch 5, dc in 1st ch.
Row 2: Ch 8, 4 dc in 2 ch, ch 2, dtr in the corner of previous row to inc 1 sp.
Row 3: Ch 8, 4 dc in 2 ch. Ch 2, sk 4 dc, 4 dc in 2 ch. Ch 2, dtr in the corner of previous row to inc 1 sp.
Row 4: Ch 23, dc in 9th ch from hook, (ch 2, sk 2 ch, 1 dc) 4 times. Ch 2, sk 3 sts, 4 dc in 2 ch. Ch 5, tr in the middle of 2 ch, ch 5, 4 dc in 2 ch. Ch 2, dtr in corner.
②: Work up to 3rd row same as for ①.
Row 4: Join thread in where indicated, ch 18, cut thread off. Work the other side as for ① up to new sts, (ch 2, sk 2 sts, 1 dc) 6 times, ch 14, sl st to the corner of ① 4th row.
③: Work as for ②, sl st to corner of ② 4th row.
④: Work up to 3rd row same as for ①.
Row 4: Join thread in as for ②, ③, ch 18, cut thread off. Ch 8 the other side, 4 dc in 2 ch. Work following sts as for ②, ③, sl st to corner of ③ 4th row.
Row 5: Ch 8, 4 dc in 2 ch. Ch 5, sc in left edge of 5-ch lp. Sc in tr, sc in right edge of next 5-ch lp. Ch 5, 4 dc in 2 ch. Ch 2, sk 3 sts, 13 dc, (ch 2, sk 2 ch, 1 dc) 5 times, 12 dc. Work in same manner across to end.
Row 6: Begin as for previous row. Having worked 3 dc in last sp, draw through 4th dc and tr tr at a time.
Rows 7–161: Following chart, work ch 2, sk 2 sts, 1 dc for each sp, 3 dc for each bl, increasing or decreasing both sides.
Rows 162–165: Part into 4, work decreasing respectively.
EDGING: Sc in 1st st of beg ch, 5-ch p, 3 sc, 5-ch p at the corner, 3 sc, 3 sc in base of 2nd row, 5-ch p on corner, 3 sc. Continue in same manner, making p at corners. Where at straight side, work 3 sc in 3 ch, 5-ch p, 3 sc in cross side of dc. Continue, so that p comes between rows. Work in same manner all around.

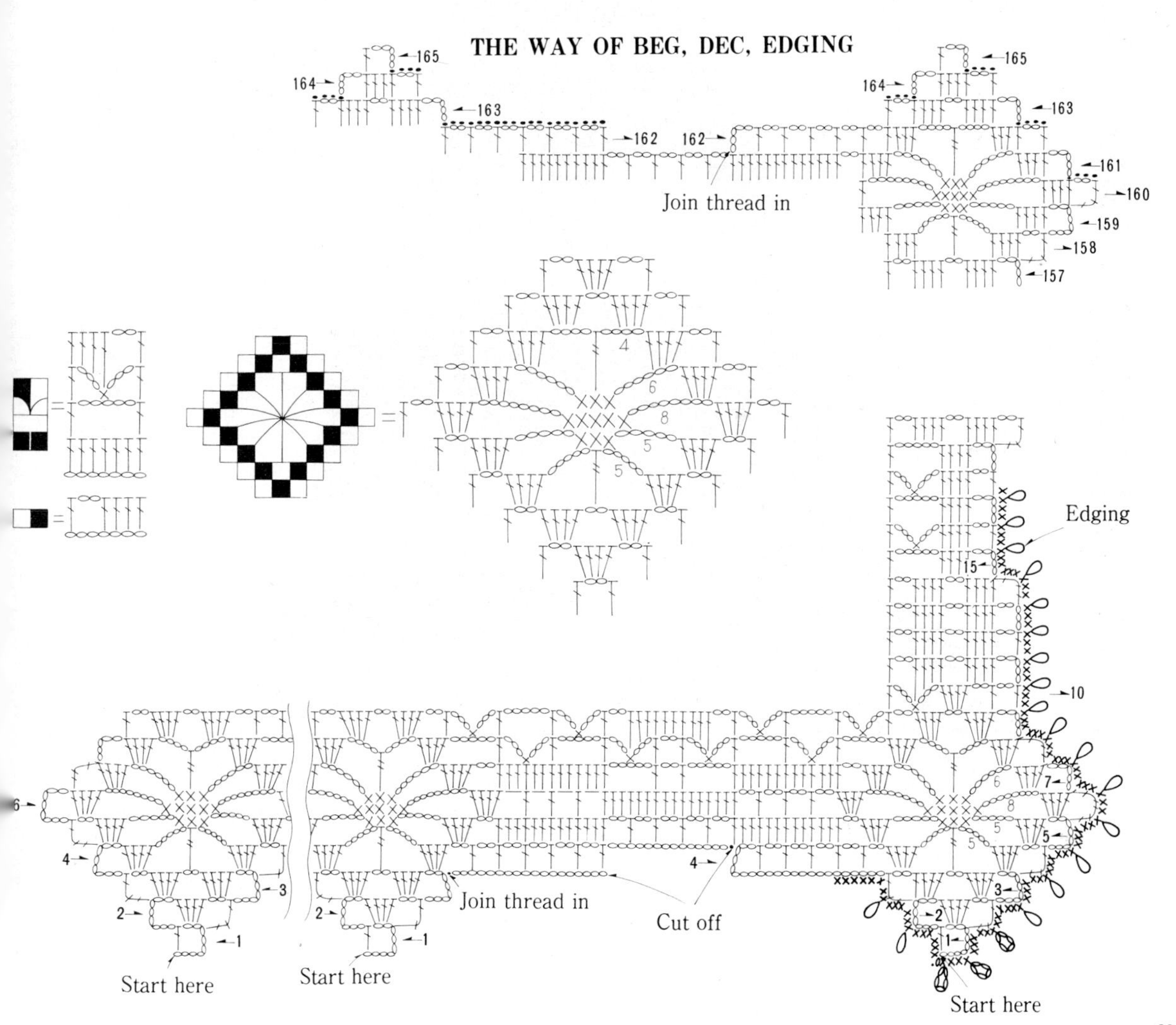

3 CUSHION

YOU'LL NEED (for each): Crochet cotton No. 20 7 20-gram balls Beige. Steel crochet hook size 0.90. Bemberg for inner case 92 cm by 47 cm Brown. Kapok 550 gram.

FINISHED SIZE: 45 cm square

GAUGE: 10 cm of filet crochet = 18 squares; 10 cm = 20.5 rows.

MAKING INSTRUCTIONS:

(A)'S FRONT: Ch 244. **Row 1:** Ch 5, dc in 9th ch from hook, (ch 2, sk 2 ch, dc in next ch) 80 times.

Row 2: Ch 5, sk 2 ch, dc in dc. Dc in each st up to 1 sp this side, ch 2, sk 2 ch, dc in next ch.

Row 3: Ch 5, sk 2 ch, dc in dc. 6 dc, (ch 2, sk 2 ch, 4 dc) 38 times, 3 dc, end ch 2, sk 2 ch, dc in 3rd st.

(A)'S FRONT

Row 4: Work as for previous row.
Row 5: Ch 5, sk 2 ch, dc in dc. 9 dc, (ch 3, sk 2 dc, dc in next dc. Ch 3, sk 2 dc, dc in next dc) 4 times, (ch 2, sk 2 dc, dc in next dc) 56 times, (ch 3, sk 2 dc, dc in next dc. Ch 3, sk 2 dc, dc in next dc) 4 times. Ch 2, sk 2 dc, 10 dc, end ch 2, sk 2 ch, dc in next ch.
Row 6: Ch 5, sk 2 ch, dc in dc, (3 dc, ch 2, sk 2 dc, dc in dc) 2 times, (ch 5, sk 2 lps, dc in dc) 4 times, 48 dc. Ch 2, sk 2 ch, dc in dc, 114 dc. Ch 2, sk 2 ch, 1 dc, (ch 5, sk 2 lps, dc in dc) 4 times, (3 dc, ch 2, sk 2 sts, 1 dc) 2 times.
Rows 7–94: Work as for rows previous referring to chart.

CONTINUED ON PAGE 43

(B)'S FRONT

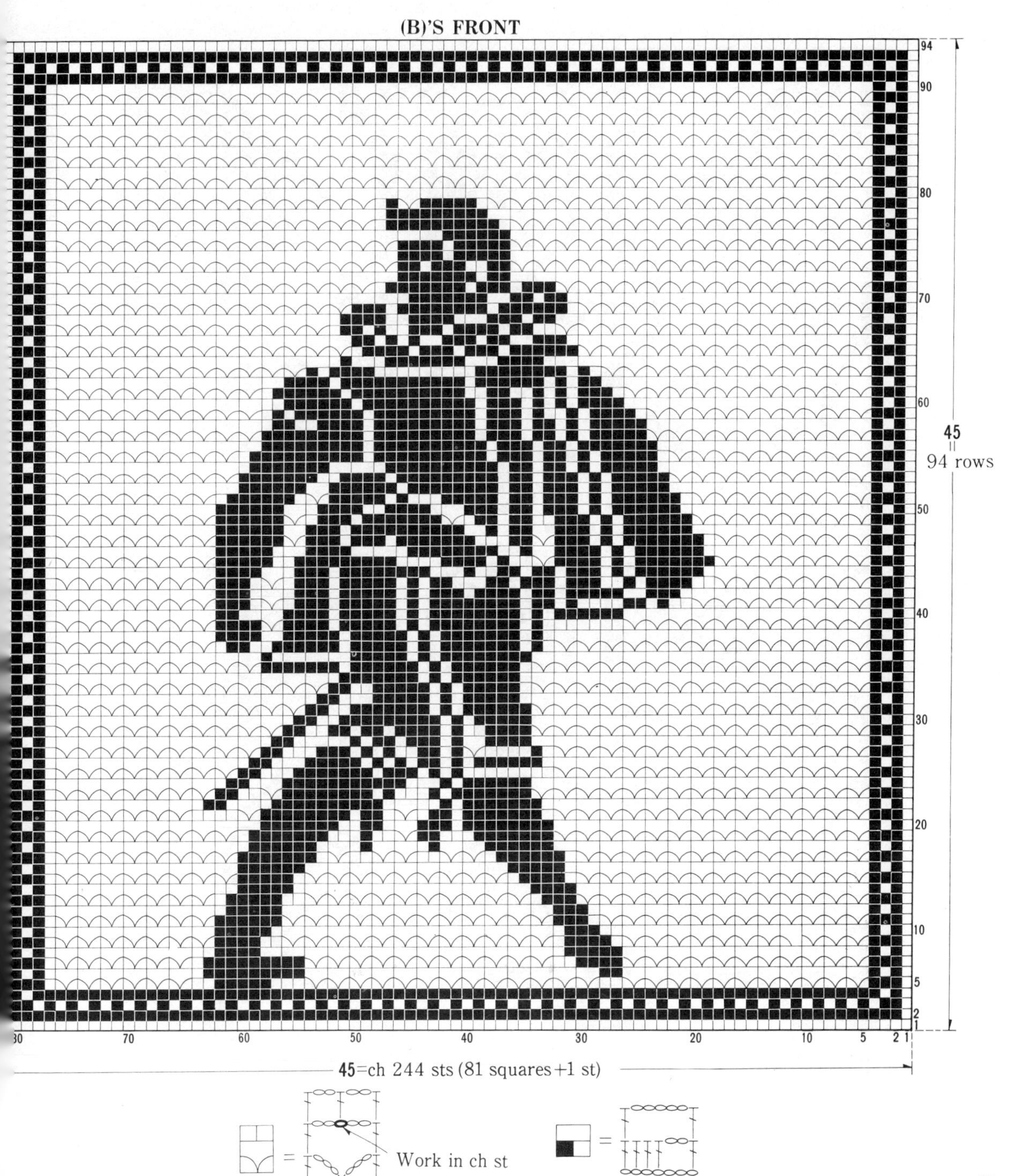

4 CENTERPIECE

YOU'LL NEED: Crochet cotton No. 20 6 20-gram balls White. Steel crochet hook size 0.90.

FINISHED SIZE: 71.5 cm by 38.5 cm

GAUGE: 10 cm of filet crochet = 20 squares; 10 cm = 23 rows.

MAKING INSTRUCTIONS:

①: Ch 28. **Row 1:** Ch 3, dc in each st across.

Row 2: Ch 6, dc in 5th ch from hook, dc in each st across.

Row 3: Ch 3, 15 dc, (ch 2, sk 2 dc, dc in next dc) 3 times. Dc in each st across to end, inc 3 sts in the manner of dc.

Row 4: Ch 6, dc in 5th ch from hook, 8 dc, (ch 2, sk 2 dc) 2 times, 3 dc, (ch 2, sk 2 sts, 1 dc) 2 times. Dc in each st remaining.

②: Ch 22. **Row 1:** Ch 3, dc in each st across.

Row 2: Ch 6, dc in 5th ch from hook, dc in each st across, inc 3 sts in the manner of dc.

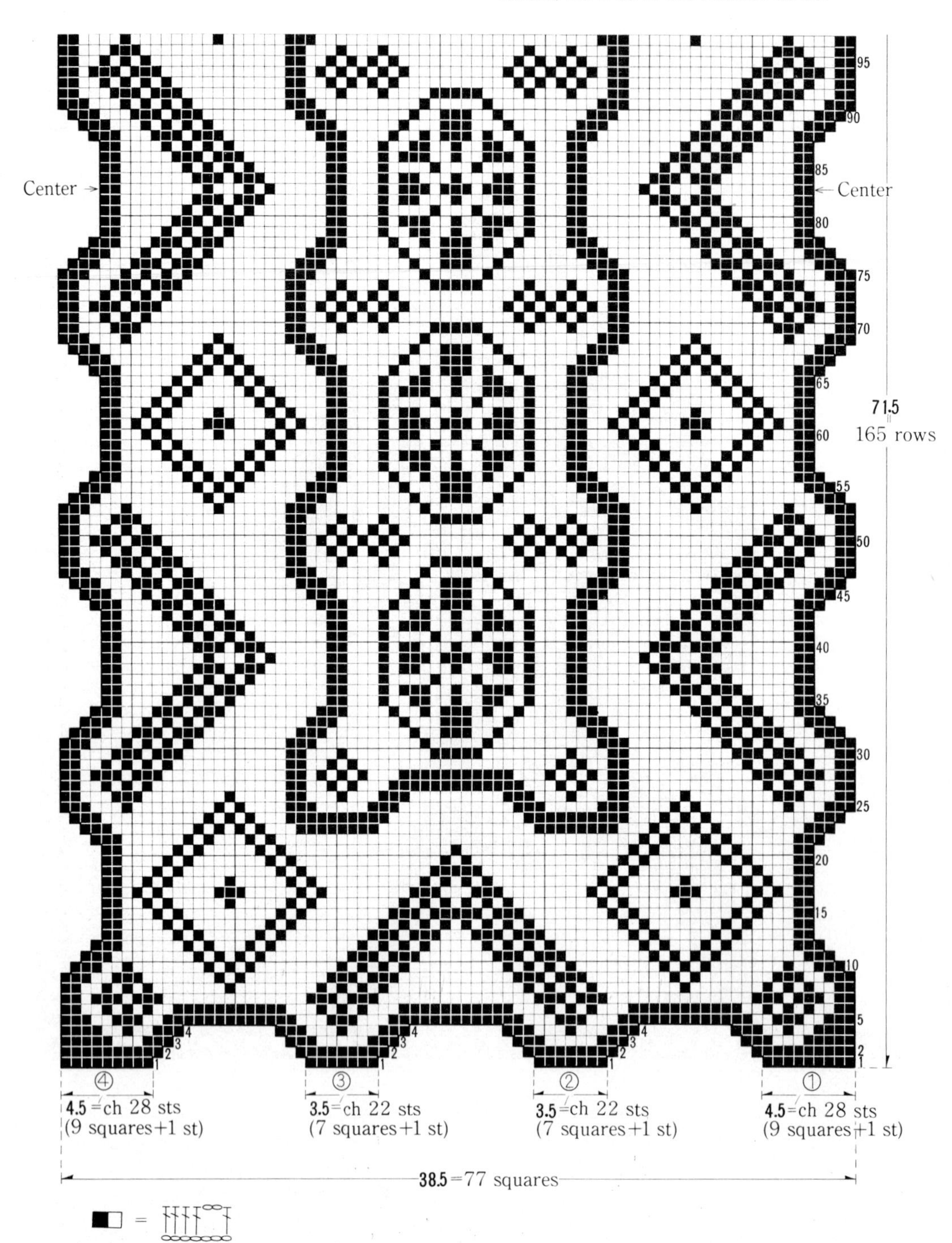

■□ =

ows 3–4: Work as for rows previous. Having in-
reased 3 sts at the end of 4th row, ch 26, sl st to top
f beg ch 4th row of ①.
): Work as for ②, sl st to top of beg ch 4th row of
).
): Ch 28. **Rows 1–4:** Work correspondingly to ①.
ow 4: Ch 3, 12 dc, (ch 2, sk 2 sts, 1 dc) 2 times. 3 dc, (ch 2, sk 2 sts, 1 dc) 2 times, 6 dc. Inc 3 sts in the manner of dc, ch 26, sl st to top of beg ch 4th row of ③.

Rows 5–165: Work referring to chart (1 sp=ch 2, sk 2 sts, 1 dc; 1 bl=3 dc). Crochet so that patterns top and bottom finished in symmetry at 83rd row.

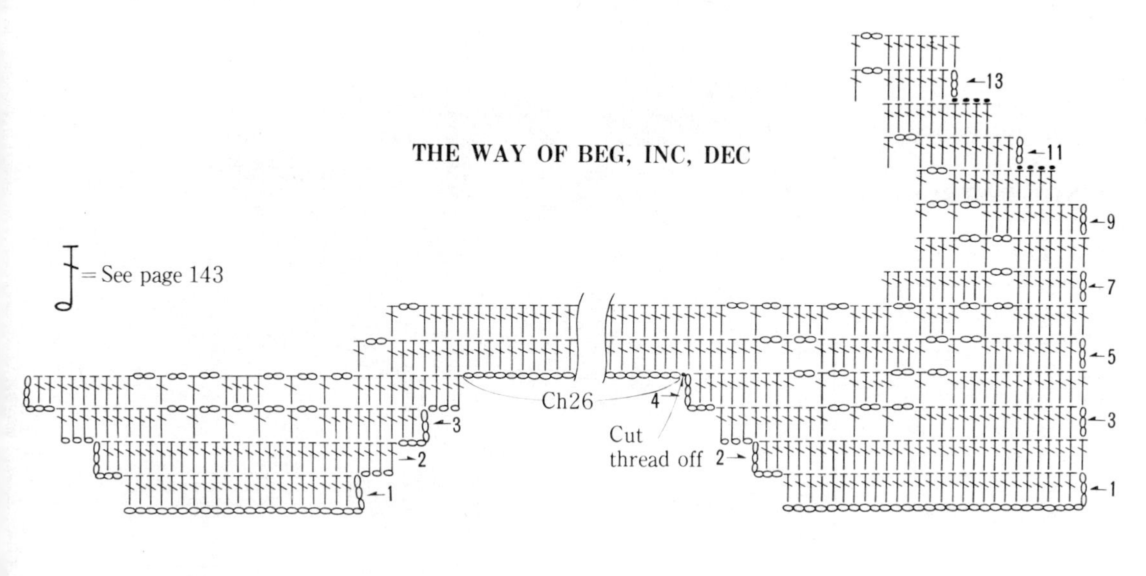

---

ontinued from page 41

ACK OF (A) & (B): Ch 244. **Rows 1–4:** Work as
r front.
ows 5–94: Work ch 2, sk 2 sts, 1 dc for each sp,
dc for each bl, referring to chart.
)'S FRONT: Ch 244. **Rows 1–4:** Work same as
r (A).
ow 5: Ch 5, sk 2 ch, 1 dc. 9 dc, (ch 3, sk 2 dc, sc in
xt dc, ch 3, sk 2 dc, dc in next dc) 11 times, (ch 2,
2 dc, 1 dc) 2 times, (ch 3, sk 2 dc, sc in next dc. Ch 3, sk 2 dc, dc in next dc) 13 times, (ch 2, sk 2 dc, dc in next dc) 3 times. 15 dc, (ch 2, sk 2 dc, dc in next dc) 2 times, (ch 3, sk 2 dc, sc in next dc. Ch 3, sk 2 dc, dc in next dc) 6 times. Ch 2, sk 2 dc, 10 dc. Ch 2, sk 2 ch, dc in next ch.

Rows 6–94: Work straight referring to chart.

FINISHING: Put front and back wrong sides together, join with 1 row of sc, putting kapok cased in between.

BACK (for each)

45 = 94 rows

45 = ch 244 sts (81 squares+1 st)

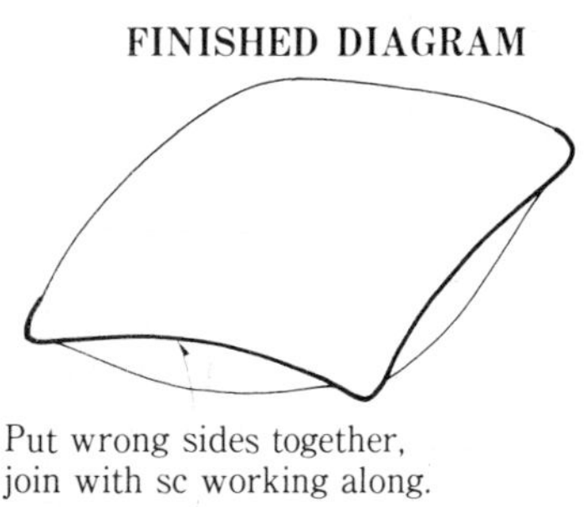

FINISHED DIAGRAM
Put wrong sides together,
join with sc working along.

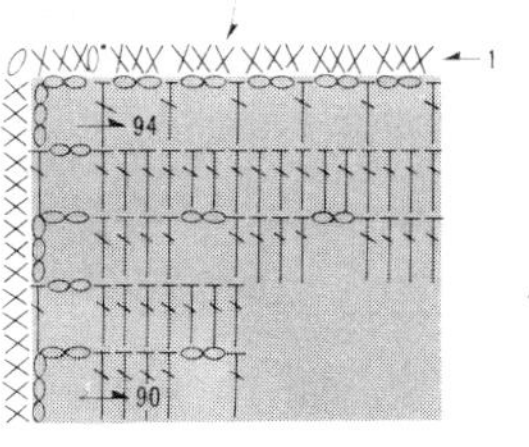

5 CENTERPIECE

YOU'LL NEED: Crochet cotton No. 4 soft twist 10 50-gram balls White. Steel crochet hook size 1.75.

FINISHED SIZE: 122 cm by 85 cm

GAUGE: 10 cm of filet crochet = 15 squares; 10 cm = 15 rows.

MAKING INSTRUCTIONS:

Ch 514. **Row 1:** Ch 5, dc in 9th ch from hook, (ch 2, sk 2 ch, dc in next ch) 170 times.

Row 2: Ch 5, sk 2 ch, dc in dc, (ch 2, sk 2 ch, dc in dc) 14 times. 3 dc, (ch 2, sk 2 ch, dc in dc) 139 times. 3 dc, *ch 2, sk 2 ch, dc in dc, repeat from *to end.

Row 3: Ch 5, sk 2 ch, dc in dc, (ch 2, sk 2 ch, dc in dc) 5 times. 3 dc, (ch 2, sk 2 ch, dc in dc) 7 times. 9 dc, *ch 2, sk 2 ch, dc in dc, repeat from * up to 154th square. 9 dc, (ch 2, sk 2 ch, dc in dc) 7 times. 3 dc, *ch 2, sk 2 ch, dc in dc, repeat from * to end.

Rows 4–121: Work straight referring to chart (1 sp = ch 2, sk 2 sts, dc in dc; 1 bl = 3 dc).

EDGING: Row 1: Join thread in 3rd dc from edge, ch 3, 3 dc. Ch 2, sk 2 ch, 2 dc in top of edge dc. Ch 3, 2 dc in same edge dc. Ch 2, dc in base of dc, 2 dc in 2 ch, dc in top of dc. Repeat in same manner all around, working 2 dc, ch 3, 2 dc at every corner. **Row 2:** Ch 3, 3 dc, *ch 2, sk 2 sts, 4 dc, repeat from * around, working 2 dc, ch 3, 2 dc at every corner. **Row 3:** Work as for row 2. **Row 4:** Sc in each st around, working 4 sc in corner lps.

EDGING
4
3
2
1
2.5 = 3 rows
121
110
100
90
80
70
60
50
40
30
20
10
5
2
1
80
121 rows
=
80
70
60
50
40
30
20
10
5
2 1
(Edging)
2.5
3 rows
107 = ch 514 sts (171 squares+1 st)

7 CENTERPIECE & CHAIR BACK

YOU'LL NEED: Crochet cotton No. 20 White 7½ 20-gram balls for table center, 11 20-gram balls for chair back. Steel crochet hook size 0.90.

FINISHED SIZE: Refer to chart.

GAUGE: 10 cm of filet crochet = 22 squares; 10 cm = 22 rows.

SIZE OF MOTIF: Refer to chart.

MAKING INSTRUCTIONS:

TABLE CENTER: Ch 16. **Row 1:** Ch 5, dc in 9th ch from hook, (ch 2, sk 2 ch, dc in next ch) 4 times.

Row 2: Ch 11, dc in 9th ch from hook. Ch 2, sk 2 ch, dc in dc, 15 dc. Ch 2, dtr in corner of previous row, ch 2, dtr in the middle of previous dtr to inc 2 squares.

Row 3: Ch 11, dc in 9th ch from hook. Ch 2, sk 2 ch, dc in dtr. 6 dc, (ch 2, sk 2 dc, dc in next dc) 5 times. 6 dc, ch 2, dtr in corner of previous row. Ch 2, dtr in the middle of irevious dtr to inc 2 squares.

Rows 4–6: Work in same manner, increasing each side.

Rows 7–198: Work straight referring to chart (1 sp = ch 2, sk 2 sts, 1 dc; 1 bl = 3 dc).

Row 199: Work sl st up to 7th st from edge, ch 5, sk 2 dc, dc in next dc. Ch 2, sk 2 dc, dc in next dc. 6 dc, (ch 2, sk 2 sts, dc in dc) 5 times. 9 dc, (ch 2, sk 2 sts, dc in dc) 5 times. 6 dc, (ch 2, sk 2 dc, dc in next dc) 2 times. Leave the sps following.

Rows 200–203: Dec in same manner as for row 199. Make 3 pieces.

JOINING MOTIFS: Join thread in left corner of row 198, ch 7, sk 2 rows, 1 sc, *ch 7, sk 2 rows, 1 sc, repeat from * to 7th row. Ch 3, dc in corner of 6th row, cut thread off. Join thread in right corner of row 6 of the center motif, ch 3, sl st in the dc of right motif, ch 3, sc in between 6th and 7th row. Ch 3, sl st to the middle of lp right side. Ch 3, sk 2 rows, 1 sc. Repeat. Join left motif in same manner.

EDGING: Join thread in corner of row 198 of right motif, sc in each st around. Work 6 sc in every corner sp, 3 sc in each row length side.

CHAIR BACK: Ch 16. Work as for table center, referring to chart. Make 9 pieces, join, finish with 1 row of edging.

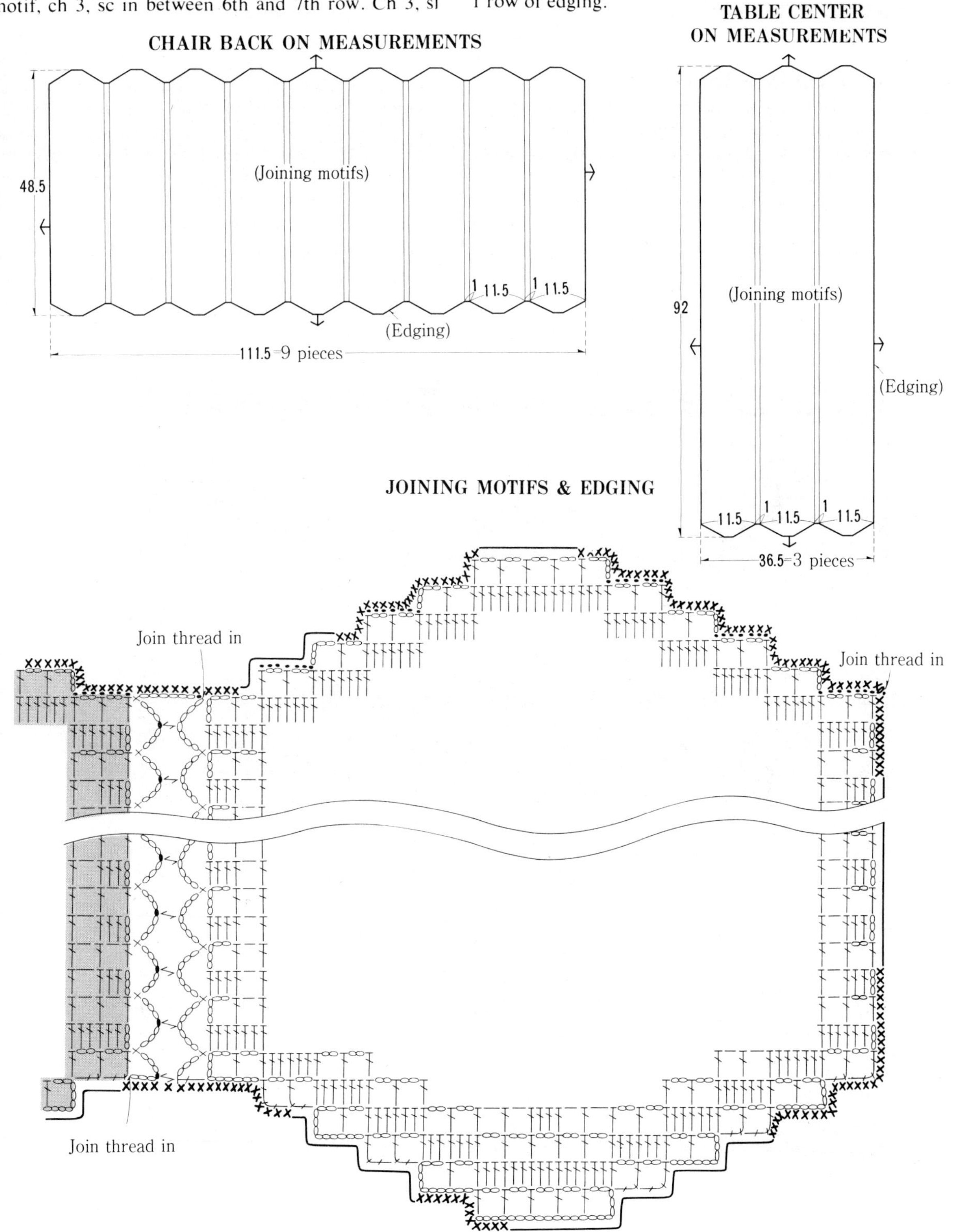

8 CUSHION

YOU'LL NEED: Crochet cotton No. 20 7½ 20-gram balls White. Steel crochet hook size 0.90. Satin for inner case 87 cm by 44.5 cm Blue. Kapok 550 gram.

FINISHED SIZE: 44 cm square

GAUGE: 10 cm of filet crochet = 20 squares; 10 cm = 20 rows.

MAKING INSTRUCTIONS:

Ch 256. **Row 1:** Ch 5, dc in 5th ch from hook, (ch 2, sk 2 ch, dc in next ch) 84 times.

Row 2: Ch 5, sk 2 ch, dc in dc, *ch 2, sk 2 ch, dc in dc, repeat from *to end.

Row 3: Ch 5, sk 2 ch, dc in dc, (ch 2, sk 2 ch, dc in dc) 9 times. 3 dc, (*ch 2, sk 2 ch, dc in dc, repeat from *9 times, 3 dc) 8 times. *Ch 2, sk 2 ch, dc in dc, repeat from *to end.

Rows 4–85: Work ch 2, sk 2 sts, 1 dc, for each sp 3 dc for each bl.

EDGING: Make 2 pieces, work edging putting wrong sides together. **Row 1:** Join thread in corner of 85th row, work 1 sc. Ch 1, 3 sc in cross side of dc *ch 1, 2 sc in 2 ch, ch 1, 2 sc in cross side of dc repeat from *around. Work 3 sc, ch 1, 3 sc in every corner sp. **Row 2:** Ch 1, sc in corner ch, ch 5, sc in same corner ch. Ch 3, sk 3 sc, sc in next sc. *Sk 2 sc (1 dc, ch 1) 3 times and 1 dc in same ch, 1 sc in next ch. Ch 2, sk 2 sc, sc in ch, ch 3, 1 sc. Repeat from *around, working 1 sc, ch 3, sk 3 sc, sc in ch, ch 5 sc in same ch, ch 3, sk 3 sc, sc in ch at every corner.

Note: Where at the opening, work edging on front piece only, sew closed after the kapok cased is stuffed.

FRONT & BACK (COMMON)

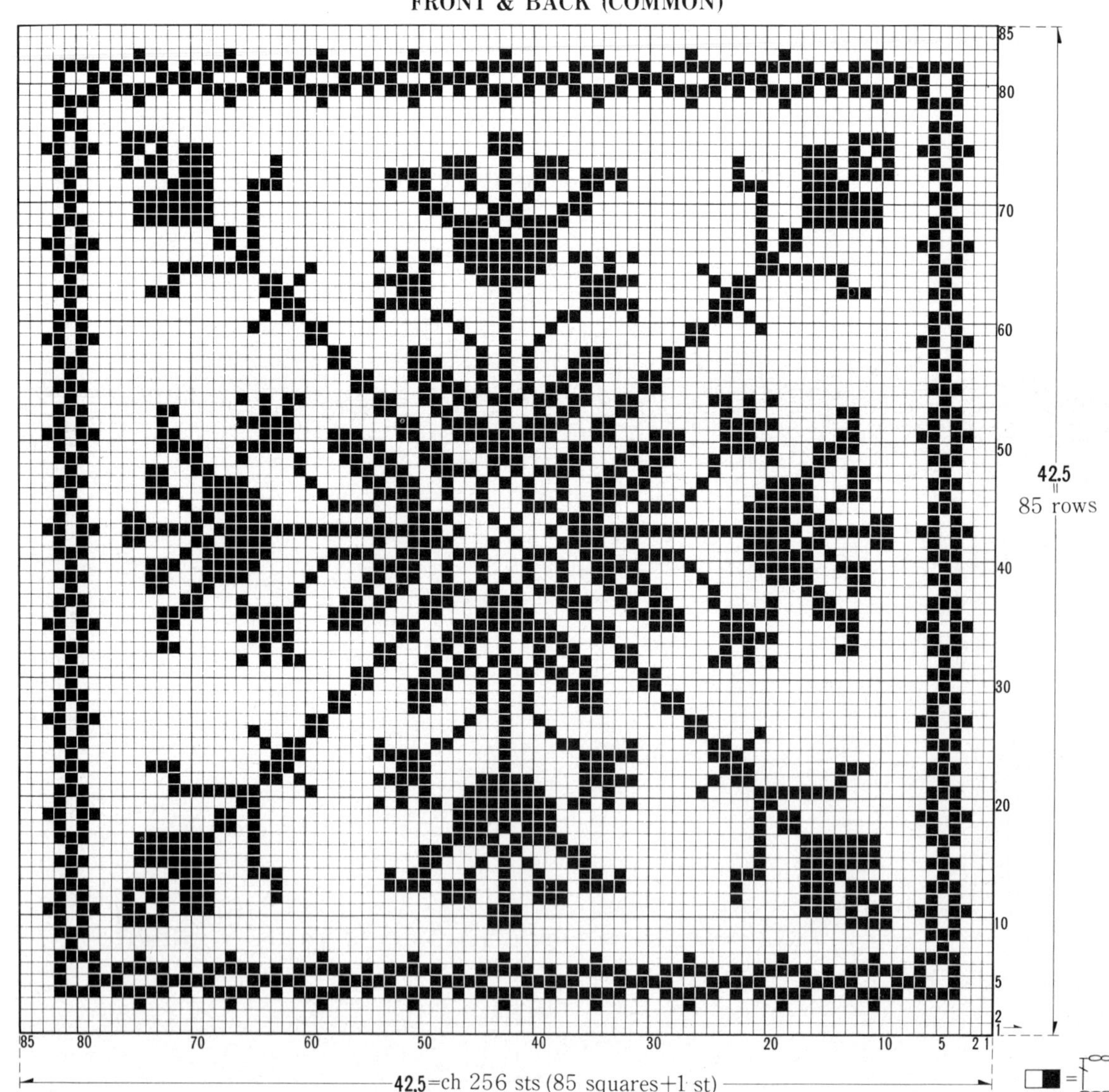

FINISHED DIAGRAM

Opening
(55 squares)

Edging: work edging putting 2 pieces wrong sides together (where at the opening, work in front piece only). close opening kapok stuffed in.

EDGING

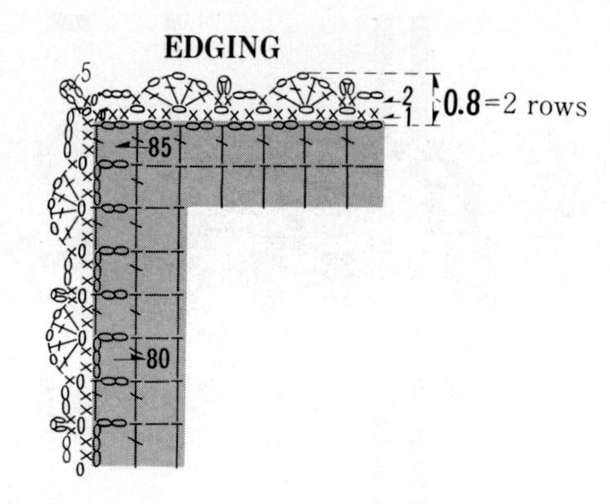

6 TABLECLOTH

YOU'LL NEED: Crochet cotton No. 20 15 20-gram balls White. Steel crochet hook size 0.90.
FINISHED SIZE: 105 cm by 102 cm
GAUGE: 10 cm of filet crochet = 15.5 squares; 10 cm = 16 rows.
MAKING INSTRUCTIONS:
①: Ch 22. **Row 1:** Ch 3, dc in each st across.
Row 2: Ch 12, dc in 5th ch from hook. 8 dc, (ch 2, sk 2 dc, 1 dc) 6 times, 3 dc.
Row 3: Ch 3, 3 dc. Ch 2, sk 2 ch, dc in dc, 15 dc, (ch 2, sk 2 dc, dc in dc) 3 times. Inc 3 sts in the manner of dc.
Row 4: Ch 6, dc in 5th ch from hook. 2 dc, ch 2, sk 2 dc, 1 dc, 9 dc, (ch 2, sk 2 dc, 1 dc) 4 times. 3 dc, ch 2, sk 2 ch, 1 dc, 3 dc.
②: Ch 16. **Row 1:** Ch 3, dc in each st across.
Row 2: Ch 12, dc in 5th ch from hook. 8 dc, (ch 2, sk 2 dc, 1 dc) 5 times. Inc 9 sts in the manner of dc.
Row 3: Ch 6, dc in 5th ch from hook. 2 dc, (ch 2, sk 2 dc, 1 dc) 3 times. 15 dc, (ch 2, sk 2 dc, 1 dc) 3 times. Inc 3 sts in the manner of dc.
Row 4: Ch 6, dc in 5th ch from hook, 2 dc. Ch 2, sk 2 dc, 1 dc. 9 dc, (ch 2, sk 2 dc, 1 dc) 5 times, 9 dc. Ch 2, sk 2 dc, 1 dc. Inc 3 sts in the manner of dc, ch 10, sl st to top of beg ch 4th row of ①.
③–⑦: Work as for ②, join all together.
⑧: Ch 22. Work correspondingly to ①, join to ⑦ on 4th row in same manner as for ②.
Rows 5–163: Work referring to chart (1 sp=ch 2, sk 2 sts, dc in next dc; 1 bl=dc in 3 sts).

THE WAY OF BEG, INC, DEC

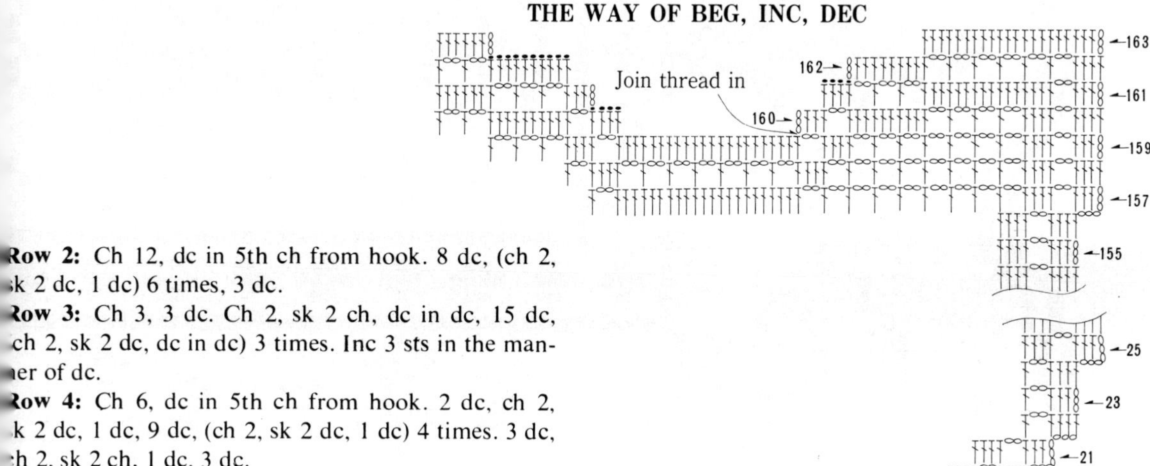

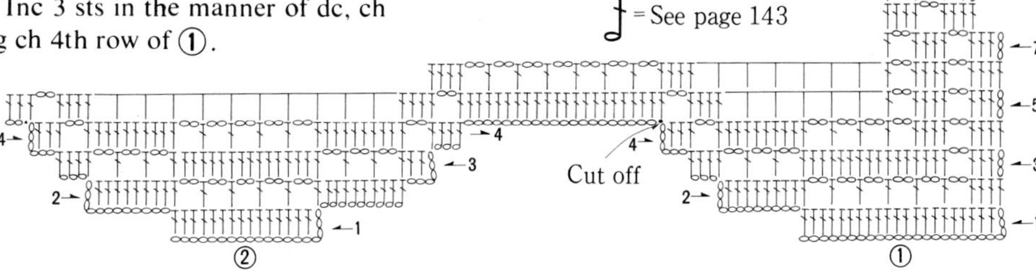

Center
⑧
4.5=
ch 22 sts (7 squares+1 st)
17 squares
⑦
3=◎
17 squares
⑥
3=◎
17 squares
⑤
3=◎
105=163

105
100
95
90
85
← Center
80
75
70
65
102
=
163 rows
60
55
50
45
40
35
30
25
20
15
10
5
4
3
2
1
④
③
②
①
17 squares
3=◎
ch 16 sts (5 squares+1 st)
◎
4.5=
ch 22 sts (7 squares
+1 st)

9 CENTERPIECE

YOU'LL NEED: Crochet cotton No. 20 1½ 20-gram balls Beige. Steel crochet hook size 0.90.
FINISHED SIZE: 32 cm square
GAUGE: 1 row of dc=0.6 cm
MAKING INSTRUCTIONS:
Make a loop at thread end. **Row 1:** Ch 5, dc in lp, (ch 2, 1 dc in lp) 6 times, ch 2, sl st in 3rd st of beg ch.
Row 2: Ch 3, dc 2 in 2 ch, dc in dc. Dc in 2 ch, dc in dc, ch 3, dc in same dc. Work in same manner around, hdc in 3rd st of beg ch.
Row 3: Ch 3, 2 dc in hdc, dc in the st of beg ch, (ch 2, sk 2 dc, dc in de) 2 times. 3 dc in 3-ch corner lp, ch 3, dc in same lp. Work in same manner around, end ch 1, hdc in 3rd st of beg ch.
Rows 4–7: Work as for rows up to 3rd, increasing sts at 4 corners.
Row 8: Ch 3, 2 dc in hdc, dc in ch. (ch 2, sk 2 sts, dc in dc) 3 times, 6 dc. Ch 3, sk 2 dc, dc in next dc. Ch 3, sk 2 dc, 7 dc, (ch 2, sk 2 sts, dc in dc) 3 times, 3 dc in 3-ch lp, ch 3, 3 dc in same lp. Work in same manner around, end ch 1, hdc in 3rd st of beg ch.
Row 9: Ch 3, 2 dc in hdc, dc in ch, (ch 2, sk 2 sts, dc in dc) 3 times, 6 dc. Ch 2, sk 2 sts, dc in dc. Ch 5, sk 2 lps, dc in dc. Ch 2, sk 2 sts, dc in dc. 6 dc, (ch 2, sk 2 sts, dc in dc) 3 times, 3 dc in 3-ch lp, ch3, 3 dc in same lp. Work in same manner around, ch 1, hdc in 3rd st of beg ch.
Rows 10–21: Work as for rows 8–9. Work 21 st row, ending ch 3, sl st in 3rd st of beg ch, cut thread off.
Rows 22–28: Join thread in where indicated, work across respectively.
(A) **Row 22:** Join thread in last dc of 21st row, ch 3, 5 dc in 3-ch lp, 4 dc, (ch 2, sk 2 ch, dc in dc) 3 times, 3 dc, (ch 3, sk 2 sts, sc in next st, ch 3, sk 2 sts, dc in dc) 3 times, 9 dc, (ch 2, sk 2 sts, dc in de) 3 times, 3 dc.
Row 23: Ch 3, turn wrong side facing to you, work up to this side of corner dc in same manner as for previous row.
Rows 24–28: Work across in same manner refering to chart.

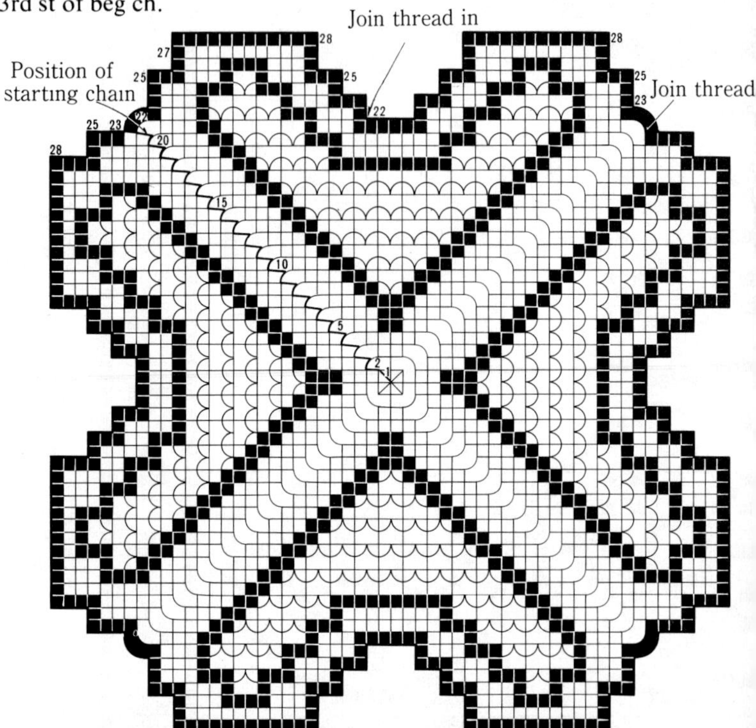

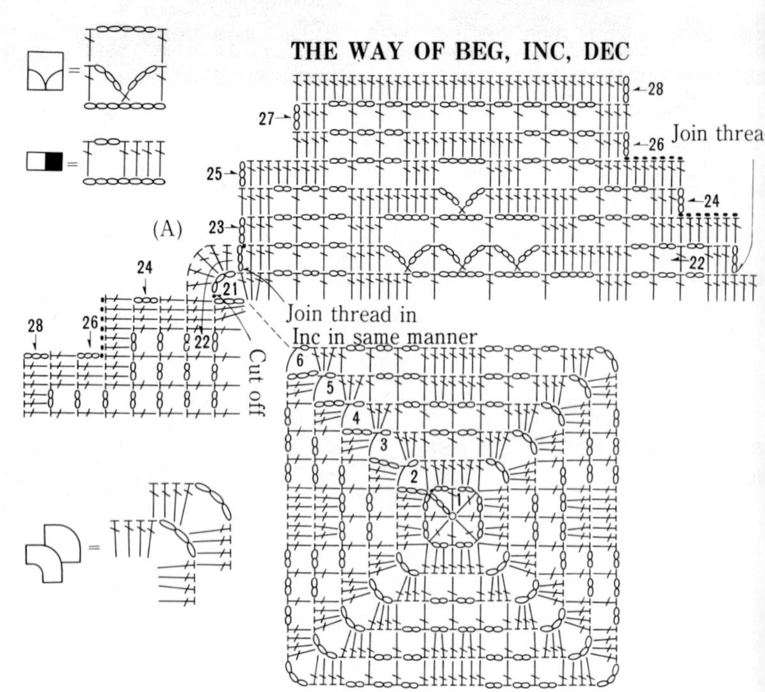

18 DRESSER MAT

YOU'LL NEED: Crochet cotton No. 20 1¼ 20-gram balls White. Steel crochet hook size 0.90.
FINISHED SIZE: 32 cm in diameter
GAUGE: 1 row of dc = 0.5 cm.
MAKING INSTRUCTIONS:
Ch 6, sl st in 1st ch to form ring. **Row 1:** Ch 3, 2 dc in ring, (ch 1, 3 dc in ring) 5 times, ch 1, sl st in 3rd st of beg ch.
Row 2: Ch 3, 2 dc in dc. Dc in next dc, ch 2, dc in ch. Ch 2, dc in dc, 2 dc in next dc, dc in next dc. Work in same manner around, end sl st in 3rd st of beg ch.
Row 3: Ch 3, dc 3. Ch 2, sk 2 ch, dc in dc, ch 2, dc in same dc. Ch 2, sk 2 ch, dc 4 in 4 dc. Work in same manner around, sl st in 3rd st of beg ch.
Row 4: Ch 3, dc 3. Ch 2, sk 2 ch, dc in dc. Ch 2, dc in the middle of 2 ch, ch 2, dc in dc. Ch 2, sk 2 ch, dc 4 in 4 dc. Work in same manner around, sl st in 3rd st of beg ch.
Rows 5–29: Work as for rows 3–4, increasing sts at 6 corners. Crochet patterns in referring to chart.
Row 30: Ch 3. Work as for rows up to 29, working 2 dc in 2 ch at every corner.
Row 31: Ch 5, sk 2 dc, dc in next dc. Continue in same manner as for previous rows, working 1 dc in each dc at corners. As for rows 32–33, join thread in where indicated, work across each row, turn.
Row 32: Ch 3, dc 69.
Row 33: Work sl st up to 22nd st from edge, ch 3, dc 27.

EDGING: Row 1: Join thread in where indicated, ch 1, sc in dc, *ch 3, sk 2 dc, sc in next dc, repeat from *around, sl st in 1st sc.

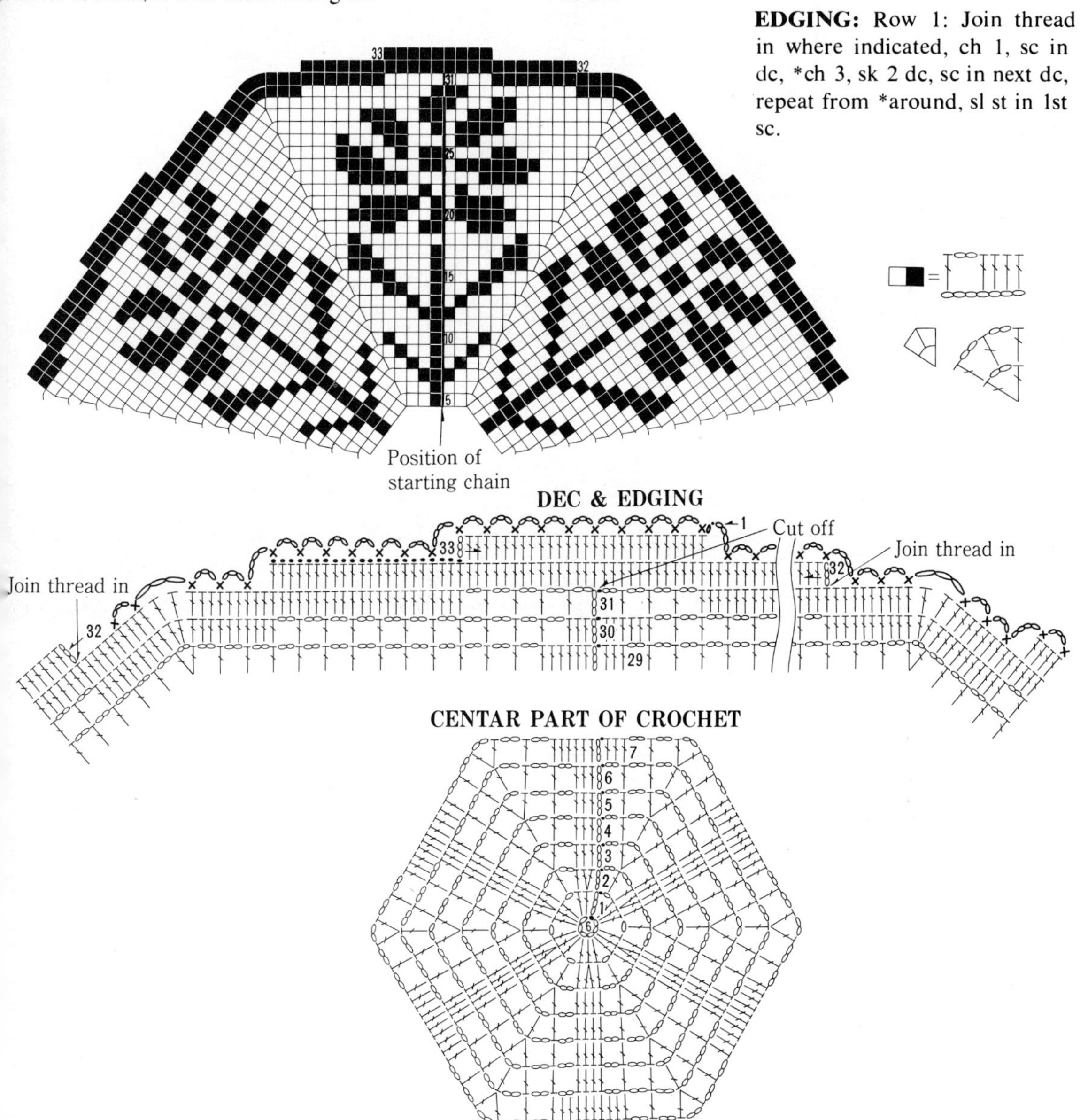

糸をつける

10 CENTERPIECE

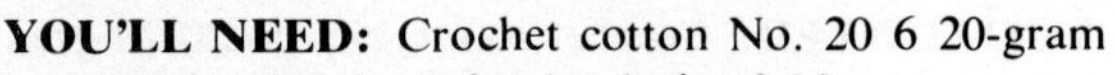

YOU'LL NEED: Crochet cotton No. 20 6 20-gram balls White. Steel crochet hook size 0.90.
FINISHED SIZE: 60 cm in diameter
GAUGE: 2 rows of dc = 1 cm
MAKING INSTRUCTIONS:
Make a loop at thread end. **Row 1:** Work 10 sc in lp.
Row 2: Ch 4, dc in sc, * ch 1, dc in sc, repeat from* around, end sl st in 3rd st of beg ch.
Row 3: Ch 3, 2 dc in 1 ch, *dc in dc, 2 dc in 1ch, repeat from* around, sl st in 3rd st of beg ch.
Rows 4–6: Work as for rows 1–3, increasing at 6 places.
Row 7: Ch 3, 2 dc in 2 ch, (dc in dc, 2 dc in 2 ch) 4 times. Dc in dc, ch 3, dc in same dc. Repeat in same manner around, ch 1, hdc in 3rd at of beg ch.
Row 8: Sc in hdc, ch 5, dc in 3rd st of beg ch. 3 dc, (ch 2, sk 2 dc, dc in dc) 3 times, 3 dc. Ch 5, sc in the middle of 3-ch lp, ch 5, dc in dc. Work in same manner around, ch 2, dc in 1st sc.
Rows 9–20: Work as for rows 1–8.
Row 21: Ch 5, sk 2 ch, dc in dc, (ch 2, sk 2 ch, dc in dc) 4 times. 2 dc in right side of 5-ch lp, dc in 3rd st of same lp. Ch 3, dc in 3rd ch of next lp, 2 dc in same lp, dc in dc, (ch 2, sk 2 sts, dc in dc) 6 times. Ch 3, sk 2 ch, sc in dc. Ch 3, sk 2 ch, dc in dc. Ch 2, sk 2 ch, dc in dc. Ch 3, sk 2 ch, sc in dc. Ch 3, sk 2 ch, dc in dc. Work in same manner around, end working 2 dc at a time in dc previous row and in 3rd st of beg ch.
Row 22: Ch 6, sc in 3rd st of beg ch previous row. Ch 3, sk 2 ch, dc in dc, (ch 2, sk 2 ch, dc in dc) 4 times, 3 dc. Ch 5, sc in the middle of 3-ch lp. Ch 5, 4 dc, (ch 2, sk 2 ch, dc in dc) 4 times. Ch 3, sk 2 ch, sc in dc. Ch 3, sk 2 ch, dc in dc. Ch 5, sk 2 lps, dc in dc. Ch 2, sk 2 ch, dc in dc. Ch 5, sk 2 lps, dc in dc. Ch 3, sk 2 ch, sc in dc. Ch 3, sk 2 ch, dc in dc. Continue in same manner around, end sl st in 3rd st of beg ch.
Rows 23–59: Work as for rows previous.
Join thread in where indicated, work straight across 1 side each. **Row 1:** Ch 3, 9 dc, (ch 2, sk 2 sts, dc in dc) 21 times, 12 dc. Ch 2, sk 2 sts, dc in dc. 12 dc, (ch 2, sk 2 sts, dc in dc) 21 times, 9 dc.
Rows 2–3: Work as for row 1.
Row 4: Work sl st up to 10th st, ch 3. Work up to 10th st from edge in same manner as for 1st row.
Rows 5–10: Work as for 4th row, decreasing both sides.

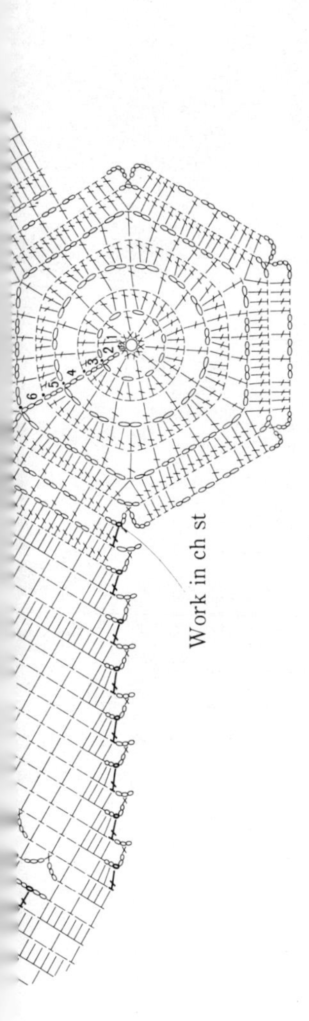

11 TABLECLOTH

YOU'LL NEED: Crochet cotton No. 20 20 20-gram balls White. Steel crochet hook size 0.90.
FINISHED SIZE: 134 cm in diameter
GAUGE: 1 row of dc = 0.5 cm
MAKING INSTRUCTIONS:
Ch 8, sl st in 1st ch to form ring. **Row 1:** Ch 1, 12 sc in ring, sl st in 1st sc.
Row 2: Ch 5, dc in sc, (ch 2, dc in sc) 11 times, sl st in 3rd st of beg ch.
Row 3: Ch 6, dc in 3rd st of beg ch previous row. Ch 2, sk 2 ch, dc in dc. Ch 2, sk 2 ch, dc in dc, ch 3, dc in same dc. Work in same manner around, sl st in 3rd st of beg ch.
Row 4: Work as for row 3.

THE WAY OF INC, DEC, EDGING

ow 5: Sl st in each of 3 ch, ch 6, dc in last sl st, ch 2, sk 2 ch, dc in dc) 3 times. Ch 2, sk 2 ch, dc in ext ch, ch 3, dc in same ch. Work in same manner round, sl st in 3rd st of beg ch.

ow 6: Work as for row 4.

ow 7: Sl st in each of 3 ch, ch 6, dc in last sl st, ch 2, sk 2 ch, dc in dc) 3 times, 6 dc. Ch 2, sk 2 ch, c in next ch, ch 3, dc in same ch. Work in same

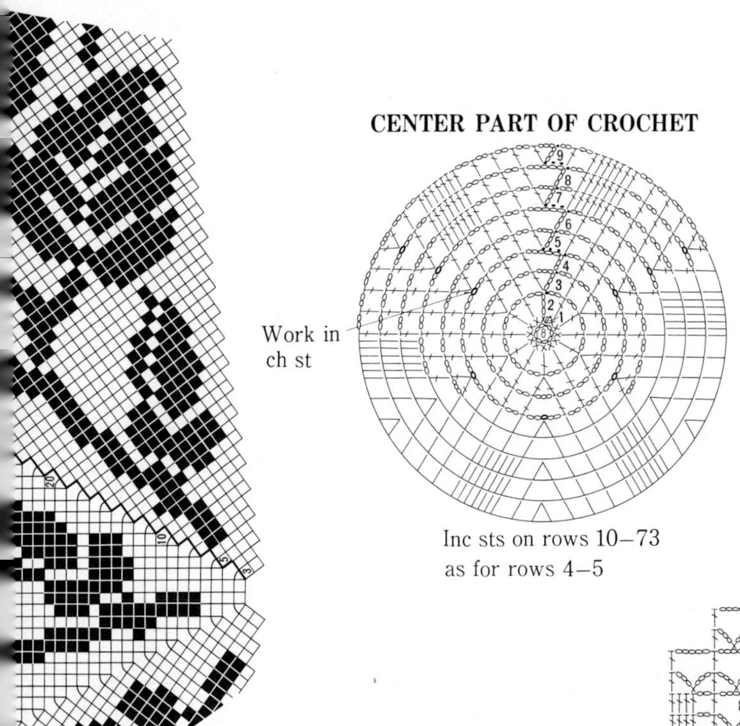

anner around, sl st in 3rd st of beg ch.

ows 8–77: Work as for rows 1–7, increasing sts at places.

ow 78: Sl st in each of 2 ch, ch 5, sk 1 ch, dc in dc, dc. Work in same manner around, sl st in 3rd st of g ch.

ow 79: Ch 5, sk 2 ch, dc in dc, 6 dc. Work in same anner around, hdc in 3rd st of beg ch.

ow 80: Ch 6, sc in 3rd st of beg ch previous row, 3, sk 2 ch, dc in dc. Ch 2, sk 2 dc, dc in next dc, dc. Work in same manner around, ch 3, sk 1 ch, st in 3rd st of beg ch.

w 81: Ch 8, sk 2 3-ch lps, dc in dc. Ch 2, sk 2 ch, dc in dc, 6 dc. Work in same manner around, end ch 1, hdc in 3rd st of beg ch.

Row 82: Ch 5, dc in 3rd st of beg ch previous row. Ch 3, sl 2 ch, sc in 3rd ch. Ch 3, sk 2 ch, dc in dc. Ch 3, sk 2 ch, dc in dc. Ch 3, sk 2 ch, sc in dc. Ch 3, sk 2 dc, dc in dc. Work in same manner around, end ch 2, sl st in 3rd st of beg ch.

Row 83: Ch 5, sk 2 ch, dc in dc, (ch 5, sk 2 3-ch lps, dc in dc) 2 times, 6 dc. Continue in same manner around, ch 1, hdc in 3rd st of beg ch.

Edging

Row 84: Ch 6, sc in 3rd st of beg ch previous row, ch 3, sk 2 ch, dc in dc. Ch 3, sk 2 ch, sc in next ch, ch 3, sk 2 sts, dc in dc. Work in same manner around, ch 3, sl st in 3rd st of beg ch.

Rows 85–103: Work as for rows up to 84.

Row 104: Work each row across up to 134th row one side each. Ch 3, 2 dc in hdc, dc in 3rd st of beg ch previous row. Ch 2, sk 2 ch, dc in dc, (ch 3, sk 2 ch, sc in next ch, ch 3, sk 2 ch, dc in dc) 50 times. Ch 2, sk 2 ch, dc in dc, 3 dc in 3 ch.

Row 105: Ch 3, 3 dc. Ch 2, sk 2 ch, dc in dc, (ch 5, sk 2 3-ch lps, dc in dc) 50 times. Ch 2, sk 2 ch, dc in dc, 3 dc.

Rows 106–134: Repeat rows 104–105, decreasing both sides referring to chart.

EDGING: Sc in each st around (3 sc in each row of dc).

13 CUSHION

YOU'LL NEED (for each): Crochet cotton No. 20 10 20-gram balls White. Steel crochet hook size 0.90. Bemberg for inner case 88 cm by 56 cm Beige. Kapok 450 gram.

FINISHED SIZE: Refer to chart.

GAUGE: 1 row of dc = 0.5 cm

MAKING INSTRUCTIONS:

FRONT: Make a loop at thread end. **Row 1:** Ch 3 2 dc in lp. (ch 2, 3 dc in lp) 5 times. Ch 1, sc in 3rd st of beg ch

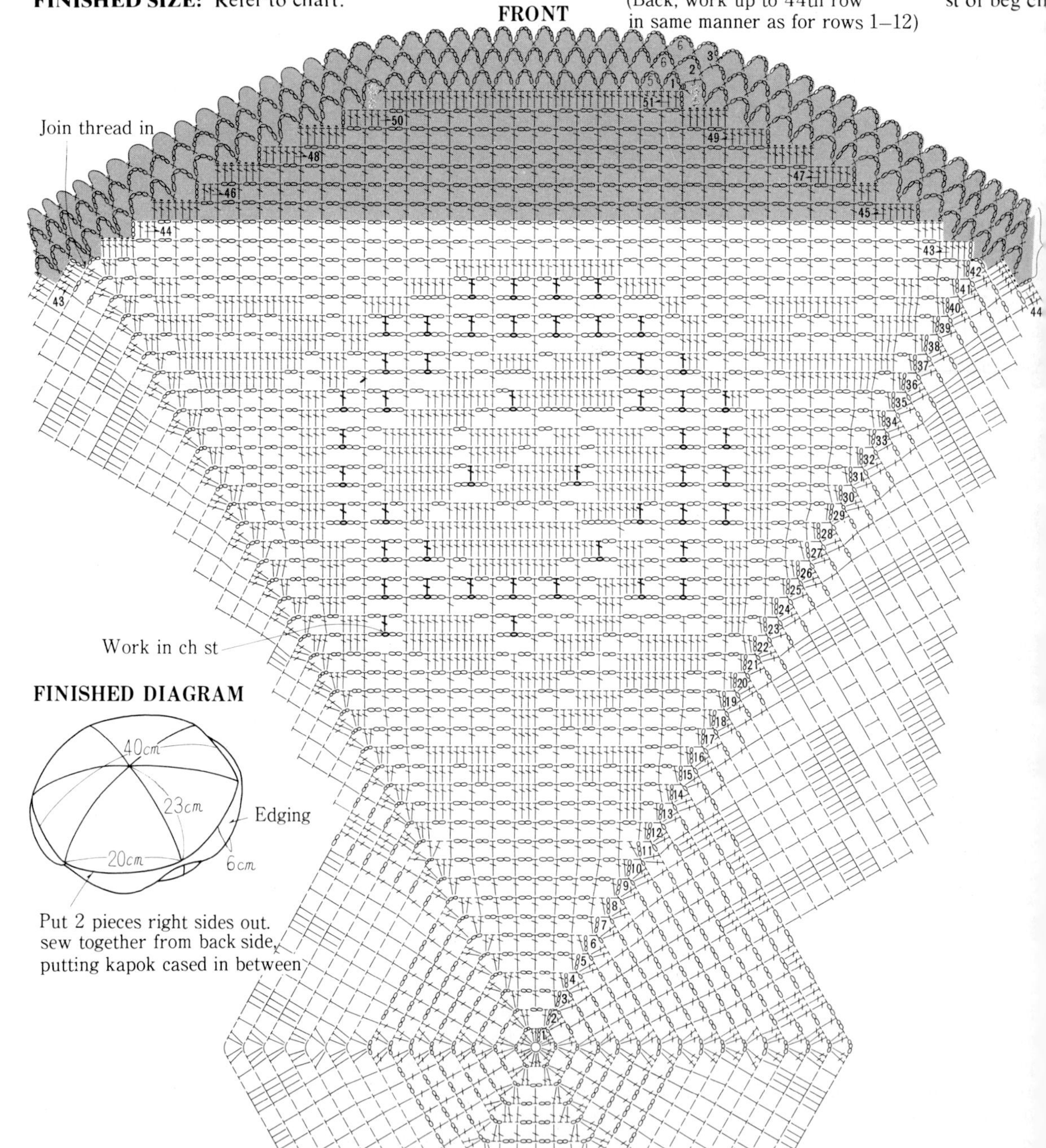

Row 2: Ch 3, dc in sc. Ch 2, sk 3 sts, 2 dc in 2 ch, ch 2, 2 dc in same ch. Continue in same manner, end 2 dc in 1 ch, ch 1, sc in 3rd st of beg ch.
Row 3: Ch 3, dc in sc. Ch 2, dc in the middle of 2 ch. Ch 2, 2 dc in 2-ch corner lp, ch 3, 2 dc in same lp. Repeat in same manner, end ch 1, hdc in 3rd st of beg ch.
Rows 4–12: Work as for row 3, increasing sts at 6 places.
Rows 13–42: Referring to chart, crochet patterns in, increasing sts at 6 corners.
Work each row across up to 51st row. **Row 43:** Ch 3, dc 5, (ch 2, sk 2 ch, dc in dc) 38 times, dc 5.
Row 44: Work sl st up to 6th st. Ch 3, dc 3, (ch 2, sk 2 ch, dc in dc) 36 times, dc 3.
Rows 45–51: Work as for row 44, decreasing each side.
EDGING: Row 1: Join thread in where indicated, sc 1, ch 5, sk 2 dc, sc in next dc. Continue in same manner, working sc in each corner. Ch 2, dc in 1st sc at the end. **Row 2:** Sc in dc, ch 6, sc in the middle of next lp. Ch 6, sc in the middle of next lp. Repeat in same manner around, ch 3, dc in 1st sc at the end. **Row 3:** Sc 1, ch 6, sc in the middle of next lp. Continue in same manner, end with sl st in 1st sc.
BACK: Crochet as for rows 1–12 of front up to 44th row, without working patterns in.
FINISHING: Put front and back wrong sides together, join, putting the kapok cased in between.

12 TABLECLOTH

YOU'LL NEED: Crochet cotton No. 20 24 20-gram balls White. Steel crochet hook size 0.90.
FINISHED SIZE: 121 cm square
GAUGE: 10 cm of filet crochet = 18.5 square; 10 cm = 18.5 rows.
MAKING INSTRUCTIONS:
Ch 6, sl st in 1st ch to form ring. **Row 1:** Ch 8, dc in ring, (ch 2, dc in ring, ch 5, dc in ring) 3 times, ch 2, sl st in 3rd st of beg ch.
Row 2: Ch 5, dc in the middle of 5-ch lp, ch 5, dc in the middle of same lp. Ch 2, dc in dc. Ch 2, sk 2 ch, dc in dc. Ch 2, dc in the middle of 5-ch lp, ch 5, dc in the middle of same lp. Work in same manner around, end sl st in 3rd st of beg ch.
Rows 3–18: Work as for row 2, increasing at 4 corners.
Row 19: Ch 5, sk 2 ch, dc in dc, *3 dc, ch 2, sk 2 ch, dc in dc, repeat from *to corner. 3 dc in 5-ch corner lp, ch 5, 3 dc in same corner lp. Work in same manner around, end sl st in 3rd st of beg ch.

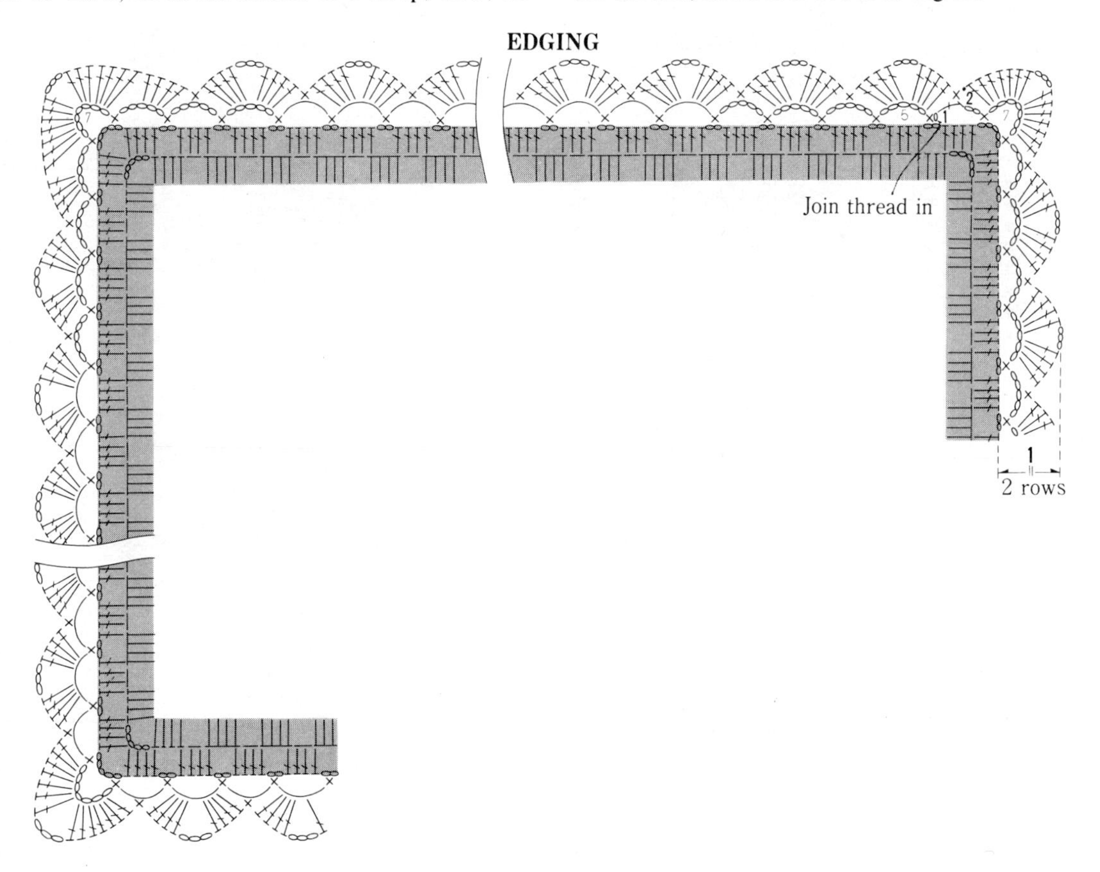

Row 20: Work as for row 19

Rows 21–110: Work as for rows previous, increasing at 4 corners. Work ch 2, sk 2 sts, 1 dc for each sp, 3 dc for each bl referring to chart, so that patterns worked as shown.

EDGING: Row 1: Join thread in where indicated, sc in the middle of 2 ch, ch 5, sk 4 dc, sc in the middle of 2 ch, repeat from *around, working sc in right edge of 5-ch lp, ch 7, sc in left edge of same lp at every corner. End ch 2, dc in 1st sc. **Row 2:** Sc in dc,

4 dc in 5-ch lp, ch 3, 4 dc in same lp. Sc in the middle of next lp. Repeat in same manner up to 1 lp this side of corner lp. Work 4 dc in the lp next to corner lp, 7 dc in corner lp, ch 3, 7 dc in same lp. Dc 4 in 5-ch lp, sc in next lp. Repeat, working dc 7, ch 3, dc 7 at every corner. End sl st in 1st sc.

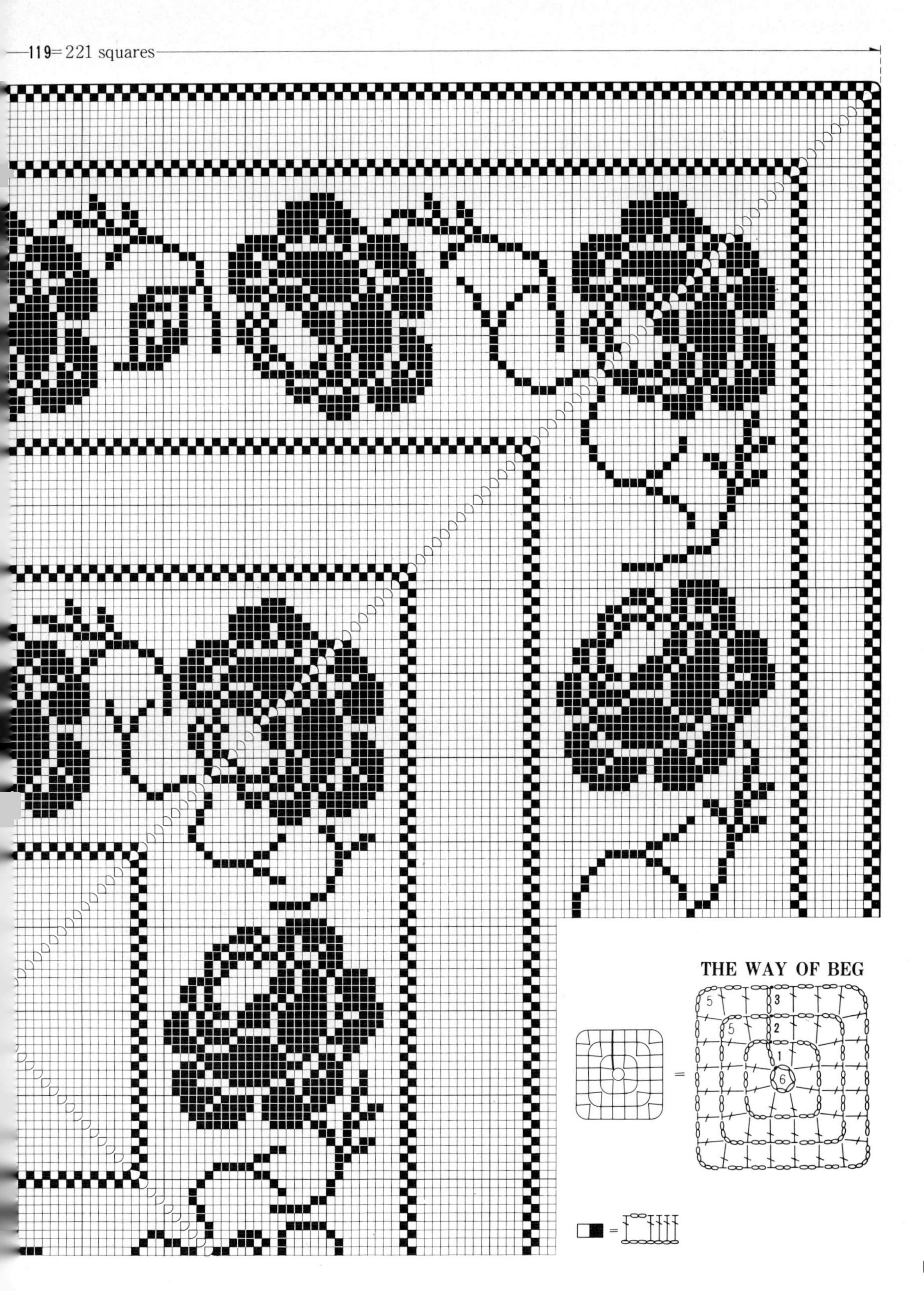

14 TABLECLOTH

YOU'LL NEED: Crochet cotton No. 4 soft twist 4 50-gram balls White. Steel crochet hook size 1.75.
FINISHED SIZE: 114 cm in diameter
GAUGE: 1 row of tr = 1 cm.
MAKING INSTRUCTIONS:
Ch 8, sl st in 1st ch to form ring. **Row 1:** Ch 4, 23 tr in ring.
Row 2: Ch 6, tr in tr, *ch 2, tr in tr, repeat from* around, sl st in 4th st of beg ch.
Row 3: Ch 6, tr in 4th st of ch previous row, (ch 2, sk 2 ch, tr in tr) 2 times. Ch 2, sk 2 ch, tr in tr, ch 2, tr in same ch. Continue in same manner, sl st in 4th st of beg ch at the end.

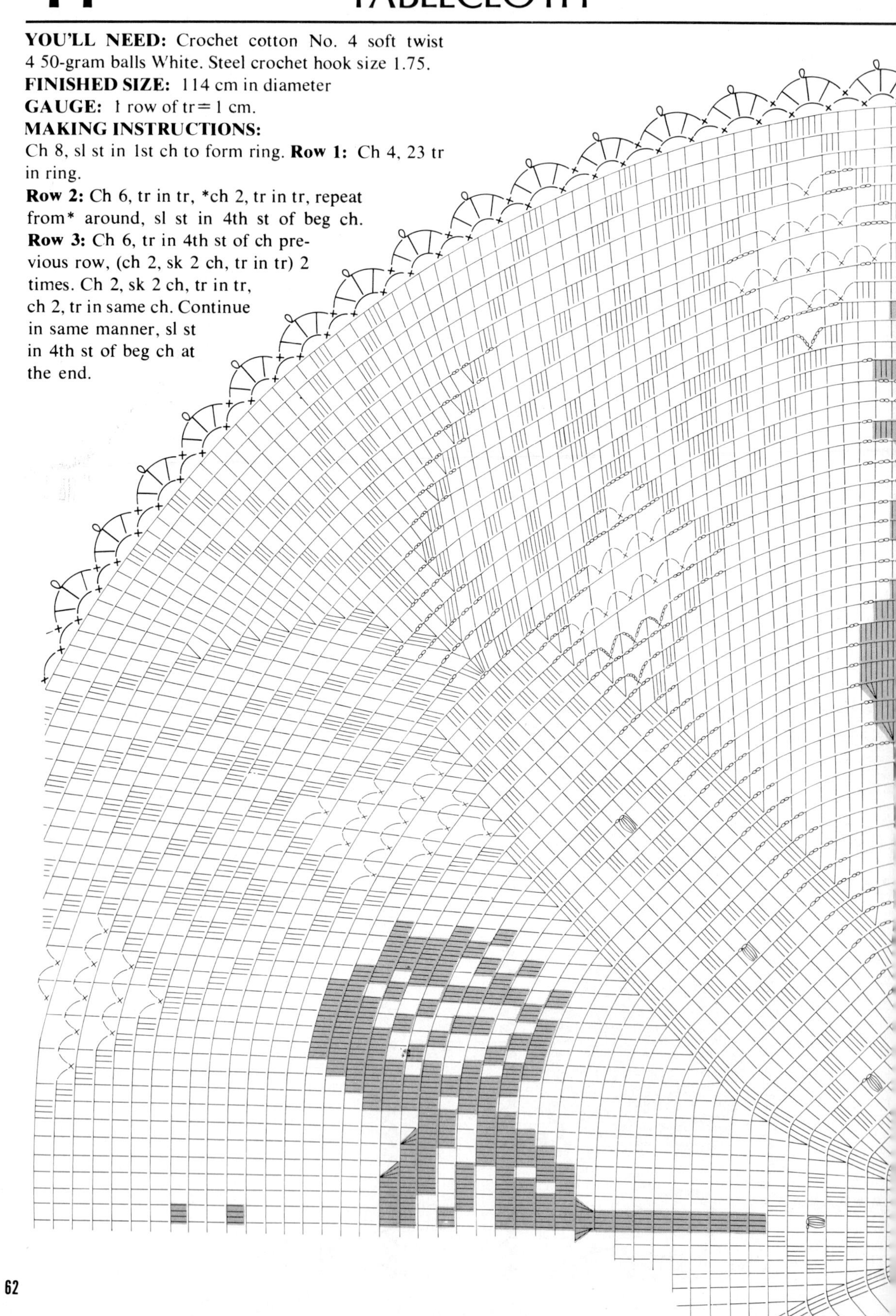

Row 4: Ch 4, 2 tr in 2 ch, tr in tr. Repeat in same manner around, end sl st in 4th st of beg ch.
Row 5: Ch 4, 1 tr each in 2 tr. Tr in tr, ch 2, tr in same tr, (ch 2, sk 2 tr, tr in next tr) 2 times. Ch 2, sk 2 tr, tr in next tr, ch 2, tr in same tr. 1 tr each in next 2 tr, tr in next tr, ch 2, tr in same tr. Repeat in same manner around, sl st in 4th st of beg ch.
Rows 6–9: Work as for rows up to 5.
Row 10: Ch 4, 1 tr each in next 3 tr. Ch 2, sk 2 ch, tr in tr. Ch 2, sk 2 ch, tr in tr, tr 3, (ch 2, sk 2 sts, tr 1) 2 times. 5-tr pop in 2 ch, ch 1, tr in next tr. Continue in same manner around, sl st in 4th st of beg ch.
Rows 11–31: Work as for rows up to 10.
Row 32: Ch 6, sk 2 tr, tr in next tr. Tr 2 in 2 ch, tr in tr. Work in same manner around, tr in 4th st of beg ch previous row, ch 2. sl st in 4th st of beg ch. 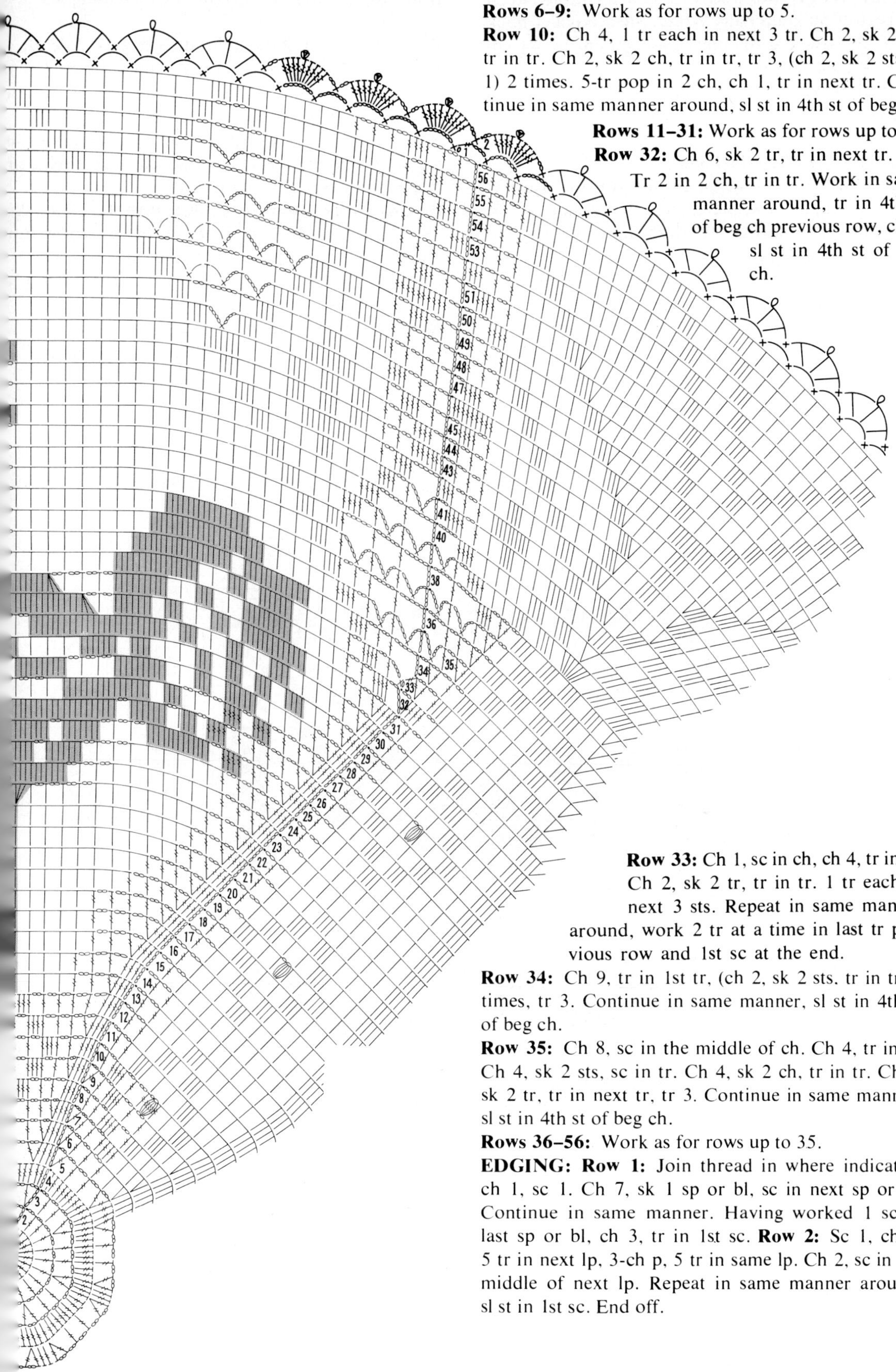
Row 33: Ch 1, sc in ch, ch 4, tr in tr. Ch 2, sk 2 tr, tr in tr. 1 tr each in next 3 sts. Repeat in same manner around, work 2 tr at a time in last tr previous row and 1st sc at the end.
Row 34: Ch 9, tr in 1st tr, (ch 2, sk 2 sts, tr in tr) 2 times, tr 3. Continue in same manner, sl st in 4th st of beg ch.
Row 35: Ch 8, sc in the middle of ch. Ch 4, tr in tr. Ch 4, sk 2 sts, sc in tr. Ch 4, sk 2 ch, tr in tr. Ch 2, sk 2 tr, tr in next tr, tr 3. Continue in same manner, sl st in 4th st of beg ch.
Rows 36–56: Work as for rows up to 35.
EDGING: Row 1: Join thread in where indicated, ch 1, sc 1. Ch 7, sk 1 sp or bl, sc in next sp or bl. Continue in same manner. Having worked 1 sc in last sp or bl, ch 3, tr in 1st sc. **Row 2:** Sc 1, ch 2, 5 tr in next lp, 3-ch p, 5 tr in same lp. Ch 2, sc in the middle of next lp. Repeat in same manner around, sl st in 1st sc. End off.

15 CUSHION

YOU'LL NEED (for each): Crochet cotton No. 4 soft twist 3 50-gram balls White. Steel crochet hook size 1.75. Bemberg for inner case 86 cm by 44 cm Black. Kapok 450 gram.
FINISHED SIZE: 42 cm square
GAUGE: 10 cm of filet crochet = 13 squares; 10 cm = 13 rows.
MAKING INSTRUCTIONS:
FRONT: Ch 12, sl st in 1st ch to form ring. **Row 1:** Ch 5, sk 2 ch, dc in next ch. Ch 5, dc in same ch. Ch 2, sk 2 ch, dc in next ch. Work in same manner, end sl st in 3rd st of beg ch.
Row 2: Ch 5, sk 2 ch, dc in dc. 3 dc in 5-ch lp, ch 5, 3 dc in same lp. Dc in next dc, ch 2, sk 2 ch, dc in dc. Work in same manner around, end sl st in 3rd st of beg ch.
Rows 3–7: Work as for row 2, increasing sts at corners.
Row 8: Ch 5, sk 2 ch, dc in dc. Ch 2, sk 2 dc, dc in 10 sts, (ch 2, sk 2 ch, dc in dc) 2 times. Ch 2, 7 dc in the middle of 5-ch lp. Ch 2, dc in dc. Work in same manner, end sl st in 3rd st of beg ch.
Rows 9–27: Work as for the rows previous, increasing sts at corners. To make 1 sp, ch 2, sk 2 sts, dc in next st; to make 1 bl, dc in 3 sts.
BACK: Work from front edge. **Row 1:** Ch 5, sk ch, dc in dc, ch 2, sk 2 ch, dc in dc, repeat from *across to corner, dec working 2 dc at a time.
Row 2: Work as for row 1, working 2 dc at a time at corners to dec.
Rows 3–16: Work as for row 2.

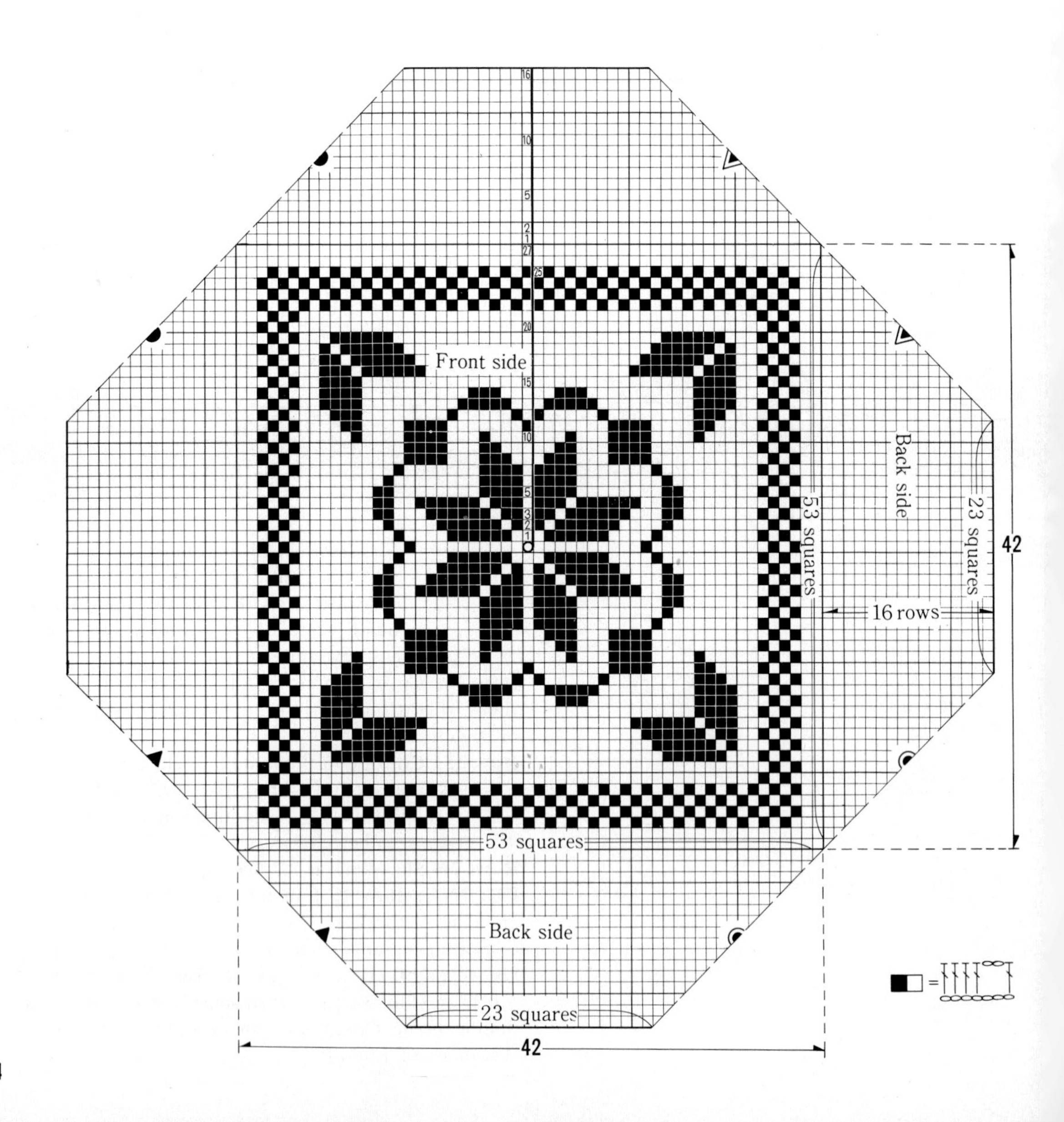

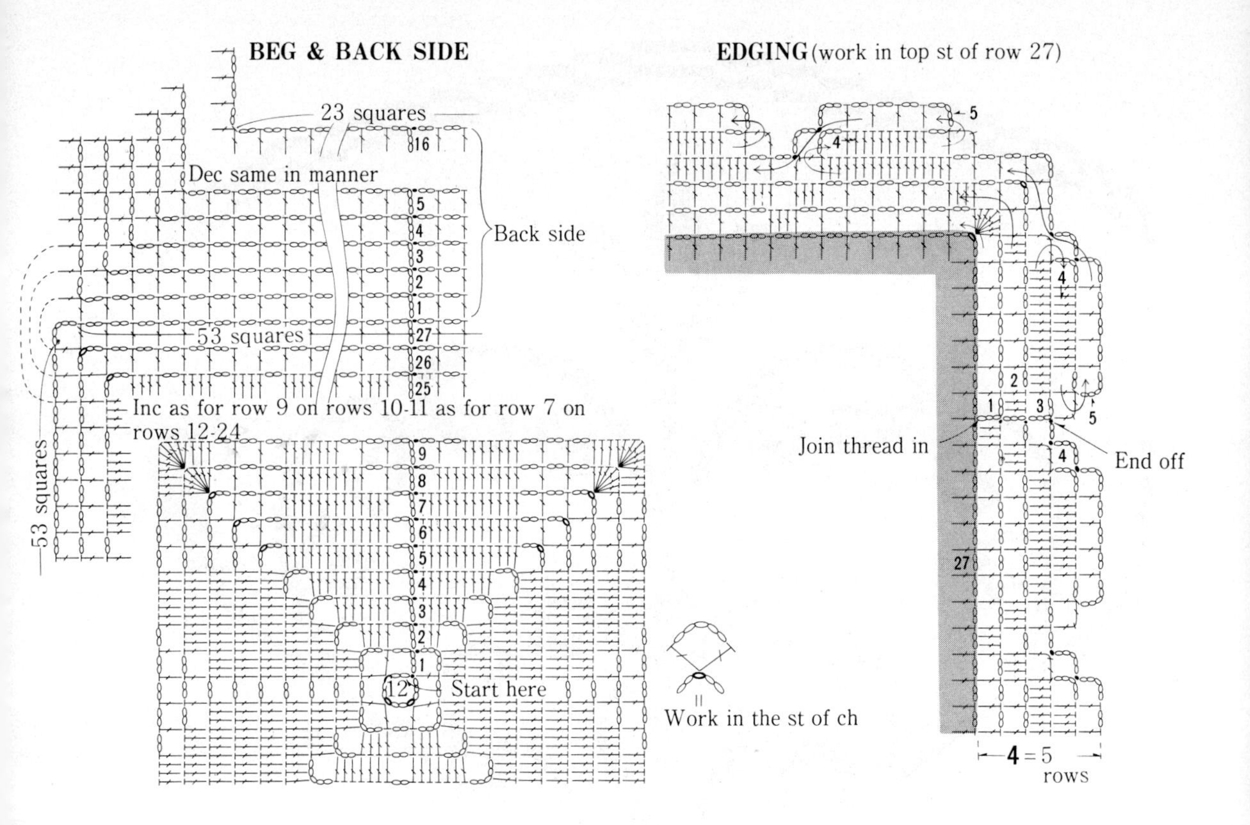

16 CENTERPIECE

YOU'LL NEED: Crochet cotton No. 20 7½ 20-gram balls White. Steel crochet hook size 0.90.
FINISHED SIZE: 70 cm in diameter
GAUGE: 1 row of dc = 0.5 cm.
MAKING INSTRUCTIONS:
Ch 10, sl st in 1st ch to form ring. **Row 1:** Ch 3, 29 dc in ring, sl st in 3rd st of beg ch.
Row 2: Ch 4, dc in dc, *ch 1, dc in dc, repeat from* around, sl st in 3rd st of beg ch.
Row 3: Ch 3, dc in each st around, sl st in 3rd st of beg ch.
Row 4: Ch 5, sk 1 dc, dc in dc, *ch 2, sk 1 dc, dc in dc, repeat from *around, sl st in 3rd st of beg ch.
Row 5: Ch 3, dc 2 in 2 ch, dc in dc. Repeat in same manner to corner, dc in dc, ch 3, dc in same dc. Work in same manner around, sl st in 3rd st of beg ch.
Row 6: Ch 5, (sk 2 dc, dc in dc) 3 times. Ch 2, dc in each lp, ch 2, dc in same lp. Repeat in same manner, and sl st in 3rd st of beg ch.
Row 7: Ch 5, work as for row 6, working dc in dc, ch 5, sk 2 ch, dc in dc at every corner.
Rows 8–30: Work increasing sts at 6 corners.
Row 31: Ch 3, dc 3, (ch 2, sk 2 ch, dc in dc) 7 times. Ch 3, sk 2 ch, sc in dc. Ch 3, sk 2 ch, dc in dc, (ch 2, sk 2 ch, dc in dc) 6 times. Work dc in dc, ch 5, sk 2 ch, dc in dc at every corner.
Row 32: Ch 3, dc 3, (ch 2, sk 2 ch, dc in dc) 5 times. Ch 3, sk 2 ch, sc in dc. Ch 3, sk 2 ch, dc in dc. Ch 5, sk 2 3-ch lps, dc in dc. Ch 3, sk 2 ch, sc in dc. Ch 3, sk 2 ch, dc in dc, (ch 2, sk 2 ch, dc in dc) 4 times. Ch 2, dc in the middle of 5-ch lp, ch 2, dc in same lp.
Rows 33–63: Work as for rows up to 32. As for rows 64–71, join thread in where indicated, work across each row, turn.
Row 64: Ch 5, sk 2 ch, dc in dc, (ch 2, sk 2 ch, dc in dc) 29 times. Dc 3, (ch 2, sk 2 ch, dc in dc) 30 times.

CENTER PART OF CROCHET

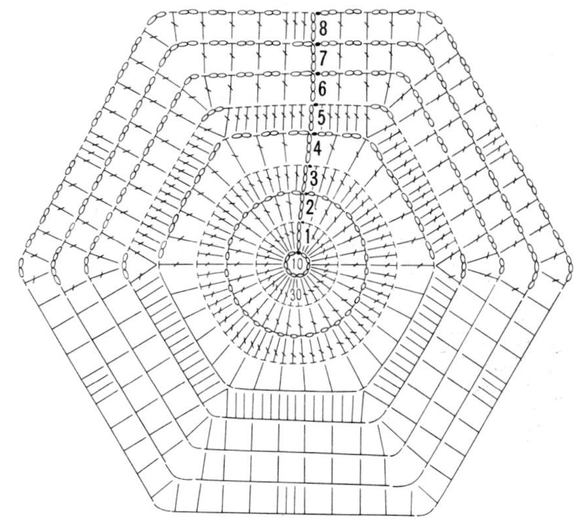

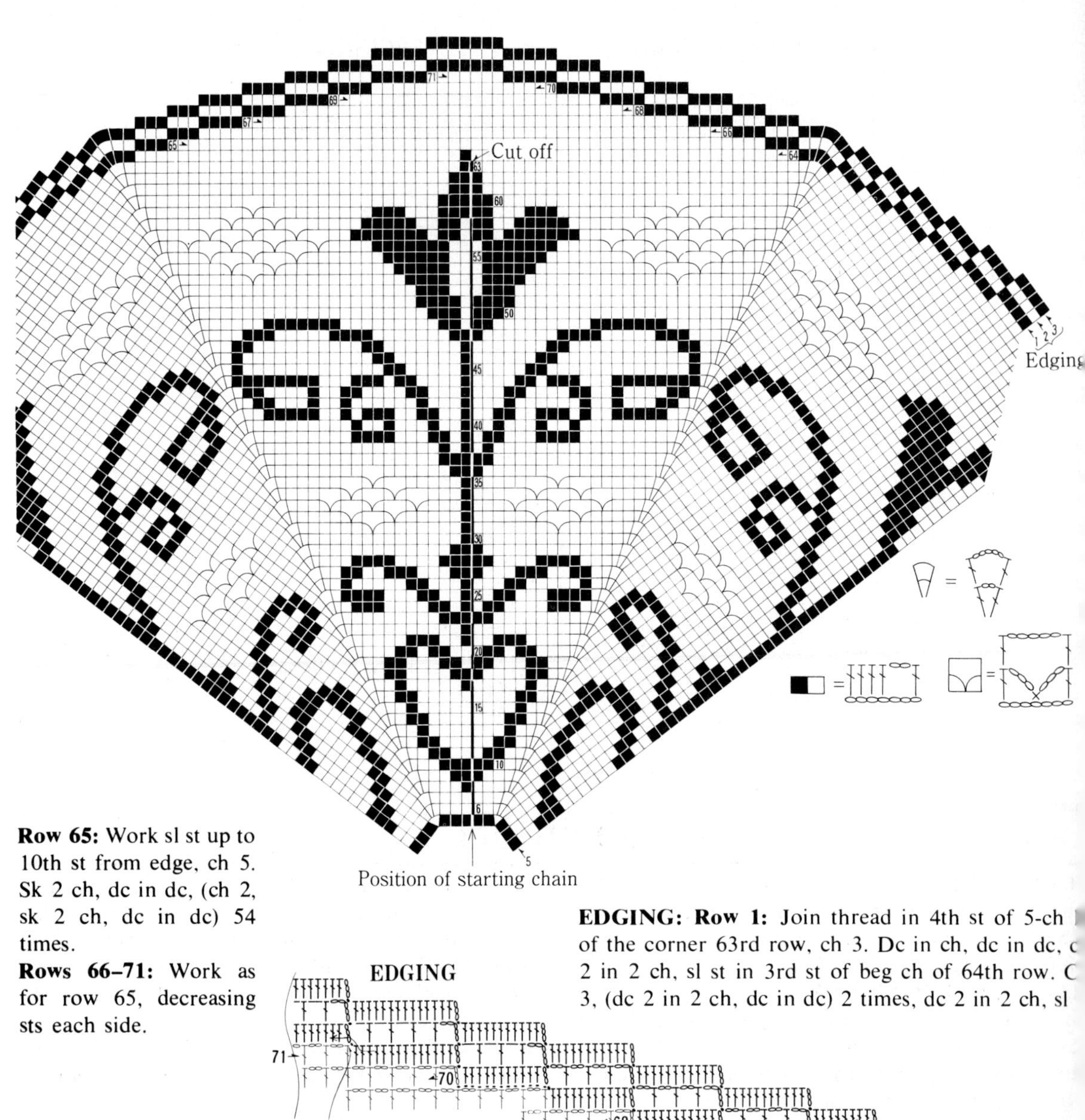

Row 65: Work sl st up to 10th st from edge, ch 5. Sk 2 ch, dc in dc, (ch 2, sk 2 ch, dc in dc) 54 times.

Rows 66–71: Work as for row 65, decreasing sts each side.

EDGING

Cut off

Join thread in

Join thread in

EDGING: Row 1: Join thread in 4th st of 5-ch of the corner 63rd row, ch 3. Dc in ch, dc in dc, c 2 in 2 ch, sl st in 3rd st of beg ch of 64th row. C 3, (dc 2 in 2 ch, dc in dc) 2 times, dc 2 in 2 ch, sl

in 1st dc of 65th row. Work in same manner arour sl st in 3rd st of beg ch. **Row 2:** Ch 5, sk 1 dc, dc next dc. Ch 2, sk 2 dc, sl st in 3rd st of beg ch p vious row. Ch 5, sk 2 dc, dc in next dc. Ch 2, sk 2 dc in next dc. Ch 2, sk 2 dc, sl st in 3rd st of beg previous row. **Row 3:** Work as for row 1.

19 TABLECLOTH

YOU'LL NEED: Crochet cotton No. 20 18 20-gram balls White. Steel crochet hook size 0.90.
FINISHED SIZE: Refer to chart.
GAUGE: 1 row of dc = 0.6 cm.
SIZE OF MOTIF: Hexagon, 4.5 cm each side.
MAKING INSTRUCTIONS:
MOTIF A: Make a loop at thread end. **Row 1:** Ch 5, 1 dc in lp, (ch 2, dc in lp) 4 times, ch 2, sl st in 3rd st of beg ch.
Row 2: Ch 5, dc in 2 ch, ch 2, dc in same dc. Ch 2, dc in dc. Work in same manner around, sl st in 3rd st of beg ch.
Row 3: Ch 5, sk 2 ch, dc in dc. Ch 5, sk 2 ch, dc in dc, (ch 2, sk 2 ch, dc in dc) 2 times. Ch 5, sk 2 ch, dc in dc. Work in same manner around, sl st in 3rd st of beg ch.
Row 4: Ch 5, sk 2 ch, dc in dc. Ch 2, dc in 5-ch lp, ch 2, dc in same lp. Ch 2, dc in dc. Ch 2, sk 2 ch, dc in dc. Work in same manner around, sl st in 3rd st of beg ch.
Rows 5–8: Work as for rows 3–4.
MOTIF B: Make a loop at thread end. **Row 1:** Ch 6, 1 dc in lp, (ch 3, dc in lp) 4 times, ch 3, sl st in 3rd st of beg ch.
Row 2: Ch 5, dc in ch 3, ch 1, dc in same ch. Ch 2, dc in dc. Work in same manner around, sl st in 3rd st of beg ch.
Row 3: Sl st in 3 sts, ch 3, 3 dc in ch, dc in dc. Ch 5, sk 2 ch, sk 1 dc, sk 2 ch, dc in dc. 3 dc in 1 ch, dc in dc. Work in same manner, end sl st in 3rd st of beg ch.

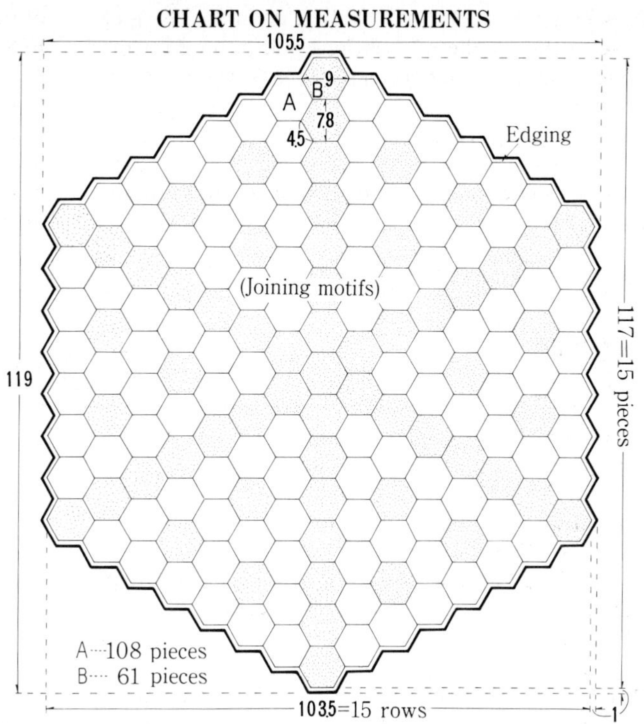

Row 4: Ch 3, dc in dc. Dc in next dc, ch 3, dc in same dc. Dc in dc twice, ch 3, sc in the middle of 5-ch lp. Ch 3, dc in dc twice. Continue in same manner around, sl st in 3rd st of beg ch.

(CONTINUED ON PAGE 68)

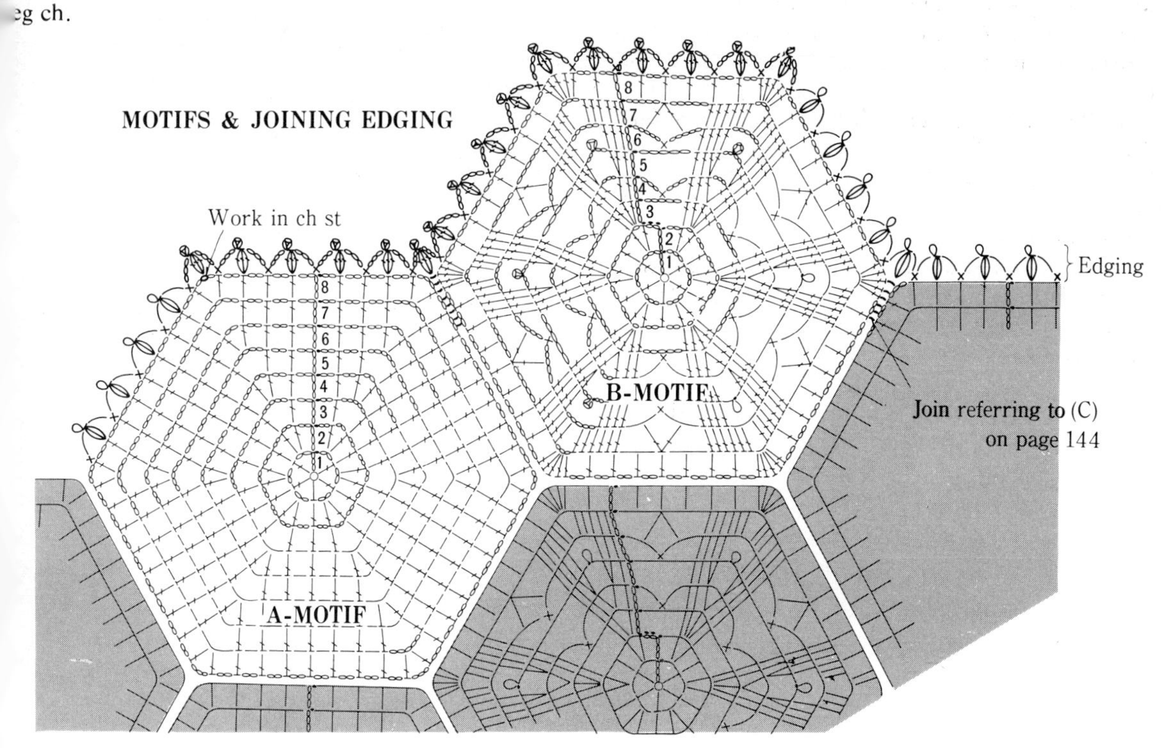

Row 5: Ch 3, dc in dc. 2 dc in next dc. Ch 2, 3-ch p, ch 2, sk 3 ch, 2 dc in dc. Dc in dc twice, ch 5, sk 2 3-ch lps, dc in dc. Dc in dc, 2 dc in next dc. Continue in same manner, end sl st in 3rd st of beg ch.
Row 6: Ch 3, dc 3. Ch 5, sk 1 lp, dc in dc. Dc 3, ch 5, sc in the middle of 5-ch lp, ch 5, dc in dc. Continue in same manner around, sl st in 3rd st of beg ch.
Row 7: Ch 3, dc in dc 3 times, 2 dc in 5-ch lp, ch 3, 2 dc in same lp. Dc in dc 4 times. Ch 5, dc in 5-ch lp and in next lp, draw through at a time, ch 5, dc in dc. Work in same manner around, sl st in 3rd st of beg ch.
Row 8: Ch 5, sk 2 dc, dc in dc. Ch 2, sk 2 dc, 5 dc in 3-ch lp, (ch 2, sk 2 dc, dc in dc) 2 times. Ch 2, dc in the middle of 5-ch lp. Ch 2, dc in the st of 2 dc at a time. Work around in same manner, sl st in 3rd st of beg ch.
FINISHING: Crochet A-motif 108 pieces, B-motif 61 pieces, join all pieces together with whip st referring to chart.
EDGING: Ch 1, sc in ch. Ch 3, sk 2 ch, 3-dc pop in dc, 3-ch p, ch 3, sk 2 ch, sc in dc. Ch 3, sk 1 dc, 3-dc pop in dc, 3-ch p, sk 1 dc, sc in dc. Continue in same manner around, sl st in 1st sc.

17 DOILY

YOU'LL NEED: Crochet cotton No. 20 2½ 20-gram balls White. Steel crochet hook size 0.90.
FINISHED SIZE: 40 cm in diameter
GAUGE: 1 row of dc = 0.5 cm.
MAKING INSTRUCTIONS:
Make a loop at thread end. **Row 1:** Ch 1, 12 dc in lp.
Row 2: Ch 5, dc in sc, (ch 2, sk 1 sc, dc in next sc. Ch 2, dc in same sc) 5 times, ch 2, sl st in 3rd st of beg ch.
Row 3: Ch 5, sk 1 ch, dc in dc. Ch 2, sk 2 sts, dc in dc. Ch 2, dc in the middle of 2 ch, ch 2, dc in dc. Continue in same manner, sl st in 3rd st of beg ch.
Row 4: Ch 5, dc in 3rd st of ch previous row. Work as for row 3, working dc in dc, ch 2, dc in same dc at corners.
Rows 5–7: Work as for rows 3–4.
Rows 8–27: Referring to chart, work patterns in, increasing sts at 6 corners. As for rows 28–39, join thread in where indicated, work across each row, turn.
Row 28: Ch 3, dc 3, (ch 2, sk 2 sts, dc in dc) 5 times. Ch 3, (ch 2, sk 2 sts, dc in dc) 5 times. Dc 27, (ch 2, sk 2 sts, dc in dc) 5 times. Dc 2 in 2 ch, dc in corner dc.
Rows 29–30: Work as for row 28.
Row 31: Work sl st up to 4th st from edge, ch 3. Dc 6, (ch 2, sk 2 ch, dc in dc) 5 times. Dc 15, (ch 2, sk 2 sts, dc in dc) 11 times, dc 6.
Row 32: Ch 3, dc 12, (ch 2, sk 2 sts, dc in dc) 17 times, dc 12.
Rows 33–39: Work as for row 31, decreasing sts each side.

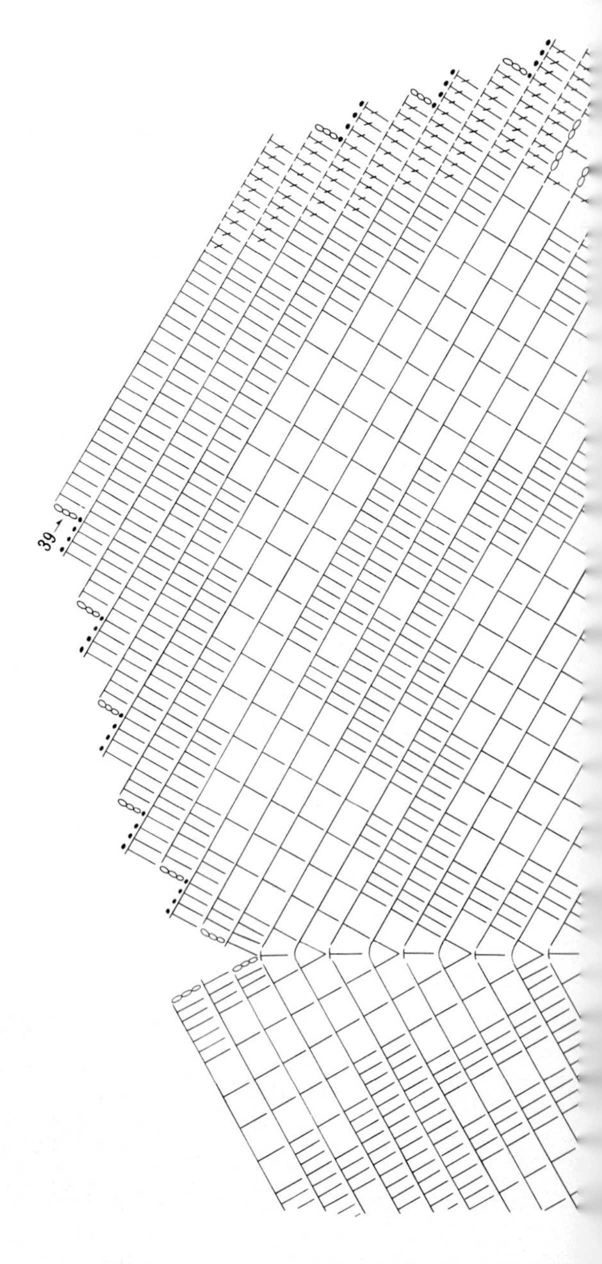

n
read in

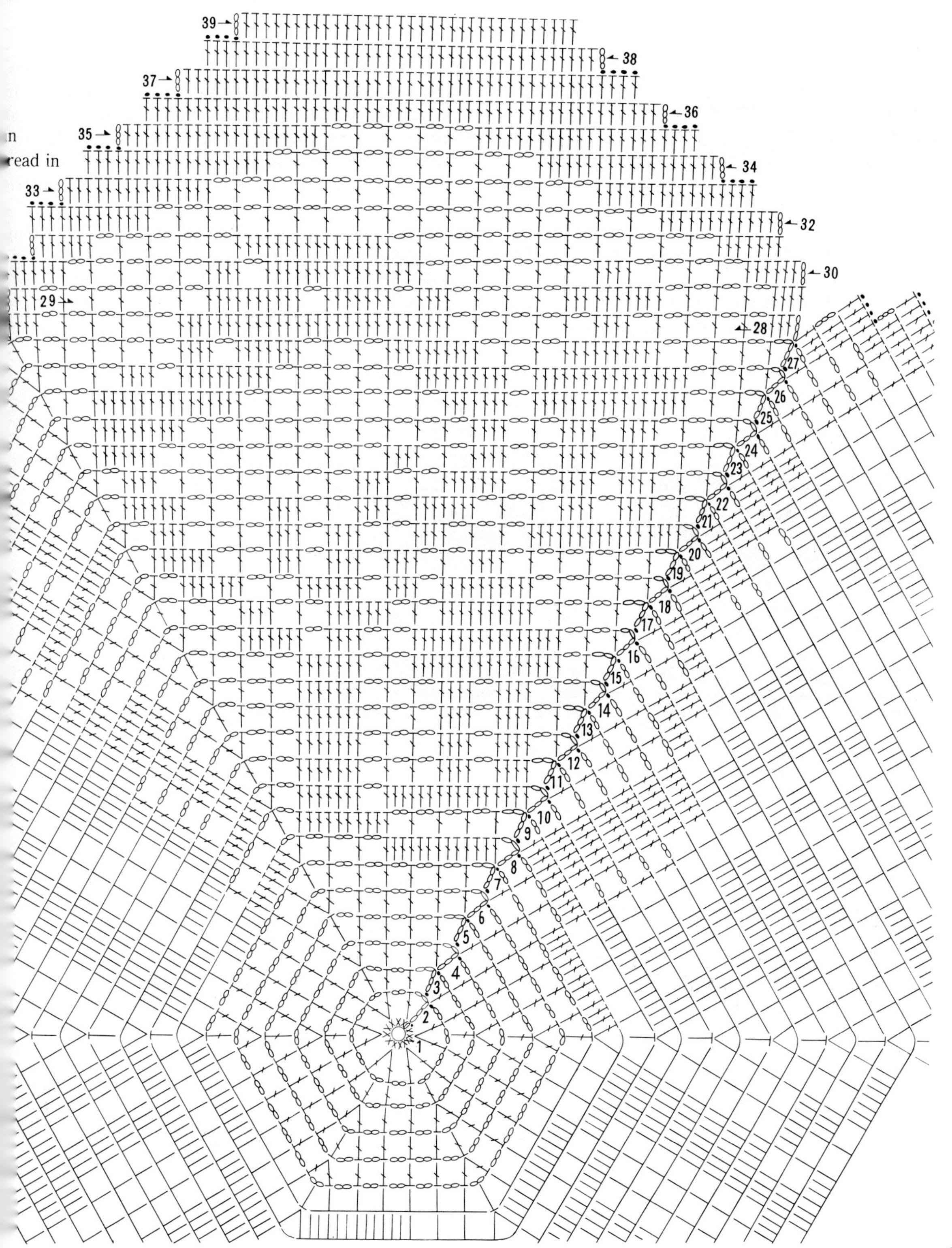

39
38
37
36
35
34
33
32
30
29
28
27
26
25
24
23
22
21
20
19
18
17
16
15
14
13
12
11
10
9
8
7
6
5
4
3
2
1

20 CUSHION

YOU'LL NEED (for each): Crochet cotton No. 20 8 20-gram balls White. Steel crochet hook size 0.90. Bemberg for inner case 90 cm by 46 cm Pink (Blue). Kapok 450 gram.
FINISHED SIZE: 44 cm square
GAUGE: 10 cm of filet crochet = 20 squares; 10 cm = 20 rows.
SIZE OF MOTIF: 14 cm square
MAKING INSTRUCTIONS:
MOTIF A: Ch 85. **Row 1:** Ch 5, dc in 9th ch from hook, (ch 2, sk 2 ch, dc in next ch) 27 times.
Row 2: Ch 5, sk 2 ch, dc in dc, (dc 2 in 2 ch, dc in dc) 6 times. (ch 2, sk 2 ch, dc in dc) 6 times. (dc 2 in 2 ch, dc in dc) 2 times. (ch 2, sk 2 ch, dc in dc) 6 times. (dc 2 in 2 ch, dc in dc) 6 times, ch 2, sk 2 ch, dc in next ch.
Rows 3–28: Work referring to chart. Ch 2, sk 2 sts, dc in next st for each sp, dc in 3 sts for each bl.

MOTIF B: Ch 85. **Row 1:** Ch 5, dc in 9th ch from hook, (ch 2, sk 2 ch, dc in next ch) 12 times. Dc 6. (ch 2, sk 2 ch, dc in next ch) 13 times.
Row 2: Ch 5, sk 2 sts, dc in dc. Dc 2 in 2 ch, dc in dc. Ch 2, sk 2 ch, dc in dc, (dc 2 in 2 ch, dc in dc) 3 times. (ch 2, sk 2 sts, dc in dc) 6 times. (dc 2 in 2 ch, dc in dc) 4 times. (ch 2, sk 2 ch, dc in dc) 6 times (dc 2 in 2 ch, dc in dc) 3 times. Ch 2, sk 2 ch, dc in dc. Dc 2 in 2 ch, dc in dc. Ch 2, sk 2 ch, dc in next ch.
Rows 3–28: Work referring to chart.
FINISHING: Crochet A-motif 10 pieces, B-motif 8 pieces. Join them into the pieces of 3 rows of 3 motifs. Put 2 pieces right sides out, work edging along, putting the kapok cased in between.
EDGING: Join thread in dc, ch 1, sc 1, (ch 2, sk 2 ch, sc in dc) 2 times. Ch 3, sc in corner. Ch 3, sc in top of dc. Ch 2, sc in ch. Work in same manner around, end sl st in 2 nd sc.

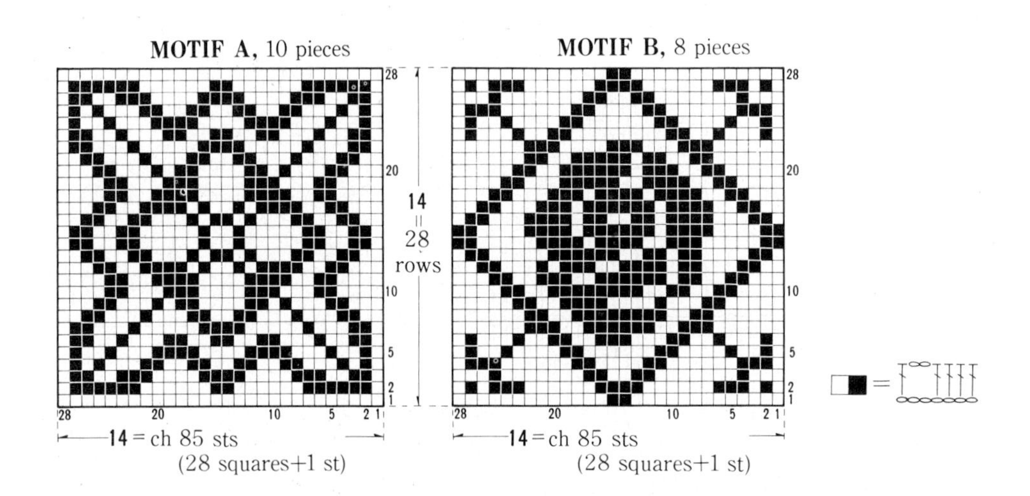

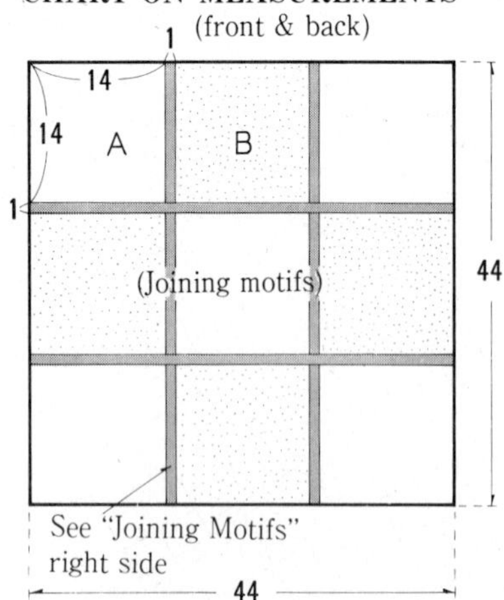

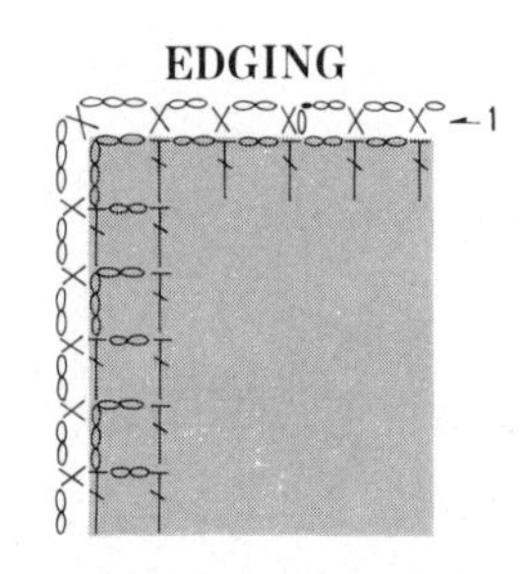

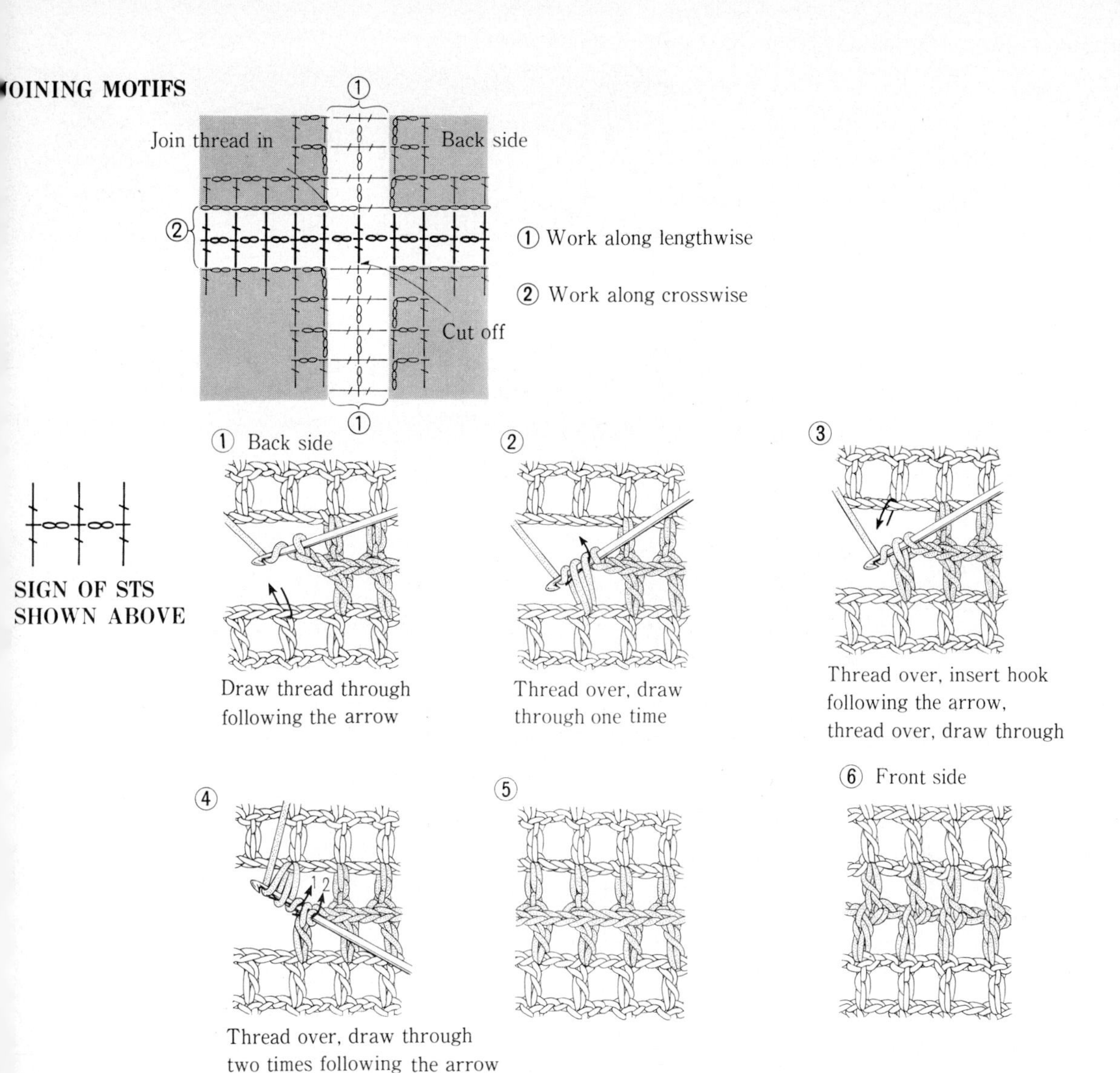
OINING MOTIFS
①
Join thread in
Back side
②
① Work along lengthwise
② Work along crosswise
Cut off
①
SIGN OF STS
SHOWN ABOVE
① Back side
②
③
Draw thread through
following the arrow
Thread over, draw
through one time
Thread over, insert hook
following the arrow,
thread over, draw through
④
⑤
⑥ Front side
1 2
Thread over, draw through
two times following the arrow

21 CENTERPIECE

OU'LL NEED: Crochet cotton No. 20 17 20-gram ılls White. Steel crochet hook size 0.90.
INISHED SIZE: 114 cm by 110 cm
AUGE: 1 row of dc = 0.5 cm.
ZE OF MOTIF: A, B=hexagon, 11 cm each side; , D=11 cm square.
AKING INSTRUCTIONS:
OTIF A: Make a loop at thread end. **Row 1:** Ch 11 dc in lp.
ow 2: Ch 5, dc in dc. Ch 2, dc in dc, ch 2, dc in me dc. Ch 2, dc in dc, ch 2, dc in next dc. Con- ıue in same manner, sl st in 3rd st of beg ch.
ow 3: Ch 5, sk 2 ch, dc in dc. Ch 2, sk 2 ch, dc in :. Ch 5, sk 2 ch, dc in dc. Continue in same manner, st in 3rd st of beg ch.
ow 4: Ch 5, sk 2 ch, dc in dc. Ch 2, sk 2 ch, dc in :. Ch 2, dc in 5-ch lp, ch 2, dc in same lp. Ch 2, : in dc. Continue in same manner around, sl st in 3rd st of beg ch.
Row 5: Ch 5, sk 2 ch, dc in dc, (ch 2, sk 2 ch, dc in dc) 2 times. Ch 5, sk 2 ch, dc in dc. Work in same manner, end sl st in 3rd st of beg ch.
Row 6: Ch 10, sk 2 ch, 1 dc, 2 ch, dtr in dc. Ch 5, sk 2 ch, 1 dc, dtr in 5-ch lp, ch 5, dtr in same lp. Work in same manner around, dtr in last 5-ch lp, ch 5, dtr in same lp, ch 2, dc in 5th st of beg ch.
Row 7: Ch 5, dc in 5th st of ch 10, ch 2, sk 2 ch, dc in next ch. Ch 2, sk 2 ch, dc in dtr. Continue in same manner, working dc in 5-ch lp, ch 2, dc in same lp at every corner.
Rows 8–14: Work as for rows 3–7.
Row 15: Ch 2, 3-ch p, hdc in 2 ch, hdc in next dc, 3-ch p. Hdc 2 in 2 ch, hdc in dc, 6-ch p. Hdc 2 in 2 ch, hdc in dc, 3-ch p. Continue in same manner, working hdc 3 in 2 ch at every corner, end sl st in 2nd st of beg ch. Crochet following pieces joining to

CHART ON MEASUREMENTS

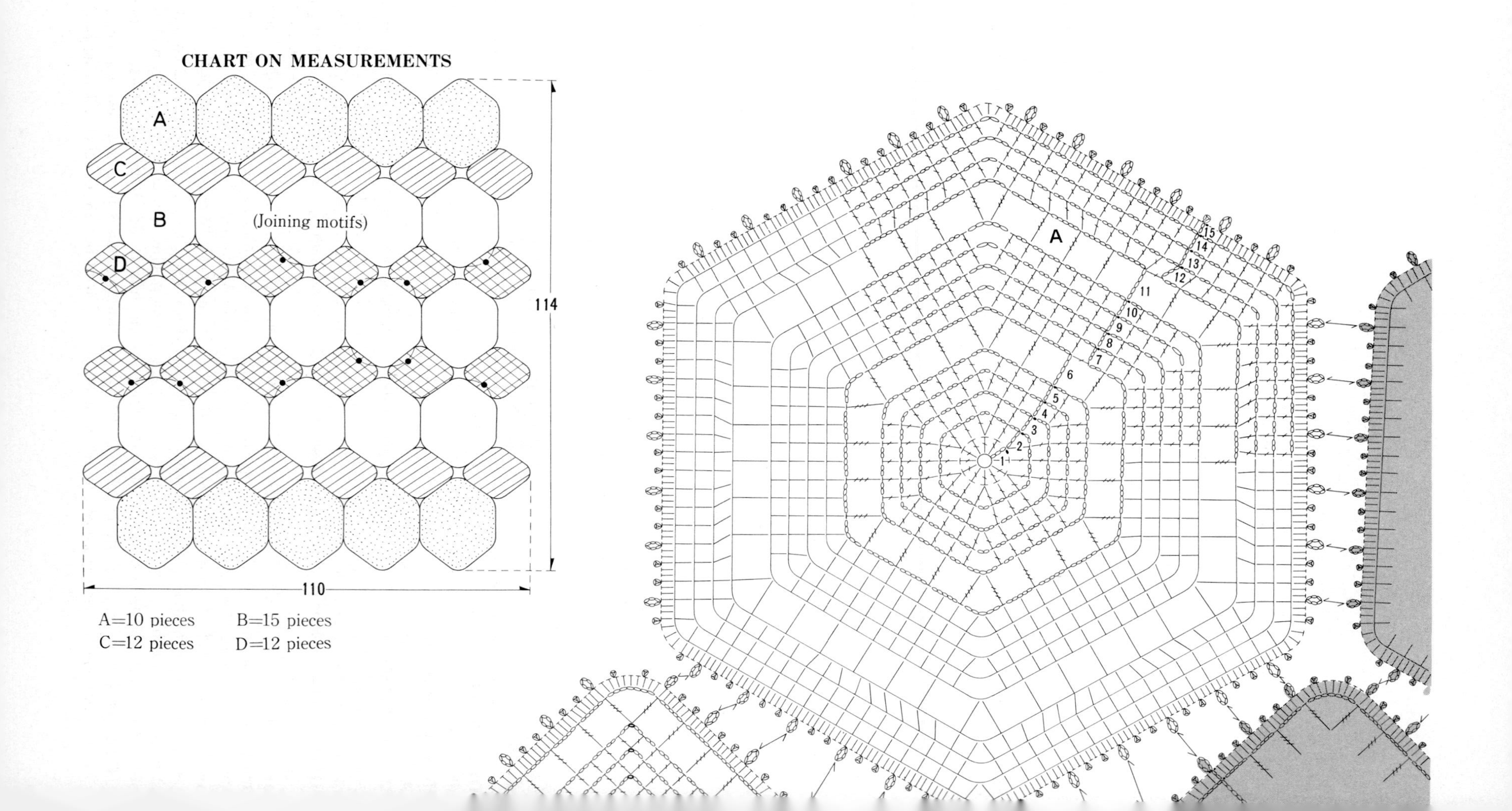

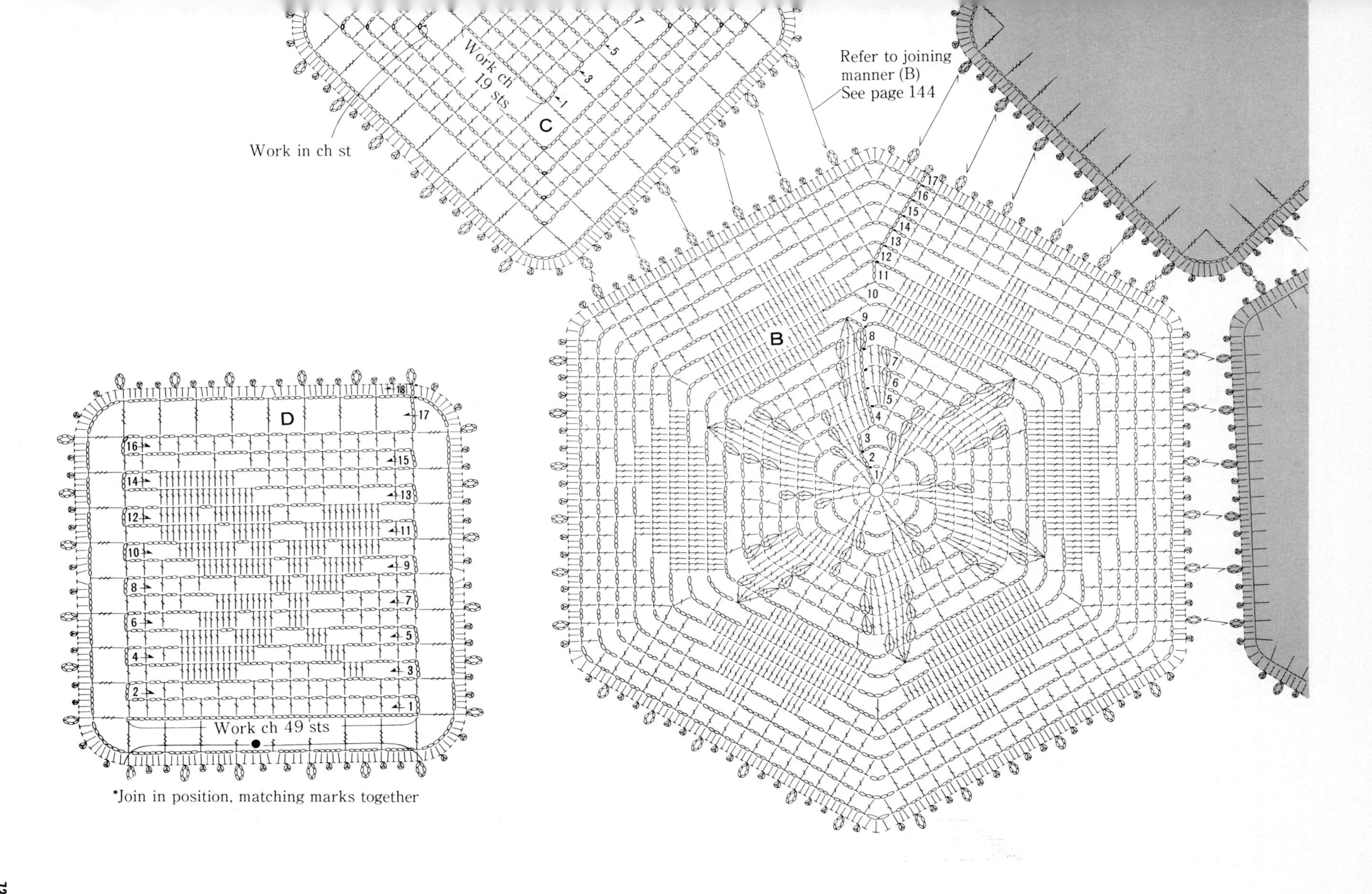
Refer to joining
manner (B)
See page 144
Work ch
19 sts
C
Work in ch st
B
D
Work ch 49 sts
*Join in position, matching marks together

previous one, referring to chart. As for the joining manner, see "sl-st joining" (b).

MOTIF B: Make a loop at thread end. **Row 1:** Ch 3, 1 dc in lp, (ch 1, 2 dc in lp) 5 times, ch 1, sl st in 3rd st of beg ch.

Row 2: Ch 3, dc in 3rd st of beg ch previous row, (dc in dc, ch 5, sk 1 ch, 2 dc in dc) 5 times, dc in dc, ch 5, sk 1 ch, sl st in 3rd st of beg ch.

Row 3: Ch 3, dc in 3rd st of beg ch previous row. Dc 2 in 2 dc, 3-dc pop in next dc, (ch 5, sk 5 ch, 2 dc in dc, 2 dc in next dc, 3-dc pop in next dc) 5 times. Ch 2, dc in 3rd st of beg ch.

Row 4: Ch 3, 2 dc in cross side of dc, dc in 3rd st of beg ch previous row. 1 dc each in 2 sts, 3-dc pop in dc, ch 2, sk 1 pop, dc in 5-ch lp, ch 2, 3 dc in same lp. 1 dc each in 3 dc, 3-dc pop in next dc. Work in same manner around, sl st in 3rd st of beg ch.

Row 5: Ch 3, 1 dc each in 5 dc, 3-dc pop in pop. Ch 2, sk 2 ch, dc in dc. Ch 2, 3 dc in 2 ch, 1 dc each in 6 dc, 3-dc pop in pop. Continue in same manner, end sl st in 3rd st of beg ch.

Row 6: Ch 3, 1 dc each in 2 dc, 3-dc pop in next dc. Ch 2, sk 1 dc, dc in dc. Ch 2, sk 1 pop, dc in dc. Ch 2, sk 2 ch, 3-dc pop in dc. 1 dc each in 5 dc, 3-dc pop in next dc, ch 2, sk 1 dc, dc in dc. Work in same manner around, sl st in 3rd st of beg ch.

Row 7: Ch 3, 1 dc each in 2 dc, 3-dc pop in pop, (ch 2, sk 2 ch, dc in dc) 3 times. Ch 2, sk 1 ch, dc in next ch. Ch 2, 3-dc pop in pop, 1 dc each in 5 dc, 3-dc pop in pop. Work in same manner around, sl st in 3rd st of beg ch.

Row 8: Ch 3, 2 dc in 3rd st of beg ch previous row, draw through 3 sts at a time to form 1 pop. 1 dc each in 2 dc, 3-dc pop in pop. Ch 5, sk 2 ch, dc in dc. Ch 5, sk 2 ch, 1 dc, 2 ch, dc in dc. Ch 5, sk 2 ch, 1 dc, 1 ch, dc in next ch. Ch 5, sk 1 pop, 2 dc, 3-dc pop in next dc. 1 dc each in 2 dc, 3-dc pop in pop. Ch 5, sk 2 ch, dc in dc. Work in same manner around, sl st in 3rd st of beg ch.

Row 9: Ch 3, 3 dc at a time in 2 dc and pop. Ch 5, 3 dc in 5 ch, dc in dc, (5 dc in 5 ch, dc in dc) 2 times. 3 dc in 5 ch, ch 5, 4 dc at a time in 1 pop, 2 dc, 1 pop. Ch 5, 3 dc in 5 ch. Work in same manner around, 3 dc in last 5 ch, ch 2, dc in 3rd st of beg ch.

Row 10: Ch 8, 3 dc in 5 ch, 1 dc each in 19 dc. Ch 5, dc in 5 ch. Ch 5, sk 4 dc at a time, 3 dc in 5 ch. Work in same manner around, dc in last dc, ch 2, dc in 3rd st of beg ch.

Row 11: Ch 8, 6 dc in 6 ch, 1 dc each in 22 dc. Ch 5, dc in the middle of 5-ch lp, ch 5, dc in dc. Continue in same manner around, sl st in 3rd st of beg ch.

Row 12: Ch 5, dc in 3rd st of beg ch previous row, ch 2, dc in the middle of 5 ch. Ch 5, sk 3 dc, 1 dc each in 22 dc. Ch 5, sk 3 dc, dc in the middle of 5 ch. Ch 2, dc in corner dc, ch 2, dc in same corner dc. Ch 2, dc in the middle of 5 ch. Continue in same manner, sl st in 3rd st of beg ch.

Row 13: Ch 8, sk 2 ch, dc in dc. Ch 2, sk 2 ch, dc in dc. Ch 2, dc in the middle of 5 ch. Ch 5, sk 3 dc, 1 dc each in 7 dc. Ch 5, sk 5 dc, 1 dc each in 4 dc. Ch 5, sk 3 dc, dc in the middle of 5 ch. Ch 5, sk 1 dc, 2 ch, dc in dc. Ch 5, sk 2 ch, dc in dc. Continue in same manner around, sl st in 3rd st of beg ch.

Row 14: Ch 5, dc in 5 ch, ch 2, dc in same 5 ch. Ch 2, dc in dc, (ch 2, sk 2 ch, dc in dc) 2 times. Ch 2, dc in the middle of 5 ch. Ch 5, sk 3 dc, 1 dc each in 4 dc. Ch 5, sk 5 ch, dc in dc. Ch 5, sk 3 dc, dc in the middle of 5 ch. Ch 2, dc in dc. Ch 2, dc in the middle of 5 ch. Ch 2, dc in dc. Ch 2, dc in 5 ch, ch 2, dc in same 5 ch. Ch 2, dc in dc. Work in same manner around, sl st in 3rd st of beg ch.

Rows 15–16: Work as for rows 13–14.

Row 17: Work as for 15th row of motif A referring to chart.

MOTIF C: Ch 19. **Row 1:** Ch 5, dc in 9th ch from hook, (ch 2, sk 2 ch, dc in next ch) 5 times.

Row 2: Ch 5, sk 2 ch, dc in dc, (ch 2, sk 2 ch, dc in dc) 5 times.

Rows 3–6: Work as for row 2.

Row 7: Ch 10, sk 2 ch, 1 dc, 2 ch, dtr in dc. Ch 5, sk 2 ch, 1 dc, 2 ch, dtr in dc. Ch 5, sk 2 ch, 1 dc, 2 ch, dtr in next ch. Ch 11, dtr in same ch. Ch 5, sk 2 ch, 1 row of dc, dtr in ch. Continue in same manner around, sl st in 5th st of beg ch.

Row 8: Ch 5, dc in the middle of 5 ch, ch 2, dc in dtr, (ch 2, dc in the middle of 5 ch, ch 2, dc in dtr) 2 times. Ch 2, sk 2 ch, dc in next st, ch 2, sk 2 ch, dc in corner ch, ch 5, dc in same ch. Work in same manner around, sl st in 3rd st of beg ch.

Rows 9–10: Work as for row 8.

Row 11: Ch 10, sk 2 ch, 1 dc, 2 ch, dtr in dc, (ch 5, sk 2 ch, 1 dc, 2 ch, dtr in dc) 3 times. Ch 5, sk 2 ch, 1 dc, 2 ch, dtr in corner ch, ch 7, dtr in same corner ch. Work in same manner around, sl st in 5th st of beg ch.

Row 12: Work as for 15th row of motif A referring to chart.

MOTIF D: Ch 49. **Row 1:** Ch 5, dc in 9th ch from hook, (ch 2, sk 2 ch, dc in next ch) 15 times.

Row 2: Ch 5, sk 2 ch, dc in dc, (ch 2, sk 2 sts, dc in dc) 2 times. (ch 5, sk 2 ch, 1 dc, 2 ch, dc in dc) 2 times, (ch 2, sk 2 ch, dc in dc) 5 times. Ch 5, sk 2 ch, 1 dc, 2 ch, dc in dc. Ch 2, sk 2 ch, dc in dc. Ch 2, sk 2 ch, dc in next ch.

Row 3: Ch 5, sk 2 ch, dc in dc. Ch 5, sk 2 ch, 1 dc, 2 ch, dc 3 in 3 ch. Dc in dc, ch 5, sk 2 ch, 1 dc, 2 ch, dc in dc, (ch 2, sk 2 ch, dc in dc) 2 times. Ch 5, sk 2 ch, 1 dc, 2 ch, dc 3 in 3 ch. Dc in dc, dc 5 in 5 ch, dc in dc. Ch 5, sk 2 ch, 1 dc, 2 ch, dc in dc. Ch 2, sk 2 ch, dc in next ch.

Rows 4–16: Work as for rows 2–3.

Row 17: Work as for row 11 of motif C.

Row 18: Work as for 15th row of motif A referring to chart.

22 LUNCHEON MAT

YOU'LL NEED (for each): Crochet cotton No. 20 2 20-gram balls White. Steel crochet hook size 0.90.
FINISHED SIZE: 44 cm by 29 cm
GAUGE: 9 cm of filet crochet=17 squares; 10 cm =17.5 rows.
SIZE OF MOTIF: Refer to chart.
MAKING INSTRUCTIONS:
MOTIF A: Ch 52. **Row 1:** Ch 5, dc in 9th ch from hook, (ch 2, sk 2 ch, dc in next ch) 16 times.
Row 2: Ch 5, sk 2 ch, dc in dc, (ch 2, sk 2 ch, dc in dc) 3 times. Ch 5, sk 2 ch, 1 dc, 2 ch, dc in dc, (ch 2, sk 2 ch, dc in dc) 5 times. Ch 5, sk 2 ch, 1 dc, 2 ch, dc in dc, (ch 2, sk 2 ch, dc in dc) 3 times. Ch 2, sk 2 ch, dc in next ch.
Row 3: Ch 5, sk 2 ch, dc in dc. Ch 2, sk 2 ch, dc in dc. Ch 5, sk 2 ch, 1 dc, 2 ch, dc in dc. Dc 5 in 5 ch, dc in dc. Ch 5, sk 2 ch, 1 dc, 2 ch, dc in dc. Ch 2, sk 2 ch, dc in dc. Ch 5, sk 2 ch, 1 dc, 2 ch, dc in dc. Dc 5 in 5 ch, dc in dc. Ch 5, sk 2 ch, 1 dc, 2 ch, dc in dc. Ch 2, sk 2 sts, dc in dc. Ch 2, sk 2 ch, dc in dc.
Rows 4–7: Work as for row 3.
Row 8: Having worked up to 7th square in same manner as for previous rows, ch 4, sk 4 dc, dc in next dc, ch 4, sk 3 dc, dc in next dc. Continue in same manner.
Row 9: Work up to 7th square referring to chart, ch 2, sk 4 ch, work 1 tr, 3 dc, 1 tr in same dc. Ch 2, sk 4 ch, dc in dc. Continue.
Row 10: Work up to 7th square, ch 4, sk 2 ch, 1 tr, 1 dc, dc in next dc. Ch 4, sk 1 dc, 1 tr, 2 ch, dc in dc. Continue.
Rows 11–47: Work as for rows up to 10. Make 2 pieces.
MOTIF B: Ch 22. **Row 1:** Ch 5, dc in 9th ch from hook, (ch 2, sk 2 ch, dc in next ch) 6 times.
Row 2: Ch 5, sk 2 ch, dc in dc, (ch 2, sk 2 ch, dc in dc) 5 times. Ch 2, sk 2 ch, dc in next ch.
Rows 3–47: Work as for row 2. Make 2 pieces.
MOTIF C: Ch 52. **Rows 1–47:** Work as for motif A. Work pattern in referring to chart. Make 1 piece.
EDGING: Ch 3 following to row 47, dc in cross side of dc, 4-ch p, dc 2 in same dc, *sk 1 row, dc 2 in cross side of dc, 4-ch p, dc 2 in same dc, repeat from* up to 1 sp this side of the corner. Work 2 dc, 4-ch p, 3 dc, 4-ch p, 2 dc at corner sp. Sk 1 sp, 2 dc in next sp, 4-ch p, 2 dc in same sp. Repeat in same manner around, sl st in 3rd st of beg ch. From 2nd piece, work joining to previous motif (refer to "sl-st joining" B. See page 144)

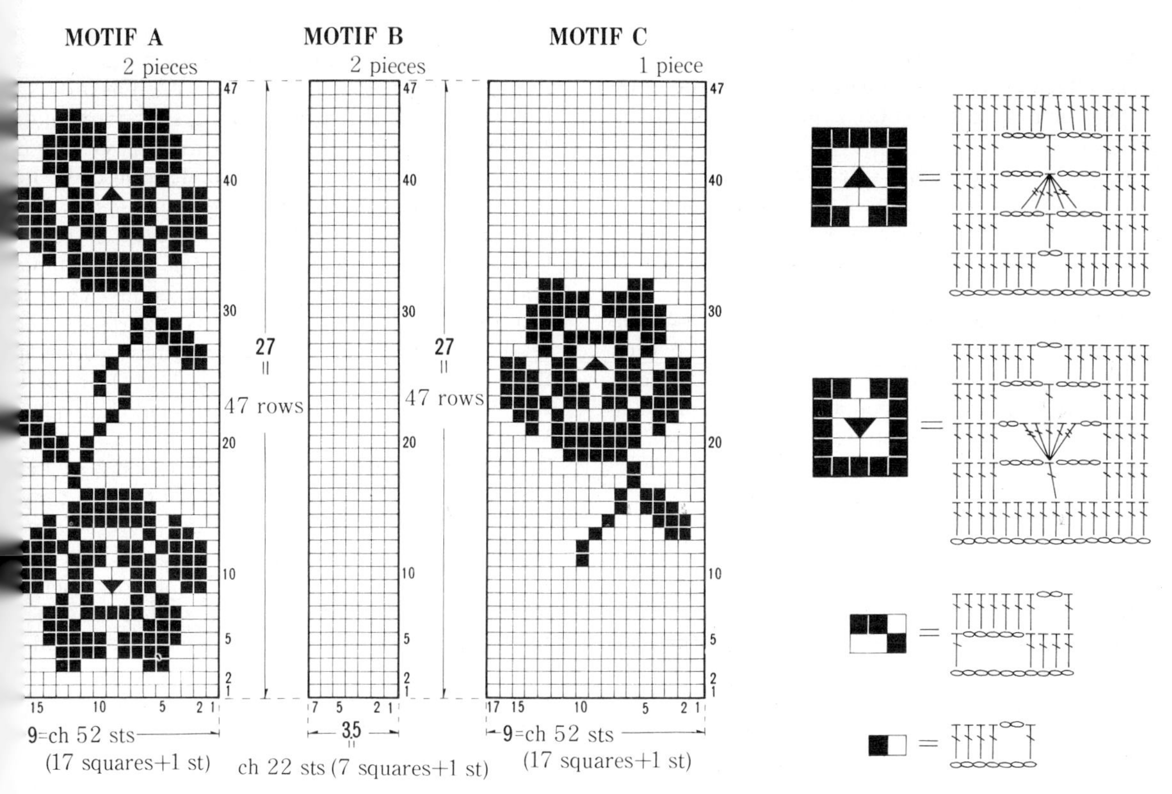

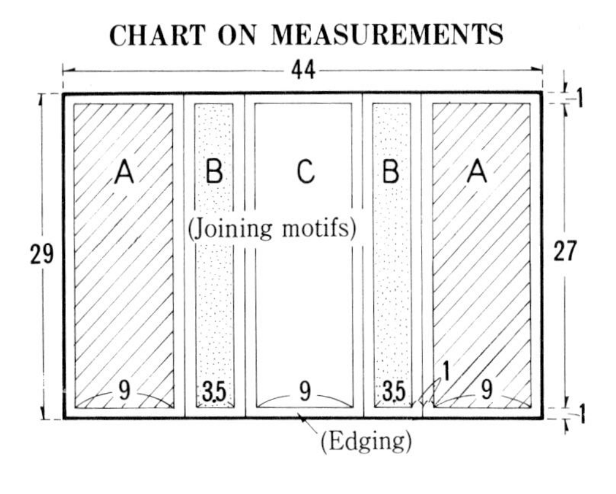

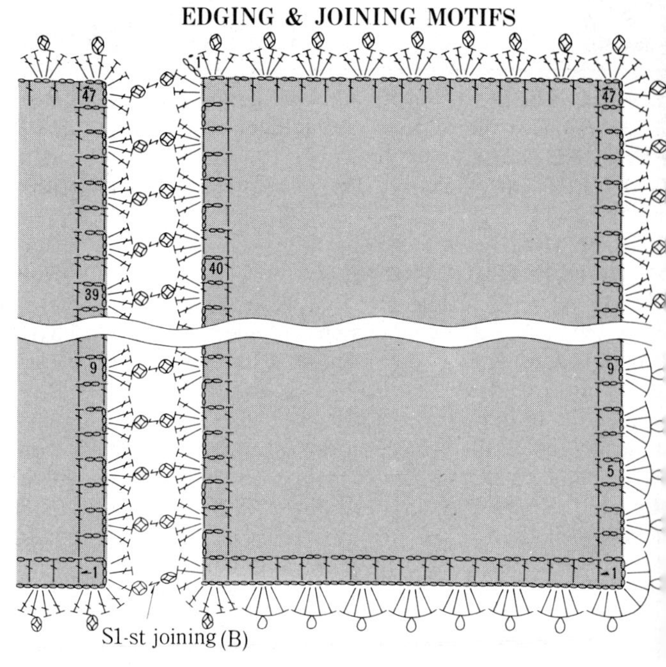

25 RUNNER

YOU'LL NEED: Crochet cotton No. 20 White 8 20-gram balls for table center, 1½ 20-gram balls for piece mat. Steel crochet hook size 0.90.

FINISHED SIZE: Table center, 86 cm by 41 cm; Piece mat, 23 cm square

GAUGE: 1 row of dc=0.5 cm

SIZE OF MOTIF: 9 cm square

MAKING INSTRUCTIONS:

Make a loop at thread end. **Row 1:** Ch 3, 4 dc in lp, (ch 3, 5 dc in lp) 3 times. Ch 1, hdc in 3rd st of beg ch.

Row 2: Ch 3, 2 dc in cross side of hdc. Ch 2, sk 1 ch, 1 dc, dc in next dc. Ch 2, sk 2 dc, 3 dc in corner lp, ch 3, 3 dc in same corner lp. Ch 2, sk 2 dc, dc in next dc. Continue in same manner around, ch 1, hdc in 3rd st of beg ch.

Row 3: Ch 3, 2 dc in cross side of hdc, ch 2, sk 1 ch, 1 dc, dc in next dc. Ch 1, sk 2 ch, dc in dc, ch 1, dc in same dc. Ch 1, sk 2 ch, dc in dc. Ch 2, sk 2 dc, 3 dc in corner lp, ch 3, 3 dc in same corner lp. Ch 2, sk 2 dc, dc in next dc. Continue in same manner. Ch 1, hdc in 3rd st of beg ch.

Row 4: Ch 3, 2 dc in cross side of hdc. Ch 2, sk 1 ch, 1 dc, dc in dc. Ch 2, sk 2 ch, dc in dc. Sk 1 ch, dc in dc, 3 dc in 1 ch, dc in dc. Sk 1 ch, dc in dc. Ch 2, sk 2 ch, dc in dc. Ch 2, sk 2 dc, 3 dc in corner lp, ch 3, 3 dc in same corner lp. Ch 2, sk 2 dc, dc in dc. Work in same manner around, ch 1, hdc in 3rd st of beg ch.

Row 5: Ch 3, 2 dc in cross side of hdc. Ch 2, sk 1 ch, 1 dc, dc in dc. Ch 2, sk 2 ch, dc in dc. Ch 2, sk 2 ch, 1 dc, 1 dc each in next 2 dc. Dc in next dc, ch 1, dc in same dc. 1 dc each in next 2 dc. Ch 2, sk 1 dc, 2 ch, dc in dc. Ch 2, sk 2 ch, dc in dc. Ch 2, sk 2 dc, 3 dc in corner lp, ch 3, 3 dc in same corner lp. Ch 2, sk 2 dc, dc in next dc. Continue in same manner around, ch 1, hdc in 3rd st of beg ch.

Row 6: Ch 3, 2 dc in cross side of hdc. Ch 2, sk 1 ch, 1 dc, dc in dc, (ch 2, sk 2 ch, dc in dc) 2 times. Sk 1 ch, dc in dc, ch 1, dc in dc. Ch 1, sk 1 dc, dc in ch, ch 1, dc in same ch. Ch 1, sk 1 dc, dc in next dc. Ch 1, dc in dc, sk 2 ch, dc in dc, (ch 2, sk 2 ch, dc in dc) 2 times. Ch 2, sk 2 dc, 3 dc in corner lp, ch 4, 3 dc in same corner lp. Ch 2, sk 2 dc, dc in next dc. Repeat around, ch 2, hdc in 3rd st of beg ch.

Row 7: Ch 3, 3 dc in cross side of hdc. Ch 2, sk 1 ch, 1 dc, dc in next dc, (ch 2, sk 2 ch, dc in dc) 2 times. Ch 1, sk 2 ch, 1 dc each in 6 sts. 3 dc in 1 ch, 1 dc each in 6 sts. Ch 1, sk 2 ch, dc in dc, (ch 2, sk 2 ch, dc in dc) 2 times. Ch 2, sk 2 dc, 4 dc in corner lp, ch 5, 4 dc in same corner lp. Ch 2, sk 2 dc, dc in next dc. Repeat in same manner around, ch 2, hdc in 3rd st of beg ch.

Row 8: Ch 3, 4 dc in cross side of hdc. Ch 2, sk 1 ch, 2 dc, dc in next dc, (ch 2, sk 2 ch, dc in dc) 3 times. Sk 1 ch, 3 dc at a time in next 3 dc, (ch 3, 3 dc at a time in 3 dc) 4 times. Sk 1 ch, dc in dc, (ch 2, sk 2 ch, dc in dc) 3 times. Ch 2, sk 3 dc, 5 dc in corner lp, ch 5, 5 dc in same corner lp. Ch 2, sk 3 dc, dc in next dc. Continue in same manner around, sl st in 3rd of beg ch.

Row 9: Sl st in dc, ch 1, sc in next dc. Ch 3, sk 2 dc, sc in the middle of 2 ch, (ch 3, sc in the middle of

2 ch) 3 times, (ch 3, sc in the middle of 3 ch) 4 times, (ch 3, sc in the middle of 2 ch) 4 times. Ch 3, sk 2 dc, sc in next dc. Ch 3, sk 2 dc, sc in corner lp, ch 5, sc in same corner lp. Ch 3, sk 2 dc, sc in next dc. Work in same manner around, sl st in 1st sc. From 2nd piece, work row 9 joining to adjacent motifs. Work ch 2, sl st in the middle of corner lp of adjacent motif, ch 2, 1 sc at every corner, ch 1, sl st in the middle of 3-ch lp of adjacent motif, ch 1, 1 sc along the side. Join motifs 36 pieces for table center, 4 pieces for piece mat as shown, work edging along.

CHART ON MEASUREMENTS

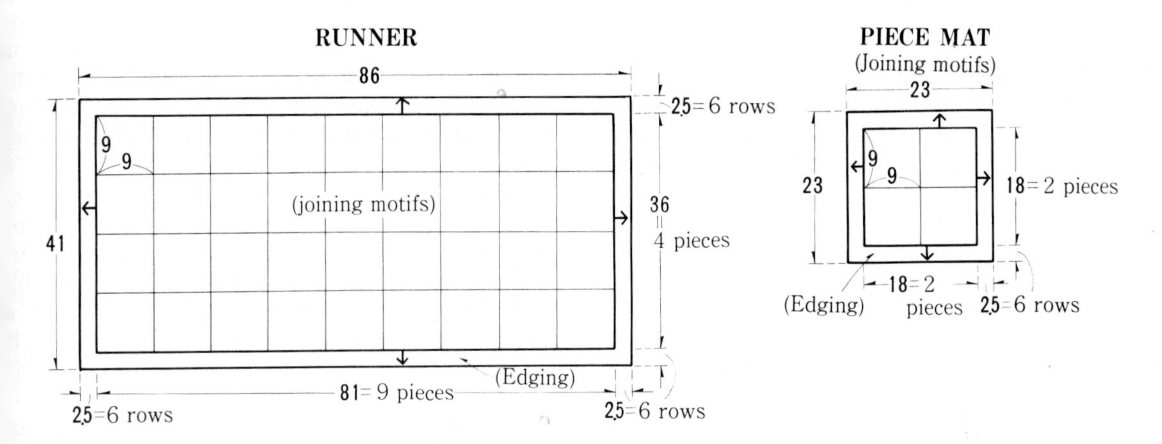

MOTIF & THE WAY OF JOINING, EDGING

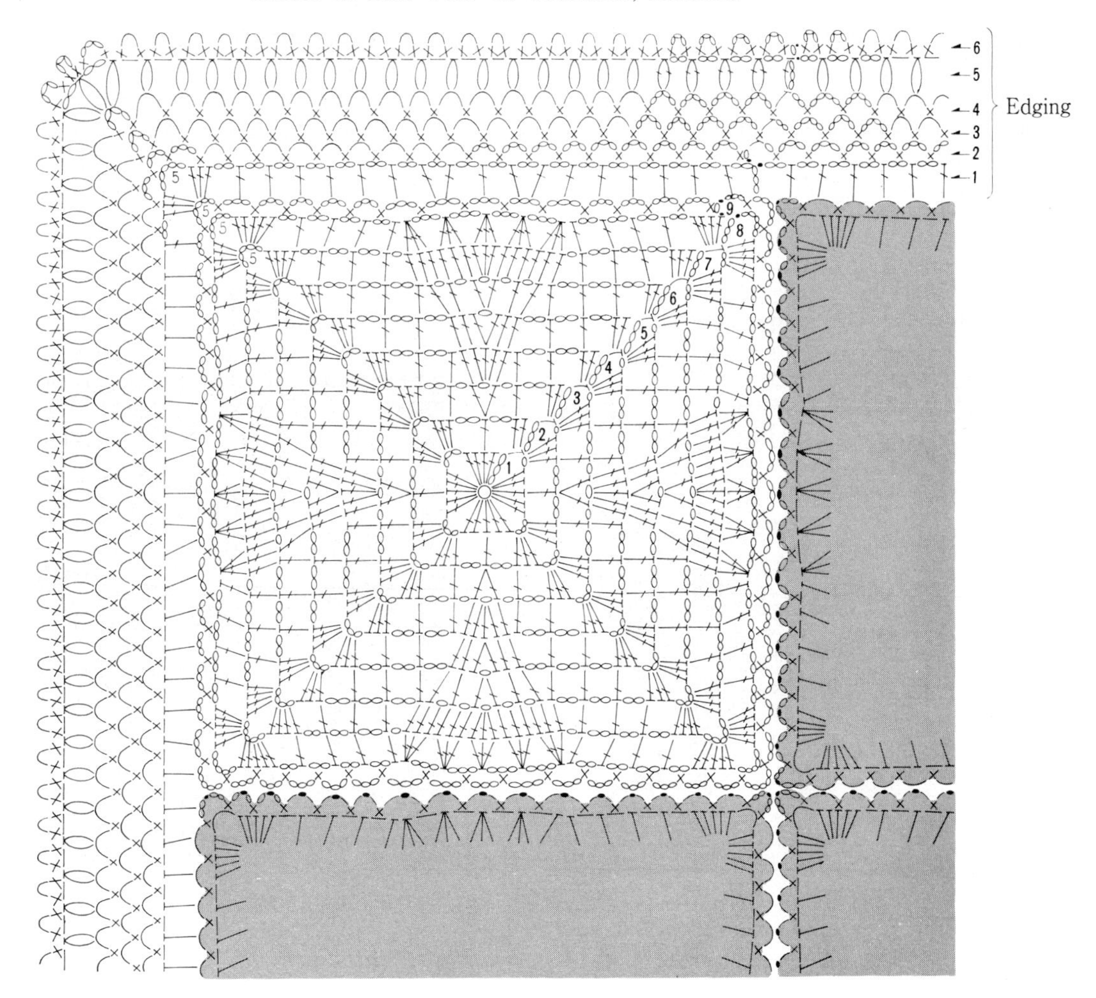

23 CUSHION

YOU'LL NEED: Crochet cotton No. 20 7 20-gram balls White. Steel crochet hook size 0.90. Satin for inner case 92 cm by 47 cm Pink. Kapok 450 gram.
FINISHED SIZE: 45 cm square
GAUGE: 10 cm of filet crochet= 19 squares; 10 cm =21 rows.
SIZE OF MOTIF: 20.5 cm square
MAKING INSTRUCTIONS:
MOTIF A: Ch 106. **Row 1:** Ch 5, dc in 9th ch from hook, (ch 2, sk 2 ch, dc in next ch) 34 times.
Row 2: Ch 5, sk 2 sts, dc in dc, (ch 2, sk 2 ch, dc in dc) 33 times. End ch2, dc in next ch.
Row 3: Ch 5, sk 2 ch, dc in dc, (ch 2, sk 2 ch, dc in dc) 2 times. (2 dc in 2 ch, dc in dc) 4 times. Ch 2, sk 2 ch, dc in dc, (2 dc in 2 ch, dc in dc) 4 times. Continue in same manner.
Rows 4–39: Work as for row 3 referring to chart.
MOTIF B: Ch 106. **Row 1:** Ch 3, dc in each st across.
Row 2: Ch 3, dc in dc 6 times, (ch 2, sk 2 dc, dc in dc) 3 times, dc in each st across.
Rows 3–39: Work referring to chart (1 sp=ch 2, sk 2 sts, dc in next st; 1 bl=dc in 3 sts).
EDGING FOR MOTIF: Row 1: Work 1 ch in last dc of row 39, 3 sc in cross side of dc, *2 sc in 3-ch row, 3 sc in dc-row, repeat from *to corner. Having worked 2 sc in last dc-row, sc in corner st. Sc in each st cross side. Continue in same manner around, sl st in 1st sc.
Row 2: Sl st in 3 sts, ch 3, dc in same sc, ch 3, 2 dc in same sc as before. Sk 3 sc, 2 dc in next sc, ch 3, 2 dc. Sk 4 sc, 2 dc in next sc, ch 3, 2 dc. Sk 3 sc, 2 dc in next sc, ch 3, 2 dc. Repeat in same manner up to corner, 2 dc in corner sc, ch 5, 2 dc. *Sk 3 sc, 2 dc in next sc, ch 3, 2 dc. Sk 4 sc, 2 dc, ch 3, 2 dc. Sk 4 sc 2 dc, ch 3, 2 dc, repeat from * cross side. Repeat in same manner all around, sl st in 3rd st of beg ch. From 2nd piece, *2 dc in sc, ch 1, sc in the middle of 3-ch lp 2nd row of edging previous motif, ch 1, 2 dc in same lp as before, repeat from * across, working ch 2, sc in corner lp of previous motif, ch 2 at corners.
EDGING: Row 1: Having joined 4 pieces together ch in the middle of 3-ch p of edging, sc in same lp. *ch 4, sc in next 3-ch lp, repeat from * across, sc in corner lp, ch 5, sc in same lp. Ch 4, sc in the middle of 3-ch p following. Continue in same manner around, sl st in 1st sc. **Row 2:** Sl st, ch 1, 5 sc in 4-ch lp, sk 1 sc, 5 sc in next 4-ch lp. Repeat in same manner around, working 7 sc in each corner lp, end sl st in 1st sc. **Row 3:** Sl st 3, ch 5, sk 2 sc, dc in next sc *ch 2, sk 2 sc, dc in next sc, repeat from * across. Dc in corner sc, ch 2, dc in same sc, ch 2, dc in same sc as before. *Ch 2, sk 2 sc, dc in next sc, repeat from * to next corner. Work in same manner around, end sl st 3rd st of beg ch. **Row 4:** Ch 5, sk 2 ch, dc in dc *ch 2, sk 2 sts, dc in dc, repeat from *around, sl st in 3rd st of beg ch. **Row 5:** Work as for row 4. End front side.
BACK: Continued from front. **Rows 1–2:** Work as for row 4 of front.

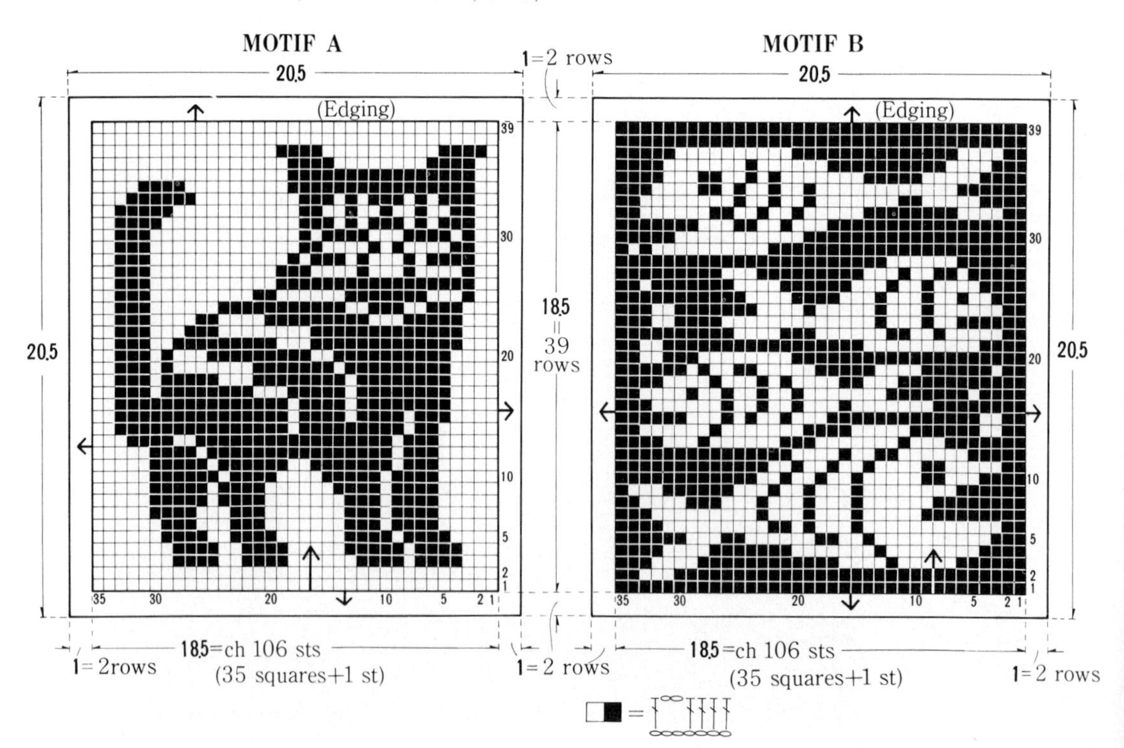

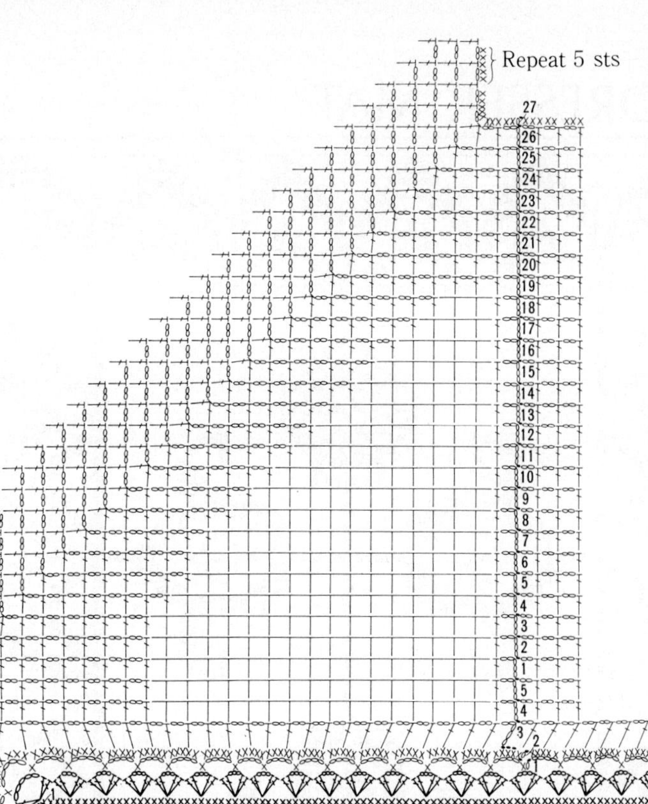

Row 3: Ch 5, sk 2 ch, dc in dc. *ch 2, sk 2 ch, dc in dc, repeat from* across to 2 sps this side of the corner. Ch 2, work 2 dc at a time in both sides of "2 ch, 1 dc, 2 ch" *ch 2, sk 2 ch, dc in dc, repeat from* up to 2 sps this side of corner. Continue in same manner around, sl st in 3rd st of beg ch.
Row 4: Ch 5, work following as for row 3. Work 2 dc at a time in both sides of "2 ch, st of 2 dc at a time, 2 ch" at every corner. End sl st in 3rd st of beg ch.
Rows 5–26: Work as for row 4.
Row 27: Ch 1, dc 2 in 2 ch, dc in dc. Sc 2 in 2 ch, sk corner dc, *sc 2 in 2 ch, dc in dc. Sc 2 in 2 ch, sk next dc, repeat from* around, sl st in 1st sc. End off. Complete, putting over the kapok cased in.

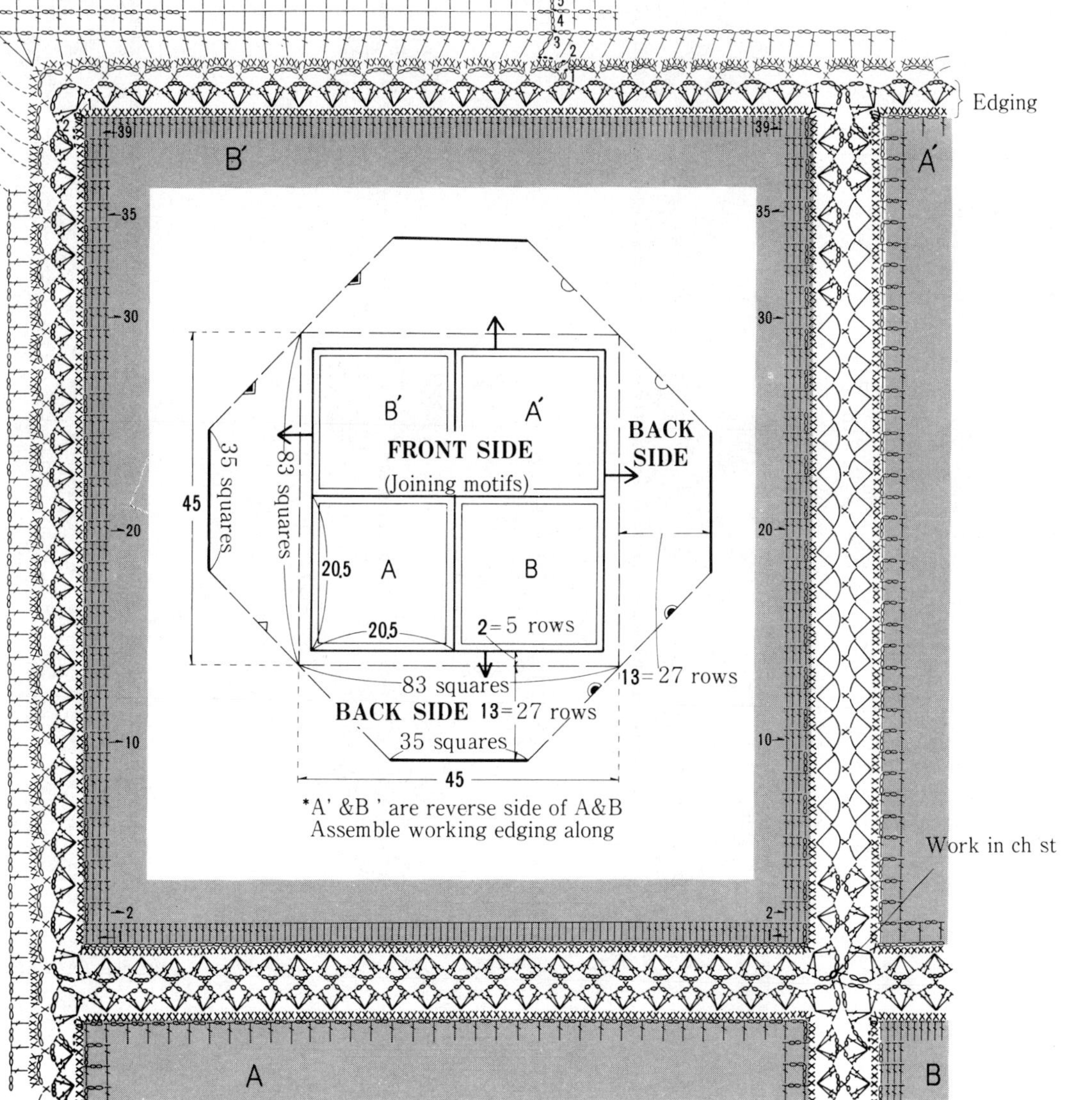

34 DRESSER MAT

YOU'LL NEED: Crochet cotton No. 20 5 20-gram balls White. Steel crochet hook size 0.90.

FINISHED SIZE: 58 cm by 32 cm

GAUGE: 10 cm of filet crochet = 23 squares; 10 cm = 25 rows.

MAKING INSTRUCTIONS:

Ch 220. **Row 1:** Ch 3, 1 dc each in 21 sts, *(ch 2, sk 2 ch, dc in next ch) 11 times, 1 dc each in 3 sts, repeat from *5 times, 1 dc each in 18 sts.

Row 2: Ch 3, 1 dc each in 24 sts, (ch 2, sk 2 sts, dc in dc) 9 times, (2 dc in 2 ch, dc in dc) 3 times. Continue in same manner.

Rows 3–15: Work as for rows 1–2, referring to chart. Work ch 2, sk 2 sts, 1 dc for each sp; 3 dc for each bl.

Row 16: Work up to 15th square in same manner as for rows previous, (ch 3, sk 2 sts, dc in dc, ch 3, sk 2 sts, dc in dc) 5 times. Work next 23 squares same as before, (ch 3, sk 2 sts, sc in dc, ch 3, sk 2 sts, dc in dc) 5 times. Repeat in same manner to end.

Row 17: Work up to 15th square in same manner as before, (ch 5, sk 2 3-ch lps, dc in dc) 5 times. Work next 23 squares same as before, (ch 5, sk 2 3-ch lps, dc in dc) 5 times. Repeat across.

Rows 18–145: Work as for rows 1–17.

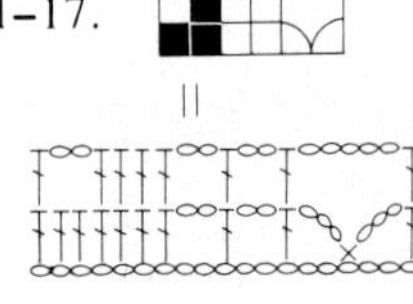

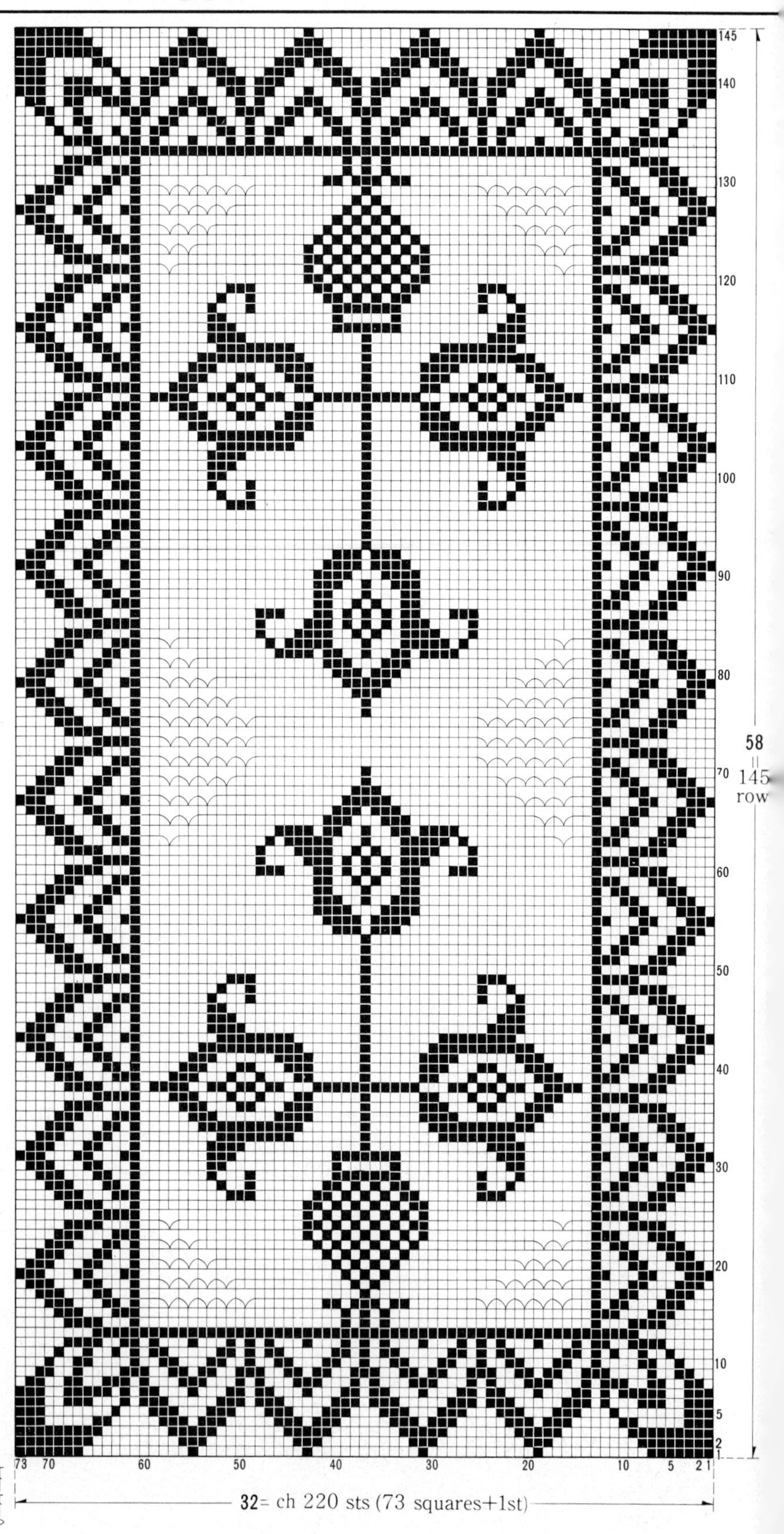

Reminiscence of Roses

37 Dresser Mat

Instructions on page 100.

38 Cushion

Instructions on page 102.

39 Tablerunner

Instructions on page 103.

40 Cushion

Instructions on page 118.

41 Centerpiece

Instructions on page 116.

42 Chair back

Instructions on page 122 .

43 Tablecloth

Instructions on page 119.

44 Runner

Instructions on page 121.

26 CENTERPIECE

YOU'LL NEED: Crochet cotton No. 20 8½ 20-gram balls Beige. Steel crochet hook size 0.90.
FINISHED SIZE: 87.5 cm by 41.5 cm
GAUGE: 10 cm of filet crochet = 18 squares; 10 cm = 16 rows.
SIZE OF MOTIF: 18 cm by 16 cm
MAKING INSTRUCTIONS:
Ch 127. **Row 1:** Ch 5, dc in 9th ch from hook, (ch 2, sk 2 ch, dc in next ch) 41 times.
Row 2: Ch 5, sk 2 ch, dc in dc, (ch 2, sk 2 ch, dc in dc) 15 times. (dc 2 in 2 ch, dc in dc) 4 times, (ch 2, sk 2 ch, dc in dc) 11 times. (dc 2 in 2 ch, dc in dc) 6 times, (ch 2, sk 2 ch, dc in dc) 4 times. End ch 2, sk 2 ch, dc in next ch.
Rows 3–41: Work as for row 2. Make 8 pieces in same manner.
EDGING ①: Join thread in where indicated, ch 3. 3 dc in 2 ch, *sk 1 dc, 2 dc in 2 ch, sk 1 dc, 2 dc in 2 ch, sk 1 dc, 3 dc in 2 ch, repeat from *up to corner. Having worked 3 dc in 2 ch, dc in dc, ch 1, dc in same dc, 3 dc in cross side of dc. 2 dc in 3 ch, 2 dc in cross side of dc. Work in same manner around, sl st in 3rd st of beg ch. Work along each of A and A'.
EDGING ②: Join thread in where indicated, ch 5, sc in dc, *ch 5, sk 3 dc, sc in next dc, repeat from* to corner, skipping 4 dc instead of 3 dc anywhere length side one time, so that sc comes in last dc next to corner ch. Work sc in dc, ch 7, sk 1 ch, sc in dc at every corner. Arrange motifs in position following to stitch directions arrow indicates, join them together working edging ② along.

MOTIF A

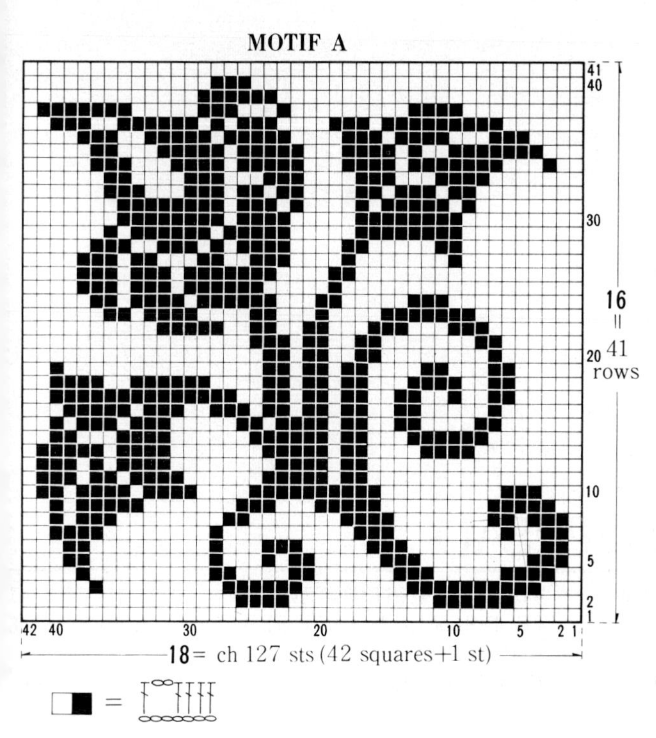

PATTERN CROCHET:
Work pattern crochet 18 rows on top and bottom side of the piece. **Row 1:** Join thread in where indicated, ch 6, sk 1 ch, 1 dc, sc in dc, *ch 3, sk 2 dc, dc in dc. Ch 3, sk 2 dc, sc in dc, repeat from *across. Where at the joint of motifs, work 1 dc in corner ch, ch 3, 1 sc in joining st, ch 3, 1 dc in corner of adjacent motif.
Row 2: Ch 8, sk 2 3-ch lps, dc in dc, *ch 5, sk 2 3-ch lps, dc in dc, repeat from *across.
Row 3: Ch 3, *5 dc in 5 ch, dc in dc, repeat from* across.
Rows 4–18: Repeat rows 1–3.
EDGING ③: Row 1: Continued on 18th row previous, work as for 1st row of pattern crochet. Having worked the last dc top corner, ch 6, sc in the base of dc, ch 3, dc in between the rows next. Continue in same manner around, dc in 3rd st of beg ch.
Row 2: Ch 11, dc in 3rd st of beg ch previous row, work following sts same as for 2nd row of pattern crochet. Having worked last dc of the row, ch 8, dc in the middle of corner lp. Work in same manner around, sl st in 3rd st of beg ch.

CHART ON MEASUREMENTS

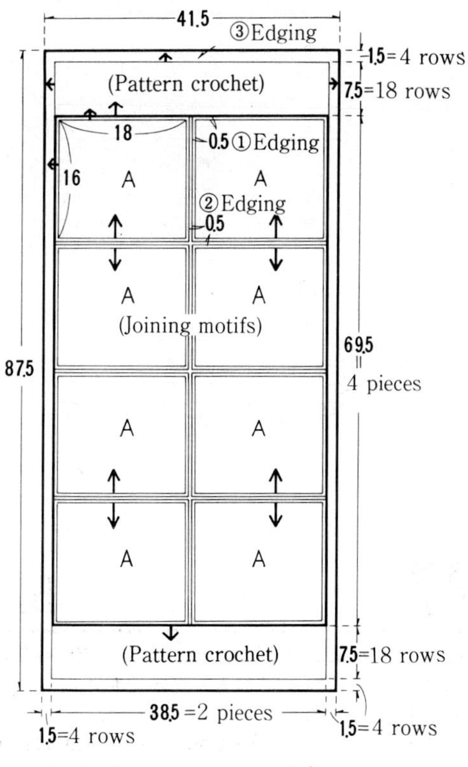

*Motif A' is reverse side of A

Row 3: Ch 3, 3 dc in 8-ch lp, dc in corner ch (3rd ch) of the lp, ch 1, dc in same ch, ch 1, dc in same corner ch, 5 dc in same 8-ch lp. Work following sts as for 3rd row of pattern crochet. Work in same manner around, end sl st in 3rd st of ch.

Row 4: Ch 1, sc in beg ch previous row, 3-ch p. 1 sc each in 6 sts, 3-ch p. 1 sc each in 8 sts, 3-ch p, *1 sc each in 6 dc, 3-ch p, repeat from *around, working 1 sc in corner dc, 3-ch p at every corner. End sl st in 1st sc.

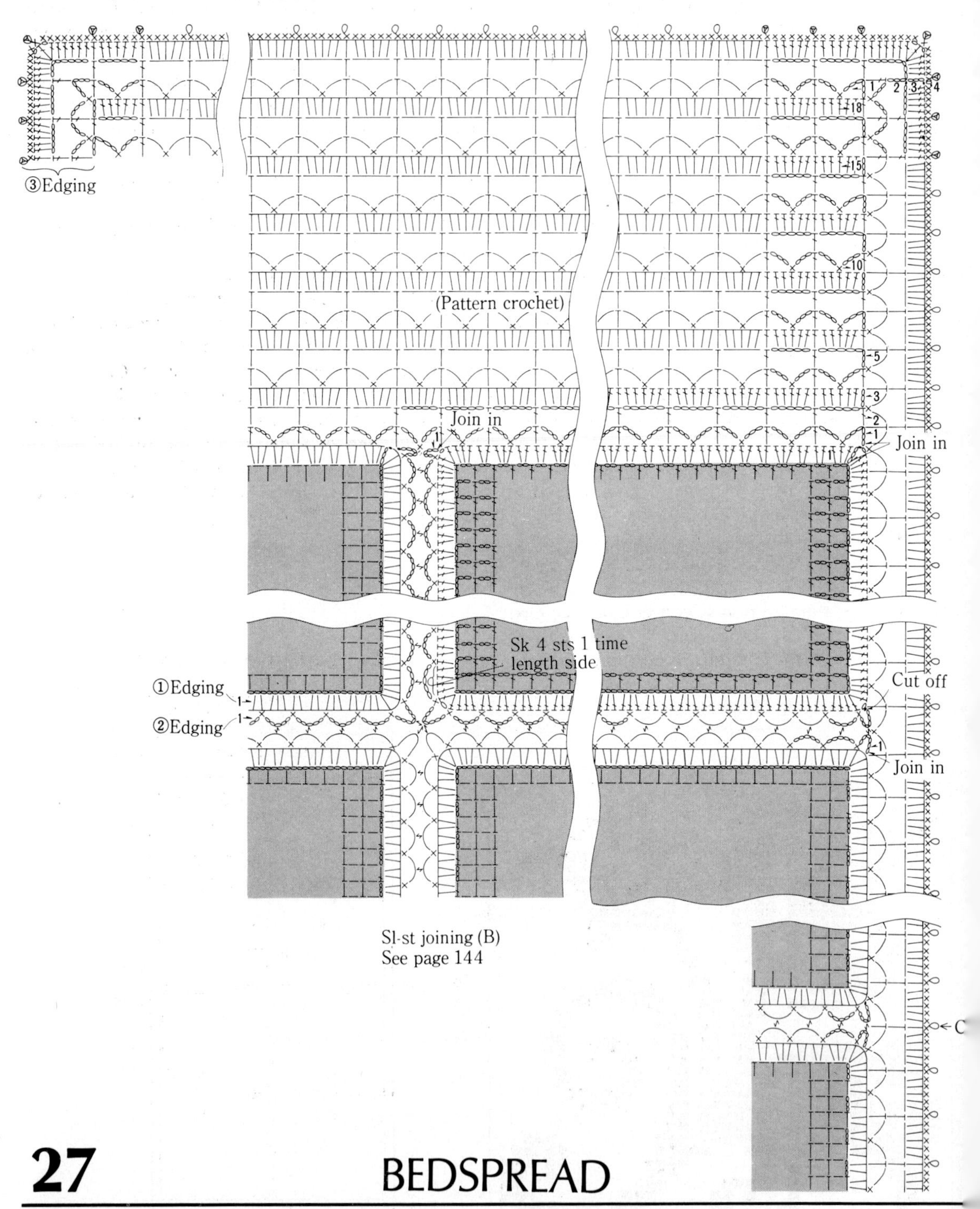

See page 144

27 BEDSPREAD

YOU'LL NEED: Crochet cotton No. 20 96 20-gram balls White. Steel crochet hook size 0.90.
FINISHED SIZE: 310 cm by 166 cm
GAUGE: 10 cm of filet crochet = 19 squares; 10 cm = 21 rows.

MAKING INSTRUCTIONS:
Ch 148. **Row 1:** Ch 3, dc in 5th ch from hook. D in each st across.
Row 2: Ch 3, dc in dc 6 times, (ch 2, sk 2 dc, dc dc, dc in dc 3 times) 23 times, end dc in last 3 dc.

Rows 3–651: Referring to chart, work ch 2, sk 2 sts, dc in next st for each sp, dc in 3 sts for each bl. Make 6 pieces.

JOINING MOTIFS: Join thread in where indicated, ch 1, sc in ch, *ch 7, sk 2 rows, 1 sc, repeat from* up to 650th row, ch 5, sc in corner st. Ch 5, sc in corner st of 651st row of adjacent motif. Ch 2, sl st in the middle of 5-ch lp corresponding, ch 2, sc in top of next row. Ch 3, sl st in the middle of 7-ch lp corresponding, ch 3, 1 sc skipping 2 rows next. Repeat in same manner, end ch 5, sl st in 1st sc. Join 4 pieces remained in same manner.

EDGING: Work edging on both sides. **Row 1:** Join thread in corner of motif, ch 5, dc in between rows next, ch 2, sk 1 row, dc in next. Repeat. **Row 2:** Ch 3, sk 2 ch, dc in dc. Ch 2, sk 2 ch, dc in dc. Repeat. **Row 3:** Ch 3, dc 2 in 2 ch, dc in dc, *ch 2, sk 2 ch, dc in dc. Dc 2 in 2 ch, dc in dc, repeat from *across. **Row 4:** Ch 3, 1 dc each in 6 sts. Work following as for row 3, ending 1 dc each in 7 sts. **Row 5:** Work as for row 3.

CHART ON MEASUREMENTS

166
(Joining motifs)
310
26
1
1
1
1
1
161
2.5=5 rows
2.5=5 rows

JOINING MOTIFS & EDGING

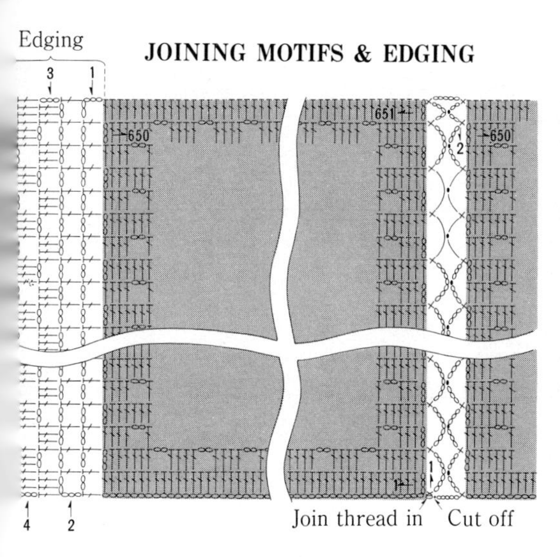

MOTIF

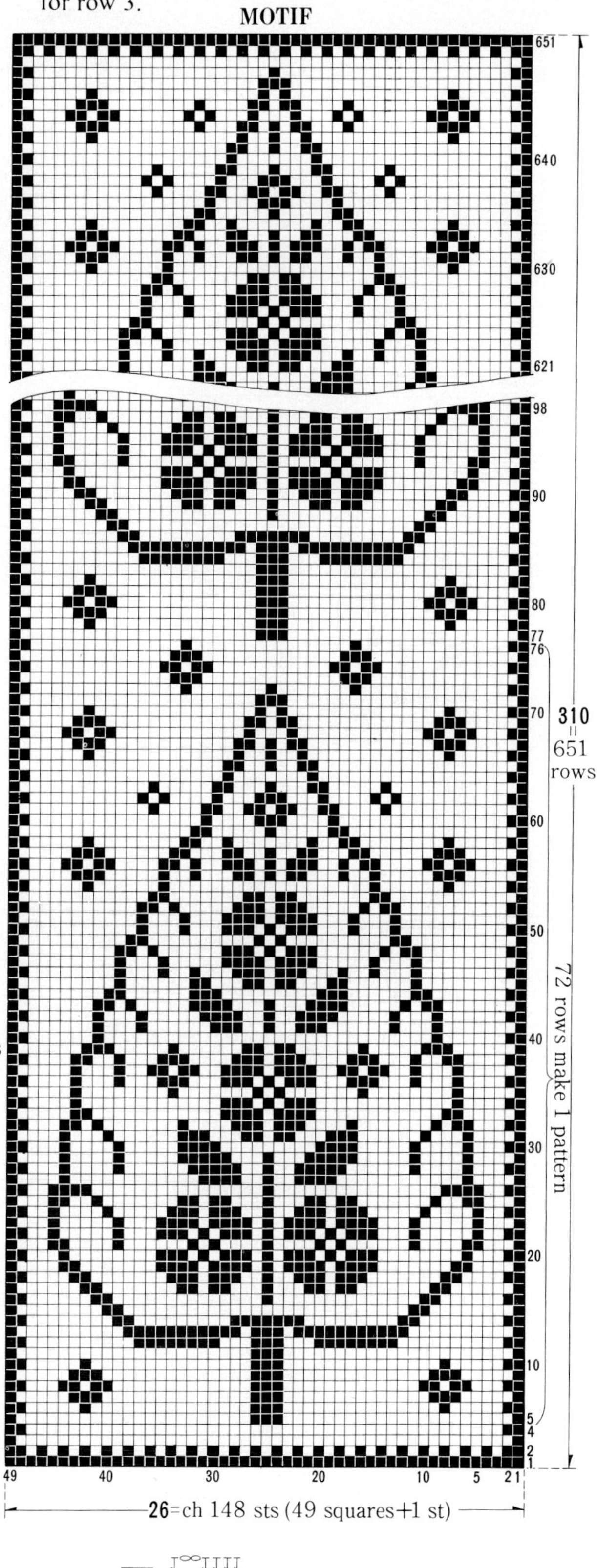

24 CHAIR BACK

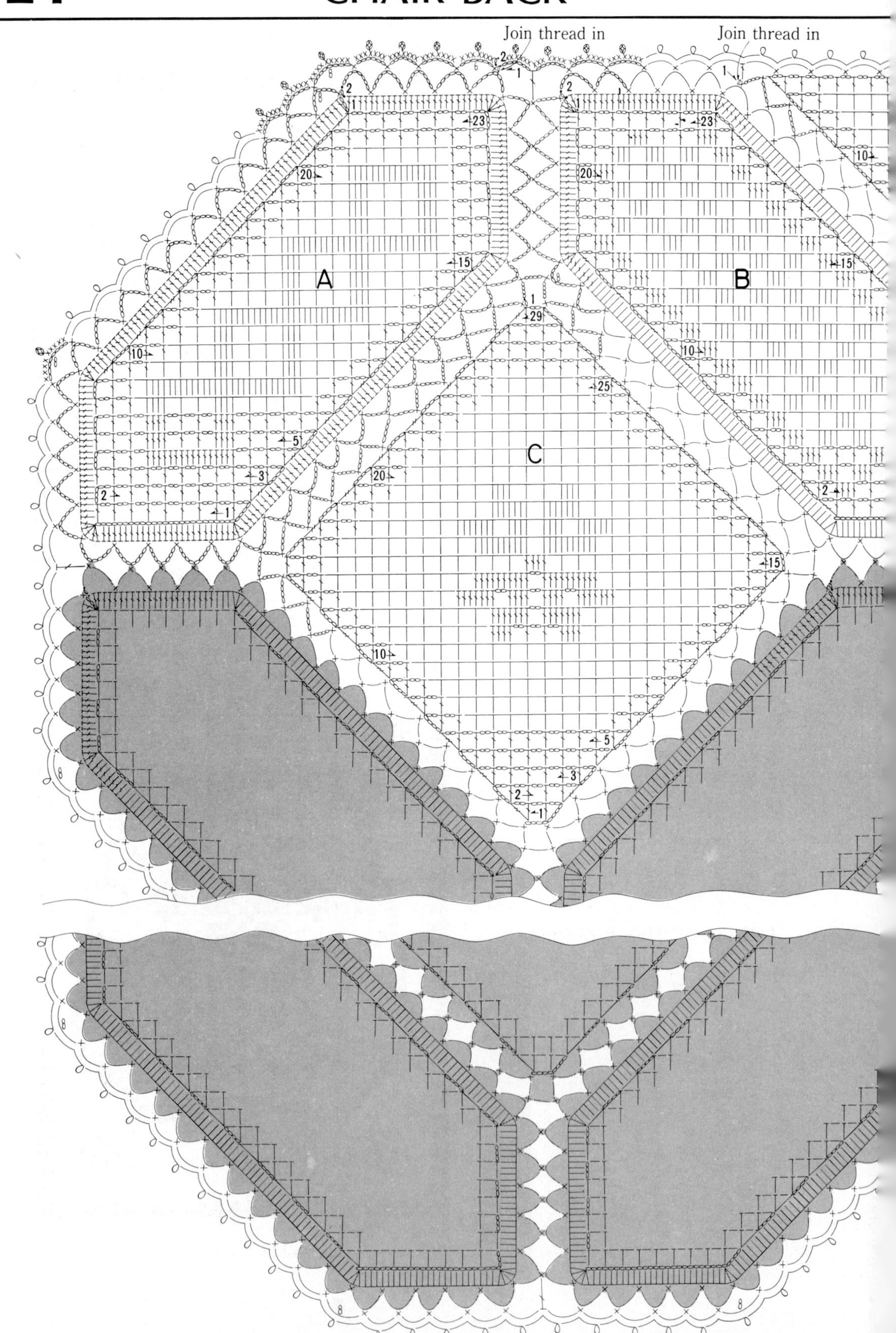

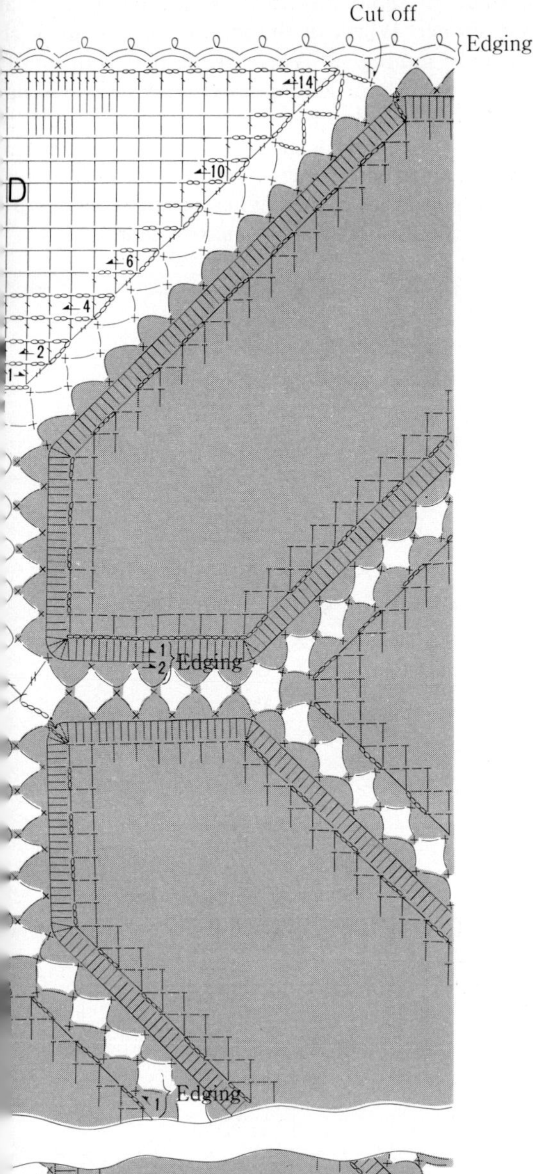

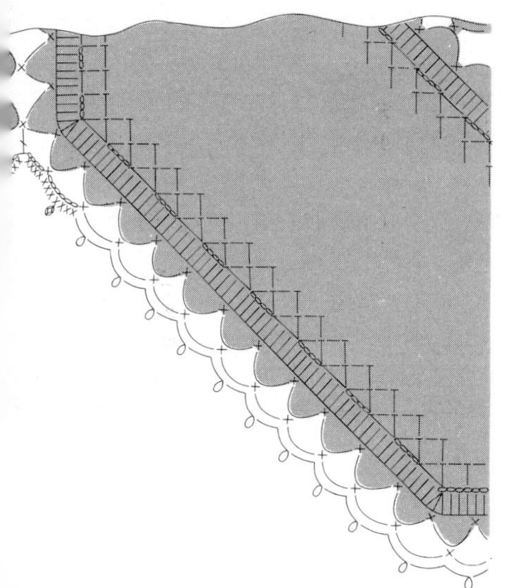

YOU'LL NEED: Crochet cotton No. 20 16 20-gram balls White. Steel crochet hook size 0.90.
FINISHED SIZE: 161 cm by 58 cm
GAUGE: 10 cm of filet crochet=21 squares; 10 cm =19 rows.
SIZE OF MOTIF: Refer to chart.
MAKING INSTRUCTIONS:
MOTIF A: Ch 25. **Row 1:** Ch 6, dc in 7th ch from hook, (ch 2, sk 2 ch, dc in next ch) 8 times.
Row 2: Ch 5, sk 2 ch, dc in dc, (ch 2, sk 2 ch, dc in dc) 7 times. Ch 2, sk 2 ch, dc in next ch, ch 2, tr in same ch.
Row 3: Ch 6, dc in tr. Work following same as for row 2.
Rows 4–8: Work as for rows 2–3, increasing sts on right side.
Row 9: Ch 6, dc in tr. Work following sts as for rows previous, dec last sp working dc and tr at a time.
Row 10: Ch 4, sk 2 ch, dc in dc. Continue in same manner, end ch 2, tr in 3rd ch from dc.
Rows 11–15: Work as for rows 9–10, increasing sts right side, while decreasing sts left side.
Row 16: Ch 4, sk 2 ch, dc in dc. Work in same manner, end ch 2, sk 2 ch, dc in next ch.
Row 17: Ch 5, sk 2 ch, dc in next ch. Continue in same manner, dec 1 sp working dc and tr at a time.
Rows 18–23: Work as for rows 16–17, decreasing sts left side.
EDGING OF A: Continued from row 23. **Row 1:** Ch 3, dc in last st of 23rd row. 3 dc in cross side of tr, dc in top of dc. Dc 3 in 4 ch, dc in top of dc and tr at a time. Work in same manner around, working 7 dc in right angled corners, 3 dc in other corners. End sl st in 3rd st of beg ch.
Row 2: Ch 1, sc in ch previous row, ch 8, sk 4 dc, sc in next dc. Ch 8, sk 5 dc, sc in next dc. Continue in same manner around, working 11 lps on long side, 5 lps on short side (note: Sk sts so that sc comes in corner dc.), end sl st in 1st sc.
MOTIF B: Ch 25. **Row 1:** Ch 5, sk 2 ch, dc in next ch, (ch 2, sk 2 ch, dc in next ch) 7 times, ch 2, tr in edge ch.
Row 2: Ch 6, dc in tr. Ch 2, sk 2 ch, dc in dc. Dc 2 in 2 ch, dc in dc, (ch 2, sk 2 ch, dc in dc) 3 times. Dc 2 in 2 ch, dc in dc, (ch 2, sk 2 ch, dc in dc) 2 times. End ch 2, sk 2 ch, dc in next ch.
Rows 3–23: Work as for motif A, reversing design.
EDGING OF B: **Row 1:** Work as for A.
Row 2: Ch 1, sc in ch previous row, ch 4, sc in the middle of 8-ch lp of adjacent motif, ch 4, sc in dc, ch 4, sc in next lp of adjacent motif. Join in same manner.
MOTIF C: Ch 4. **Row 1:** Ch 6, dc in 7th ch from hook. Ch 2, sk 2 ch, dc in next ch, ch 2, tr in same ch.
Row 2: Ch 6, dc in tr, (ch 2, sk 2 ch, dc in dc) 2 times. Ch 2, sk 2 ch, dc in next ch, ch 2, tr in same ch.
Rows 3–14: Work as for rows 1–2, increasing sts each side. Work design in following chart.

Row 15: Ch 5, sk 2 ch, dc in dc. Continue in same manner, end ch 2, sk 2 ch, dc in next ch.
Row 16: Ch 4, sk 2 ch, dc in dc. Repeat. Dec last sp, working dc and tr at a time.
Row 17: Ch 4, sk 2 ch, dc in dc. Repeat. Dec last sp, working dc and tr at a time.
Rows 18–29: Work as for rows 16–17, decreasing sts each side.
EDGING OF C: Continued from row 29. **Row 1:** Ch 1, sc in the st of 2 sts at a time. Ch 4, sc in the middle of 8-ch lp of adjacent motif, ch 4, sc in the middle of 4-ch next row. Ch 4, sc in the middle of next lp adjacent, ch 4, sk 1 row, sc in top of dc next row. Work in same manner around, sl st in 1st sc.
MOTIF D: Work motif C up to 14th row, crochet edging from hook side.

EDGING: Join motifs as shown, join thread in where indicated. **Row 1:** Ch 1, sc 1, ch 6, sc in the middle of next lp. Ch 6, sc in the middle of next lp. Continue in same manner, working ch 8, 1 sc at every corner. Where at the joint of motifs, work ch 6, 1 dc in joining sc. Where at the indent of motifs work ch 4, 1 dc in joining sc, ch 4, 1 sc in next lp.
Row 2: Ch 1, sc 4 in 6-ch lp, 4-ch p, sc 3 in same lp. Sk 1 sc, sc 4 in next 6-ch lp, 4-ch p, sc 3 in same lp. Continue in same manner, working 5 sc, 4-ch p, 4 sc in 8-ch lp at every corner. Where at the indent, work 4 sc in 4-ch lp, sk 1 dc, 4 sc in next 4-ch lp.

MOTIF (Refer to chart)

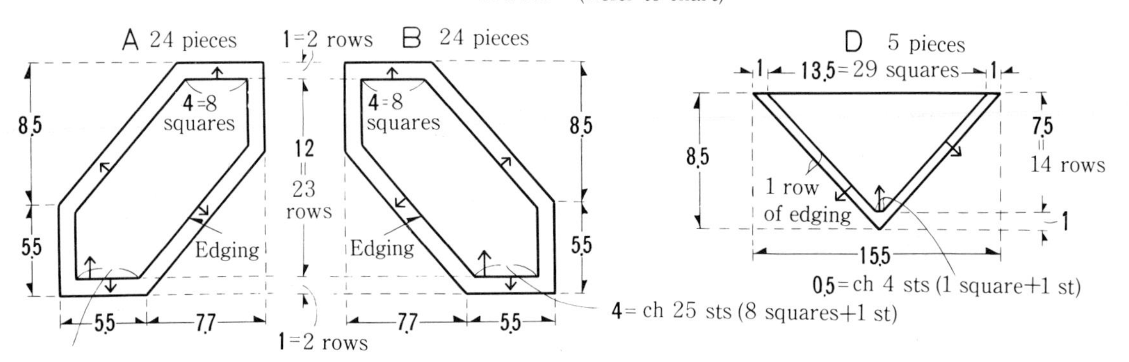

CHART ON MEASUREMENTS

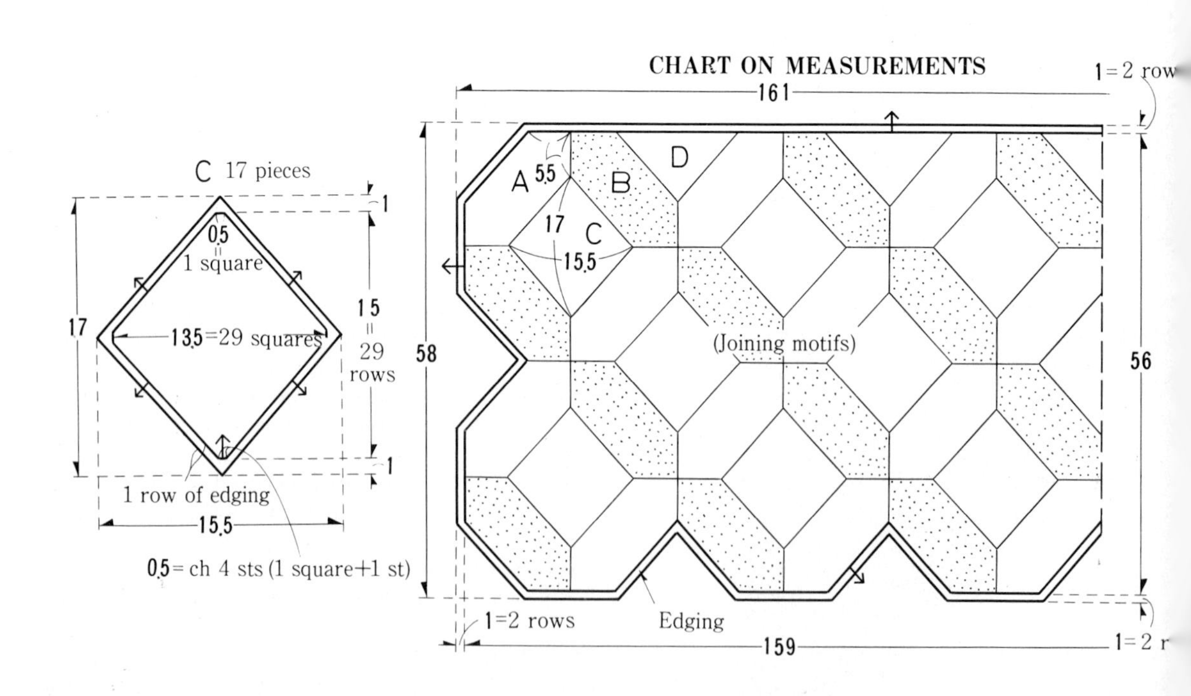

29 LUNCHEON MAT

YOU'LL NEED (for each): Crochet cotton No. 20 3 20-gram balls White. Steel crochet hook size 0.90.
FINISHED SIZE: 37.5 cm by 30 cm
GAUGE: 10 cm of filet crochet = 20 squares; 10 cm = 22 rows.
MAKING INSTRUCTIONS:
Ch 226. **Row 1:** Ch 3, dc in 3 sts, (ch 2, sk 2 ch, dc in next ch) 26 times. Dc in 3 sts, (ch 2, sk 2 ch, dc in next ch) 46 times, end dc in 3 sts.
Row 2: Work as for row 1.
Row 3: Ch 3, dc in 3 sts, (ch 2, sk 2 ch, dc in dc) 2 times, (2 dc in 2 ch, dc in dc) 2 times, (ch 2, sk 2 ch, dc in dc) 2 times, (ch 3, sk 2 ch, dc in dc. Ch 3, sk 2 ch, dc in dc) 3 times. Ch 2, sk 2 ch, dc in dc, (2 dc in 2 ch, dc in dc) 2 times. Ch 2, sk 2 ch, dc in dc, (ch 3, sk 2 ch, dc in dc. Ch 3, sk 2 ch, dc in dc) 4 times, (ch 2, sk 2 ch, dc in dc) 2 times. Dc in 3 sts, (ch 2, sk 2 ch, dc in dc) 46 times, end dc in 3 sts.
Row 4: Work up to 50th square from edge in same manner as for previous row, (ch 5, sk 2 3-ch lps, dc in dc) 4 times. Dc in 7 sts, ch 2, sk 2 dc, dc in 4 sts, (ch 5, sk 2 3-ch lps, dc in dc) 3 times. Ch 2, sk 2 ch, dc in 4 sts, (ch 2, sk 2 ch, dc in dc) 4 times. End dc in 3 sts.
Rows 5–65: Work as for rows 1–4 referring to chart.
EDGING: Join thread in 4th dc from corner, ch 1, 1 sc. Ch 2, sk 2 dc, sc in corner dc, ch 1, sc in same corner dc. *Ch 2, sc in between rows next, repeat from *to next corner. Work in same manner all around, end sl st in 1st sc.

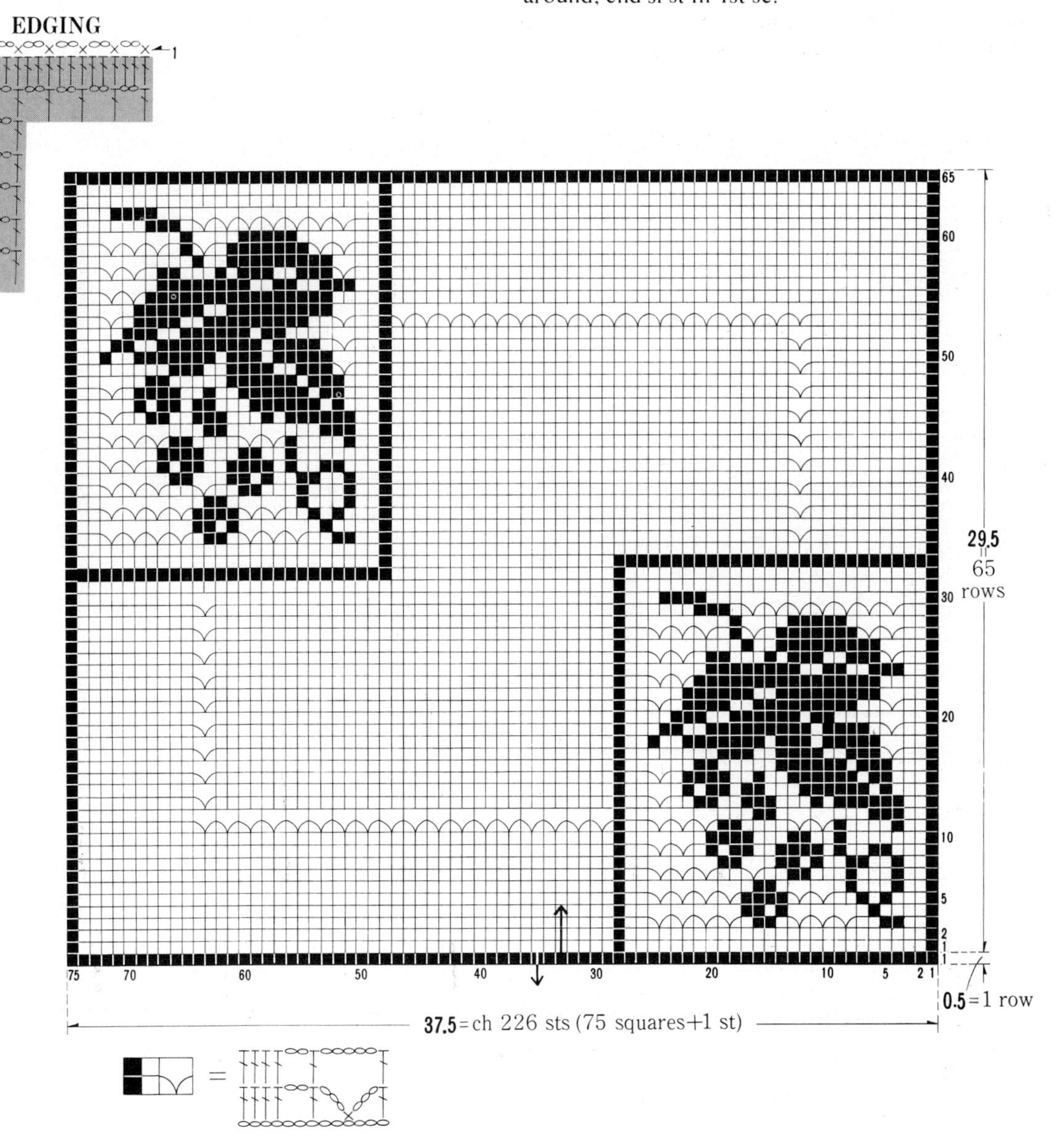

28 BEDSPREAD

YOU'LL NEED: Crochet cotton No. 4 soft twist 40 50-gram balls Beige. Steel crochet hook size 1.75.
FINISHED SIZE: 283 cm by 190 cm
GAUGE: 1 row of dc=0.9 cm
SIZE OF MOTIF: 31 cm square
MAKING INSTRUCTIONS:
Make a loop at thread end. **Row 1:** Ch 3, 15 dc in lp, sl st in 3rd st of beg ch.
Row 2: Ch 5, dc in dc, *ch 2, dc in dc, repeat from* around, sl st in 3rd st of beg ch.
Row 3: Sl st in 3rd st of beg ch. Ch 3, 4 dc in 2 ch, sl st through 5 lps to form pop st, (ch 5, sk 1 dc, 5-dc pop in 2 ch) 3 times. Ch 7, sk 1 dc, 5-dc pop in 2 ch. Work in same manner around, ch 3, tr in 1st pop.
Row 4: Ch 3, 3 dc in cross side of tr. Ch 2, dc in 5-ch lp, ch 2, dc in same lp. Ch 2, dc in 5-ch lp. Ch 2, 4 dc in 7-ch lp, ch 3, 4 dc in same lp. Work in same manner around, ch 1, hdc in 3rd st of beg ch.

CHART ON MEASUREMENTS

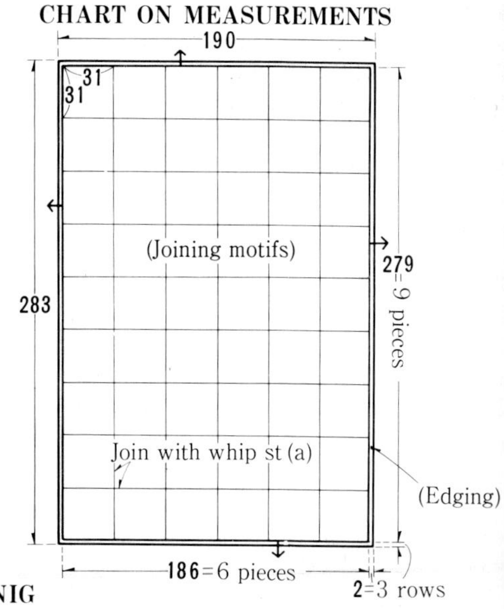

MOTIF & EDGINIG

Row 5: Ch 3, 2 dc in hdc, 1 dc each in 4 sts, (ch 2, sk 2 ch, dc in dc) 5 times. 1 dc each in 3 dc, 3 dc in 3-ch lp, ch 3, 3 dc in same lp. Work in same manner around, ch 1, hdc in 3rd st of beg ch.
Row 6: Work as for row 5.
Row 7: Ch 3, 2 dc in hdc, 1 dc each in 4 sts, (ch 2, sk 2 sts, dc in dc) 3 times. 2 dc in 2 ch, dc in dc, ch 7, sk 2 dc, dc in next dc. Work following same as for row 6.
Row 8: Ch 3, 2 dc in hdc, 1 dc each in 4 sts, (ch 2, sk 2 sts, dc in dc) 3 times. 2 dc in 2 ch, dc in dc, ch 4, sk 3 dc, sc in 7-ch lp. Ch 4, sk 3 dc, dc in dc. Work following same as for row 6.
Row 9: Ch 3, 2 dc in hdc, 1 dc each in 4 sts, (ch 2, sk 2 sts, dc in dc) 3 times. 2 dc in 2 ch, dc in dc, ch 5, sk 3 dc, sc in 4-ch lp. Ch 5, sc in 4-ch lp. Ch 5, sk 3 dc, dc in dc. Work following same as for row 6.
Row 10: Ch 3, 2 dc in hdc, 1 dc each in 4 sts, (ch 2, sk 2 sts, dc in dc) 3 times. 2 dc in 2 ch, dc in dc, ch 5, sk 3 dc, sc in 5-ch lp, (ch 5, sc in 5-ch lp) 2 times. Ch 5, sk 3 dc, dc in next dc. Work following same as for row 6.
Row 11: Ch 3, 2 dc in hdc, 1 dc each in 4 sts, (ch 2, sk 2 sts, dc in dc) 3 times. 2 dc in 2 ch, dc in dc. Ch 2, sk 2 dc, dc in next dc. 3 dc in 5-ch lp, ch 5, sc in 5-ch lp. Ch 5, sc in 5-ch lp. Ch 5, 3 dc in 5-ch lp, dc in dc. Work following same as for row 6.
Rows 12–18: Work as for row 11. Make 54 pieces, join with whip st (a) referring to chart.
EDGING: Row 1: Ch 1, sc in corner ch. Sc in each st around, working 2 sc in 3-ch lp, ch 1, 2 sc in same 3-ch lp at every corner. Where at the joint of motifs, work 2 sc in corner lp, ch 1, 2 sc in corner lp of adjacent motif. End sl st in 1st sc. **Row 2:** Sl st in 3 sc, ch 3, sk 2 sc, dc in next sc. *Ch 7, sk 2 sc, sk next sc and 2 sc, work 2 dc at a time in next sc. Repeat from* around, working 2 dc at a time in 3rd sc from corner and corner ch, ch 7, sk corner ch and 2 sc, work 2 dc at a time in next sc at every corner. Where at the joint of motifs, work 3 dc at a time in 3rd sc from corner st and joining st and the sc skipping next 2 sc. End sl st in 1st dc. **Row 3:** Ch 1, 8 sc in 7-ch lp. Work 8 sc each in each st around, end sl st in 1st sc.

30 COASTER

'OU'LL NEED (for each): Crochet cotton No. 50 ¼ 20-gram ball White. Steel crochet hook size 0.60.
'INISHED SIZE: 11 cm in diameter
;AUGE: 1 row of dc=0.4 cm
1AKING INSTRUCTIONS:
1OTIF A: Ch 19. **Row 1:** Ch 5, dc in 9th ch from ıook, (ch 2, sk 2 ch, dc in next ch) 5 times.
Row 2: Ch 11, dc in 9th ch from hook, (ch 2, sk 2 h, dc in dc) 7 times. Ch 2, dtr in 3rd st of beg ch revious row. Ch 2, dtr in the middle of dtr.
Row 3: Ch 11, dc in 9th ch from hook, (ch 2, sk 2 h, dc in dc) 4 times. (dc 2 in 2 ch, dc in dc) 4 times. :h 2, sk 2 ch, dc in dc) 2 times. Ch 2, sk 2 ch, dc in ext ch, ch 2, dtr in same ch. Ch 2, dtr in the middle f dtr.
ows 4–10: Work as for rows 1–3, increasing sts ach side.
ows 11–14: Work straight.
ow 15: Ch 5, sk 2 ch, dc in dc. Repeat in same ıanner across to 1 sp this side of the edge, sk 1 dc, ch, work 2 sts (1 dc and 1 dtr) at a time in next ch dec 1 sp.
Row 16: Ch 5, sk 2 ch, dc in dc. Work as for previous row, dec 1 sp at the end.
Rows 17–24: Work as for rows 15–16, decreasing each side. Neaten edges round. Ch 3 following to the end of row 24, sk 2 ch previous row, dc in dc. Ch 3, sc in the middle of 5-ch lp. Ch 3, hdc in dc previous row, ch 3, sc in the middle of dtr. Ch 3, sc in the middle of 5-ch lp previous row. Work in same manner, end sl st in the middle of 5-ch lp on 15th row. Neaten 3 sides remained in same manner.
EDGING: Join thread in 3rd st of beg ch of 24th row. **Row 1:** Ch 3, 2 dc in 2 ch, dc in dc; 2 dc in 3 ch. Repeat working 3 dc each in each row around, sl st in 3rd st of beg ch. **Row 2:** Ch 1, sc in beg st previous row, *ch 5, sk 2 dc, sc in next dc, repeat from *around, sl st in 3rd st of beg ch.
MOTIF B, C: Work as for motif A. Crochet each pattern referring to chart.

(DESIGN'S ON NEXT PAGE)

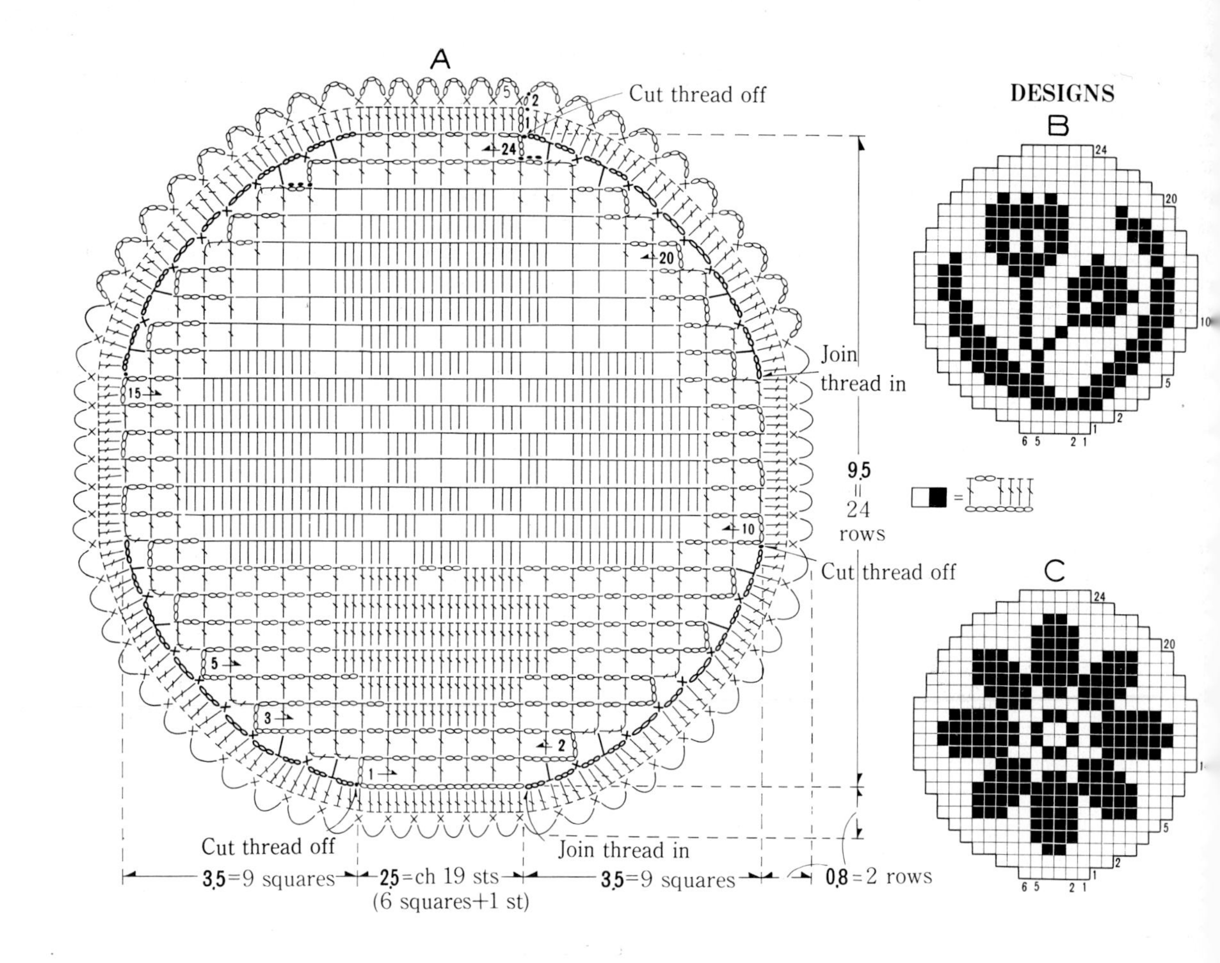

31 BELOW TRAY MAT

YOU'LL NEED: Crochet cotton No. 20 1½ 20-gram balls White. Steel crochet hook size 0.90.

FINISHED SIZE: Refer to chart.

GAUGE: 10 cm of filet crochet=20.5 squares; 10 cm=19.5 rows.

MAKING INSTRUCTIONS:

Ch 70. **Row 1:** Ch 6, dc in 7th ch from hook. 1 dc each in 18 sts, (ch 2, sk 2 ch, dc in next ch) 11 times. 1 dc in 18 sts, ch 2, tr in last ch.

Row 2: Ch 6, dc in tr. 2 dc in 2 ch, dc in dc, (ch 2, sk 2 dc, dc in dc) 6 times. (2dc in 2 ch, dc in dc) 2 times. (ch 2, sk 2 ch, dc in dc) 7 times. (2 dc in 2 ch, dc in dc) 2 times. (ch 2, sk 2 dc, dc in dc) 6 times. 2 dc in 2 ch, dc in next ch, ch 2, tr in same ch.

Rows 3–5: Work as for rows 1–2, increasing 1 sp each side.

Row 6: Ch 6, dc in tr. Work 8 squares as for previous rows, ch 5, sk 5 dc, dc in next dc. Work 13 squares as for previous row, ch 5, sk 5 dc, dc in next dc. Work 8 squares as for previous rows, ch 2, tr in 4th st of beg ch previous row.

Row 7: Ch 6, dc in tr. Work 7 squares as for previous rows, ch 3, sk 2 sts, sc in dc, ch 3, sk 2 sts, d in dc. Ch 3, sc in the middle of 5-ch. Ch 3, dc in dc Ch 3, sk 2 sts, sc in dc, ch 3, sk 2 sts, dc in dc. Continue.

Row 8: Ch 6, dc in tr. Work 8 squares as for previous rows, (ch 5, sk 2 3-ch lps, dc in dc) 3 times Work in same manner across to the end.

Rows 9–14: Work as for rows 1–8, increasing 1 s each side.

Rows 15–35: Work straight in same manner as fo rows previous.

Row 36: Ch 4, sk 2 dc, dc in next dc. 2 dc in 2 ch dc in dc. Work following in same manner, dec las sp working 2 sts (dc and tr) at a time in 4th dc fro edge and edge ch.

Rows 37–49: Work as for row 36, decreasing 1 s each side.

EDGING: Join thread in edge st of 1st row. **Row 1:** Ch 6, dc in same edge st. Ch 3, dc in between rows 1st and 2nd. Ch 3, dc in between rows next. Continue in same manner to corner, work 1 dc in corner, ch 3, 1 dc in same corner. Work ch 3, 1 dc in every 1½ rows along the straight side following. Where at even sides on top and bottom, work ch 3, sk 3 sts, 1 dc in dc. Continue in same manner around, sl st in 3rd st of beg ch. **Row 2:** Ch 4, dc in corner lp, ch 1, dc in same lp, ch 1, dc in same lp as before. Ch 1, dc in dc, *ch 1, dc in the middle of 3 ch, ch 1, dc in dc. Repeat from *around, working *ch 1, dc in 3 ch lp, repeat from *2 times, ch 1, dc in dc at every corner, end sl st in 3rd st of beg ch. **Row 3:** Ch 1, sc in beg ch previous row, *ch 3, sk 3 sts, 2 dc in dc, 3-ch p, dc in same dc. Ch 3, sk 3 sts, sc in dc, repeat from* around, sl st in 1st sc.

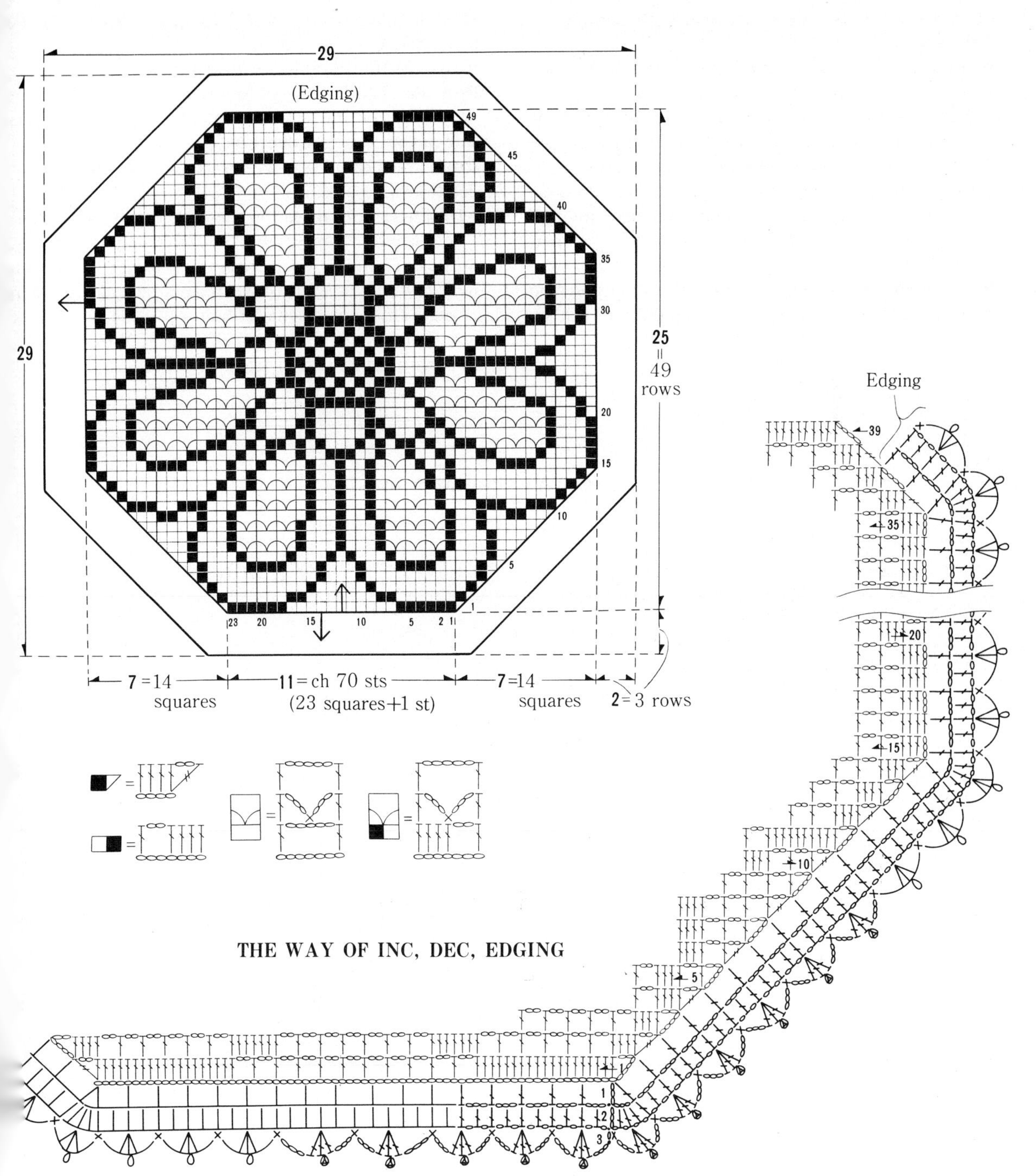

37 DRESSER MAT

YOU'LL NEED: Crochet cotton No. 20 3½ 20-gram balls White. Steel crochet hook size 0.90.
FINISHED SIZE: 64.5 cm by 34 cm in oval
GAUGE: 10 cm of filet crochet=19.5 square; 10 cm=19.5 rows.
MAKING INSTRUCTIONS:
Ch 31. **Row 1:** Ch 3, dc in 5th ch from hook. 1 dc each in 14 sts. Ch 2, sk 2 ch, dc in each st remaining.
Row 2: Ch 6, dc in 5th ch from hook. 1 dc in each of 20 sts. Ch 2, sk 2 dc, dc in each st remaining, inc 3 sts with tr.
Rows 3–6: Work as for row 2, increasing each side.
Row 7: Ch 21 with another thread, sl st in 3rd st of beg ch of row 6. Ch 24 following the end of row 6, dc in 5th ch from hook. 8 dc, (ch 2, sk 2 ch, dc in next ch) 3 times, 12 dc. Work in same manner across.
Row 8: Ch 8, 13 dc starting from edge dc, (ch 2, sk 2 ch, dc in dc) 2 times. Continue in same manner to end, ch 2, dtr in 3rd st of beg ch of previous row to inc 1 sp.
Rows 9–15: Work as for row 8, increasing sts on both sides. Work ch 2, sk 2 sts, dc in dc, for each sp; 3 dc for each bl referring to chart.
Row 16: Having worked 14 squares in same manner as for rows previous, ch 3, sk 2 sts, sc in dc, ch 3, sk 2 sts, dc in dc. Work following 10 squares same as before. Ch 3, sk 2 sts, dc in dc, ch 3, sk 2 sts, dc in dc. 6 dc, (ch 3, sk 2 sts, sc in dc, ch 3, sk 2 sts, dc in dc) 2 times. Continue in same manner to end, ch 2, dtr in 3rd st of beg ch of previous row to inc 1 sp.
Row 17: Work 16 squares same as before, (ch 5, sk 2 3-ch lps, dc in dc) 2 times, work 2 squares in same manner, ch 5, sk 2 3-ch lps, dc in dc. Work in same manner to end.
Rows 18–35: Work as for rows previous.
Row 36: Sl st from edge to 4th st, ch 3, 2 dc in 2 ch, dc in dc, continue in same manner up to 3 sts this side of the corner to dec 1 bl.
Rows 37–126: Work as for rows previous. Inc or dec following chart.
EDGING: Join thread in the edge of row 120, ch 1, 1 sc. Sc in dc 9 times, (ch 2, sk 2 ch, sc in dc) 3 times. Sc in dc 2 times, work 2 sc at a time in dc and ch next row. Ch 2, sc in between rows next. Ch 2, sc in corner, ch 2, sc in same corner. Sc in dc, work 2 sc at a time in dc and the base of next dc. Work in same manner around, sl st in 1st sc.

THE WAY OF BEG & INC

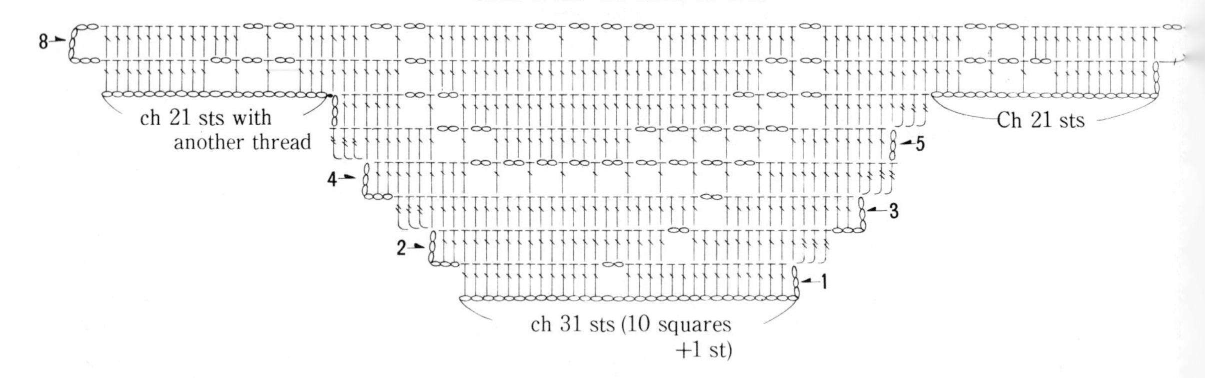

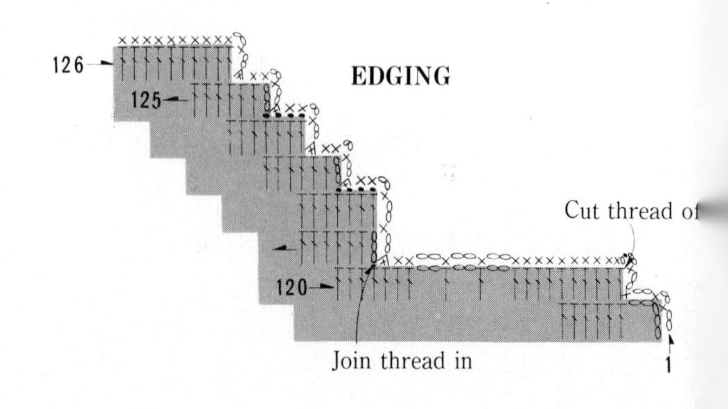

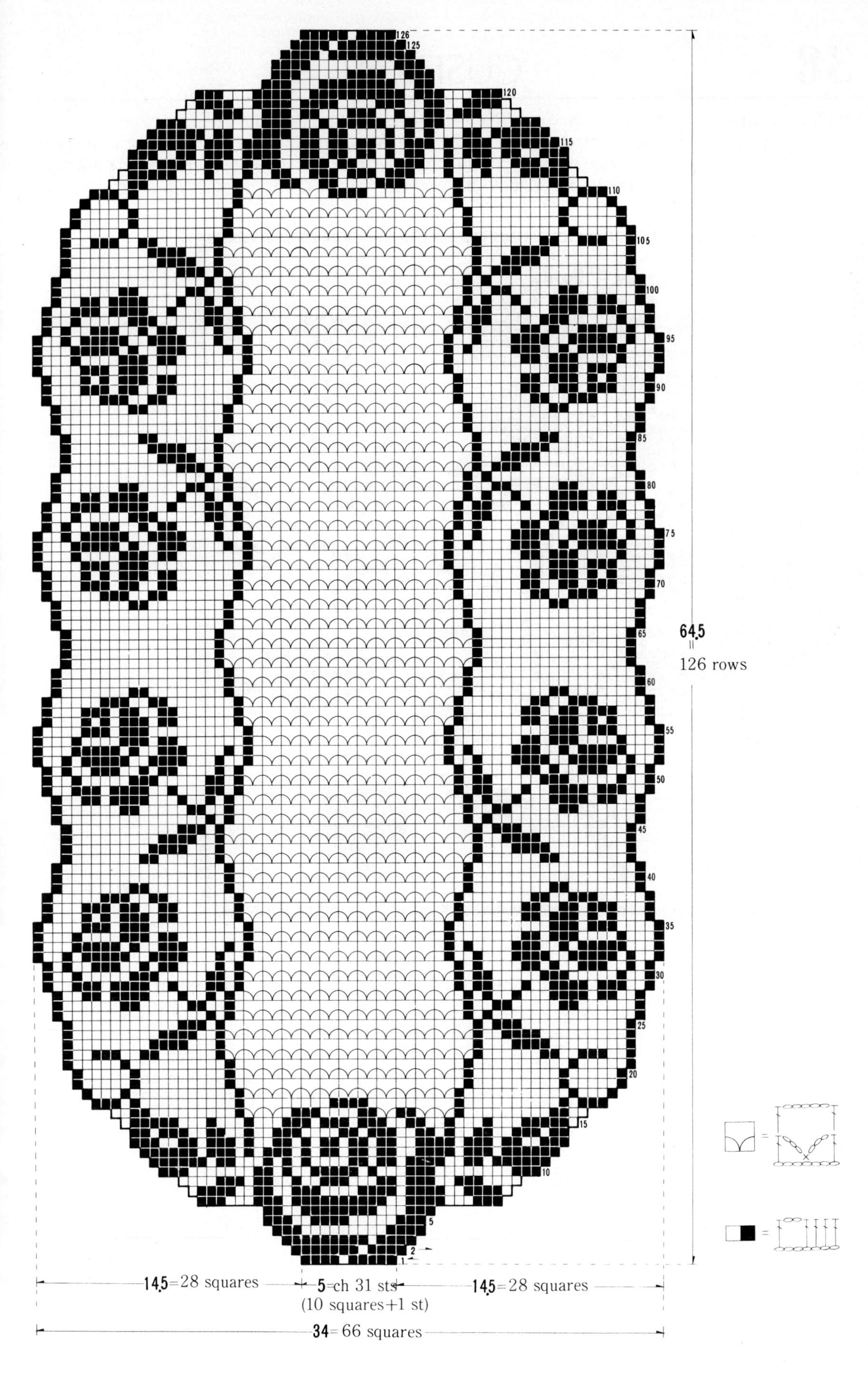
126
125
120
115
110
105
100
95
90
85
80
75
70
65
60
55
50
45
40
35
30
25
20
15
10
5
2
1
64.5
=
126 rows
14.5=28 squares
5=ch 31 sts
(10 squares+1 st)
14.5=28 squares
34=66 squares
=
=

38 CUSHION

YOU'LL NEED (for each): Crochet cotton No. 4 soft twist 2 50-gram balls White. Steel crochet hook size 1.25. Cotton print for outer case 90 cm by 70 cm. Cloth for inner case 90 cm by 40 cm. Kapok 300 gram. 33 cm long zip.
FINISHED SIZE: 39 cm by 36 cm; Frill, 7 cm wide.
GAUGE: 10 cm of filet crochet = 16.5 squares; 10 cm = 18 rows.

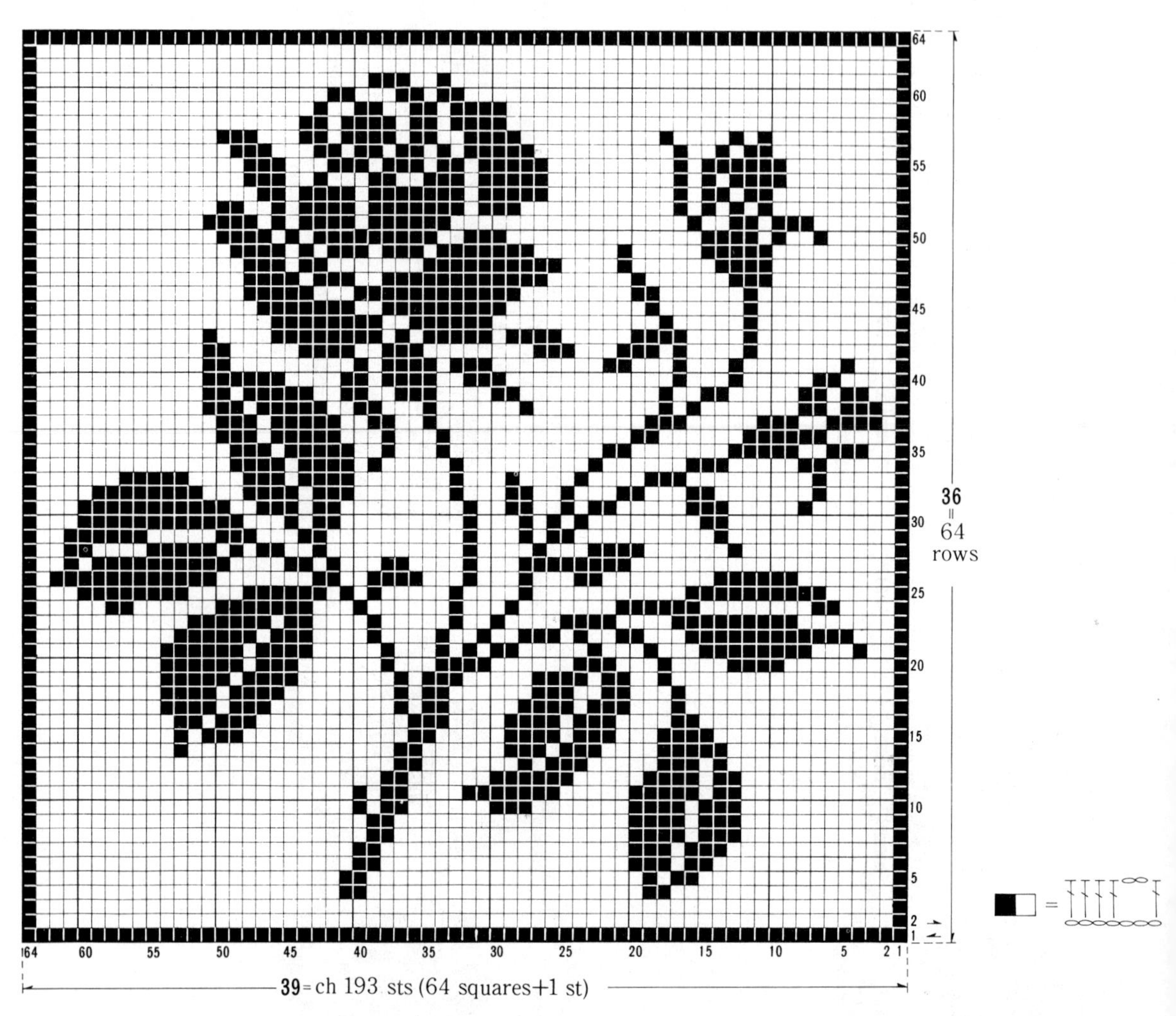

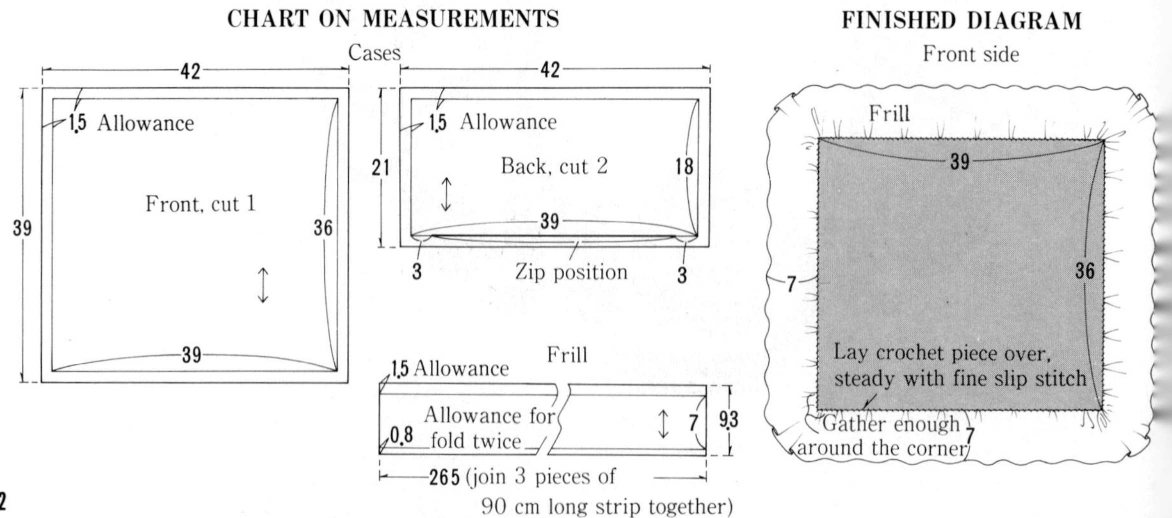

MAKING INSTRUCTIONS:
LEFT: Ch 139. **Row 1:** Ch 3, dc in 5th ch from hook. Dc in each st across to the end.
Row 2: Ch 3, dc in dc 3 times, (ch 2, sk 2 dc, dc in next dc) 62 times, dc in dc 3 times.
Rows 3–64: Work ch 2, sk 2 sts, dc in dc, for each sp; 3 dc for each bl referring to chart.
SEWING CASES: (1) Cut cotton print in size referring to chart. (2) Set zip in position back side. (3) Put front and back right sides together, insert frill between, stitch all around, turn inside out. (4) Spread crochet piece over the front, steady with slip stitch. Finish inner case 41 cm by 39 cm in size, stuff kapok.
RIGHT: Work same as for left, spread its reverse side over, steady with slip stitch.

39 TABLERUNNER

YOU'LL NEED: Crochet cotton No. 4 soft twist 15½ 50-gram balls White. Steel crochet hook size 1.50.
FINISHED SIZE: 128 cm square
GAUGE: 10 cm of filet crochet = 13 squares; 10 cm = 13 rows.
SIZE OF MOTIF: 18.5 cm square
MAKING INSTRUCTIONS:
MOTIF A: Ch 73. **Row 1:** Ch 3, dc in 5th ch from hook. 1 dc each in 17 sts, (ch 2, sk 2 ch, dc in next ch) 12 times. 1 dc each in sts remained.
Row 2: Ch 3, dc in dc 6 times, (ch 2, sk 2 ch, dc in dc) 20 times. 1 dc each in 6 sts.
Rows 3–24: Work as for rows 1–2, following chart. Crochet 18 pieces.
MOTIF B: Ch 73. Work as for A, making design shown on chart B. Crochet 18 pieces.
EDGING ①: Join thread in the corner of row 24, ch 6, dc in corner dc, *ch 3, sk 2 sts, sc in dc. Ch 3, sk 2 sts, dc in dc, repeat from *to corner. Dc in corner st, ch 2, tr in same corner, ch 2, dc in same corner. Ch 3, sc in between rows next. *Ch 3, dc in between rows next. Ch 3, sc in between rows next, repeat from *to corner. Work in same manner around, sl st in 4th st of beg ch. From 2nd piece, work joining A and B alternately, referring to joining manner.
EDGING ②: Continued on edging ①. **Row 1:** Ch 8, sk 2 ch, dc in dc. *Ch 5, sk 2 3-ch lps, dc in dc, repeat from *to corner, ch 5, dc in corner tr, ch 5, dc in dc. Work in same manner around, sl st in 3rd st of beg ch.
Row 2: Ch 5, dc in 3rd st of beg ch previous row, *ch 2, dc in the middle of 5 ch. Ch 2, dc in dc, repeat from *to corner. Dc in corner dc, ch 2, dc in same dc. Work in same manner around, sl st in 3rd st of beg ch.
Row 3: 1 sl st, sc in 4th st of beg ch previous row, ch 5, sc in ch. *Sk 4 sts, 8 dc in 2 ch, sk 4 sts, sc in 2 ch. Ch 5, sk 1 dc, sc in 2 ch, repeat from *to corner. Sc in corner ch, ch 5, sc in same corner ch. Work in same manner around, sl st in 1st sc.
Row 4: Sl st in 3 sts, sc in the middle of 5 ch, (dc in dc, ch 3, sc in dc) 7 times, dc in dc, sc in the middle of 5 ch. Work in same manner around, sl st in 1st sc.

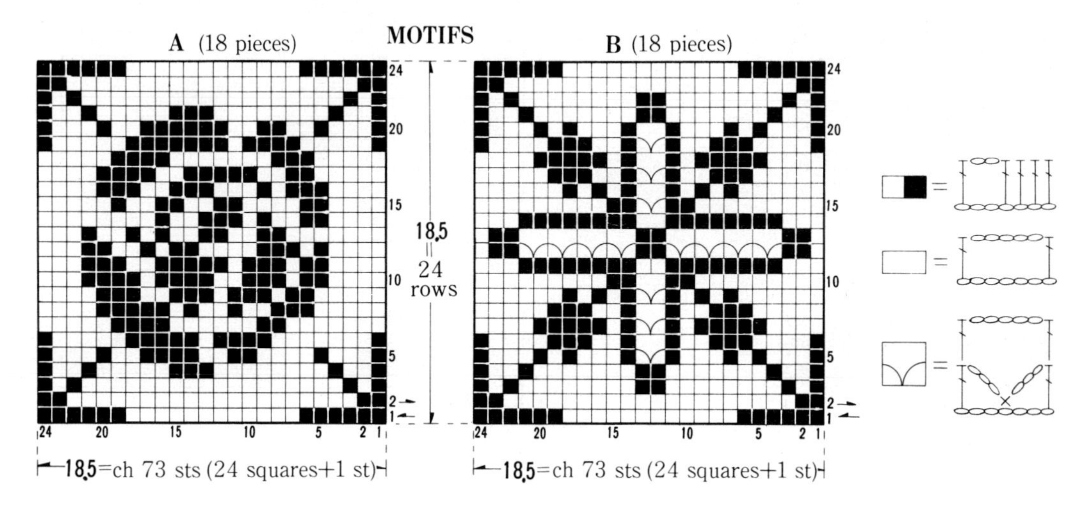

JOINING MOTIFS & EDGING

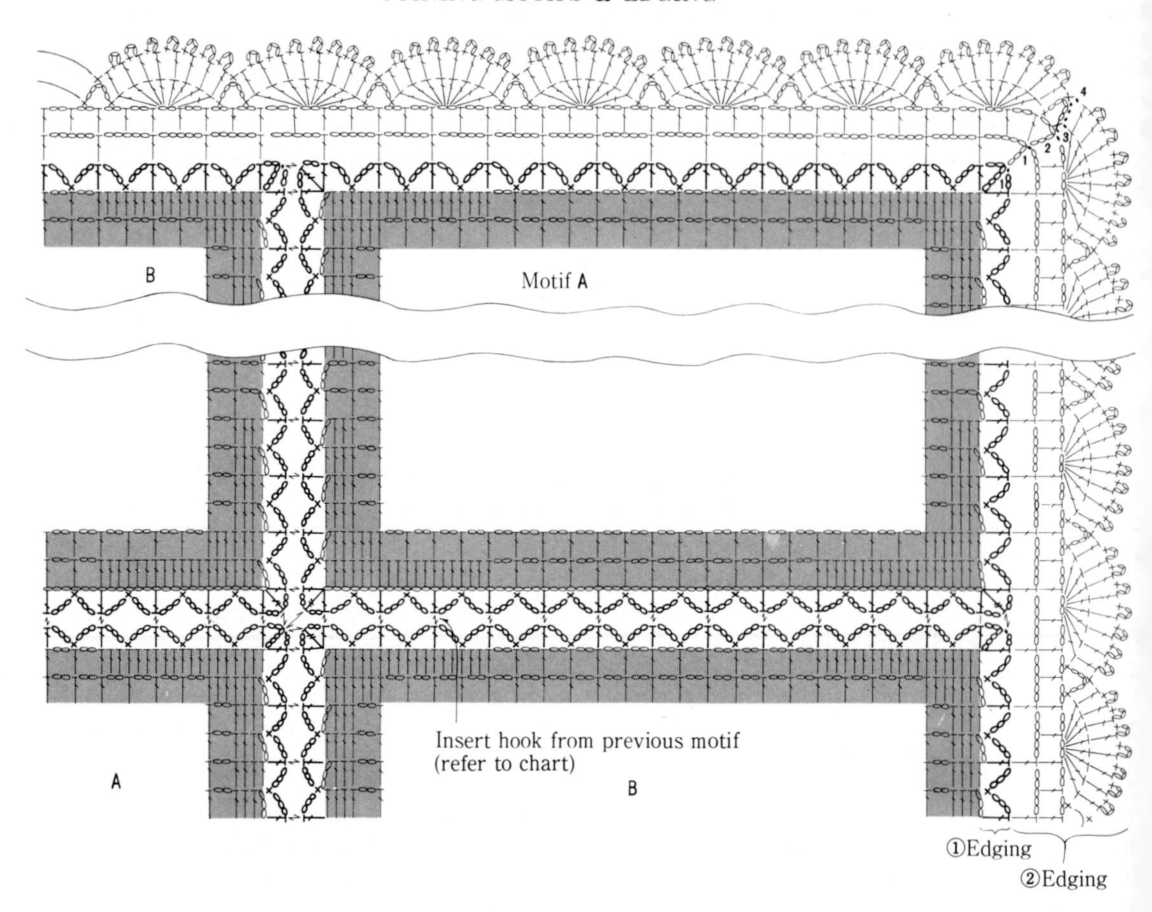

B
Motif A
Insert hook from previous motif
(refer to chart)
A
B
①Edging
②Edging

JOINING MOTIF

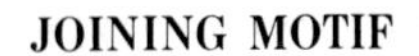

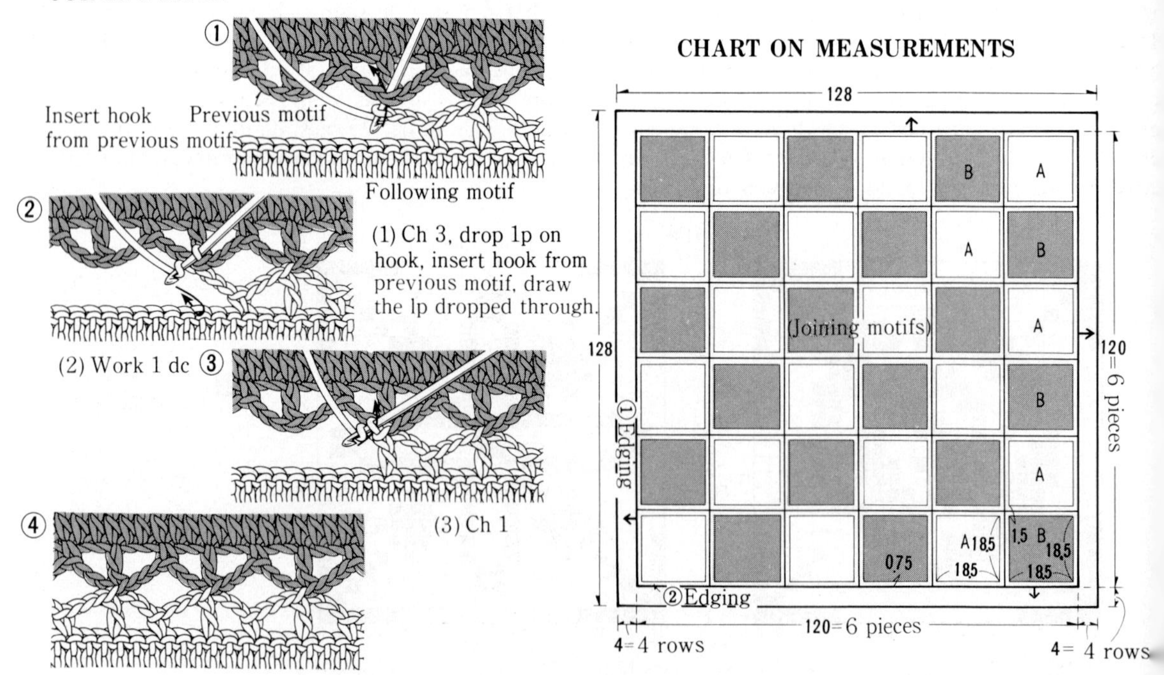

①
Insert hook from previous motif
Previous motif
Following motif
②
(1) Ch 3, drop 1p on hook, insert hook from previous motif, draw the lp dropped through.
(2) Work 1 dc
③
④
(3) Ch 1
CHART ON MEASUREMENTS
128
128
120=6 pieces
(Joining motifs)
①Edging
②Edging
120=6 pieces
4=4 rows
4= 4 rows
B
A
A
B
A
B
A
A18.5
18.5
1.5 B
18.5
18.5
0.75

YOUR ROOM ACCENTUATING

45 CENTERPIECE

Instructions on page 126.

46 CENTERPIECE

Instructions on page 128.

47 TABLECLOTH

Instructions on page 123.

48 CENTERPIECE

Instructions on page 134.

49 CENTERPIECE

Instructions on page 136.

50 CENTERPIECE

 Instructions on page 138.

51 CENTERPIECE

Instructions on page 139.

52 TABLECLOTH

Instructions on page 130

31 ABOVE TRAY MAT

YOU'LL NEED: Crochet cotton No. 20 2 20-gram balls White. Steel crochet hook size 0.90.
FINISHED SIZE: 33 cm in diameter
GAUGE: 1 row of dc=0.6 cm
MAKING INSTRUCTIONS:
Ch 6, sl st in 1st ch to form ring. **Row 1:** Ch 3, 1 dc in ring, (ch 2, 2 dc in ring) 7 times, ch 2, sl st in 3rd st of beg ch.
Row 2: Ch 3, dc in 3rd st of beg ch, 2 dc in next dc. Ch 2, sk 2 ch, 2 dc in dc, 2 dc in next dc. Repeat in same manner, sl st in 3rd st of beg ch.
Row 3: Ch 3, 1 dc each in 3 dc. Ch 2, dc in the middle of 2 ch. Ch 2, 1 dc each in 4 dc. Work in same manner around, sl st in 3rd st of beg ch.
Row 4: Ch 3, 1 dc each in 4 dc. Ch 2, sk 2 ch, dc in dc, ch 2, dc in same dc. Ch 2, sk 2 ch, 1 dc each in 4 dc. Continue in same manner around, sl st in 3rd st of beg ch.
Row 5: Ch 3, 1 dc each in 3 dc. Ch 2, sk 2 ch, dc in dc. Ch 2, dc in the middle of 2 ch, ch 2 dc in dc. Ch 2, sk 2 ch, 1 dc each in 4 dc. Continue in same manner around, sl st in 3rd st of beg ch.
Rows 6–23: Work as for rows 4–5, increasing sts at 8 places.
Rows 24–29: Join thread in where indicated, work across each side.

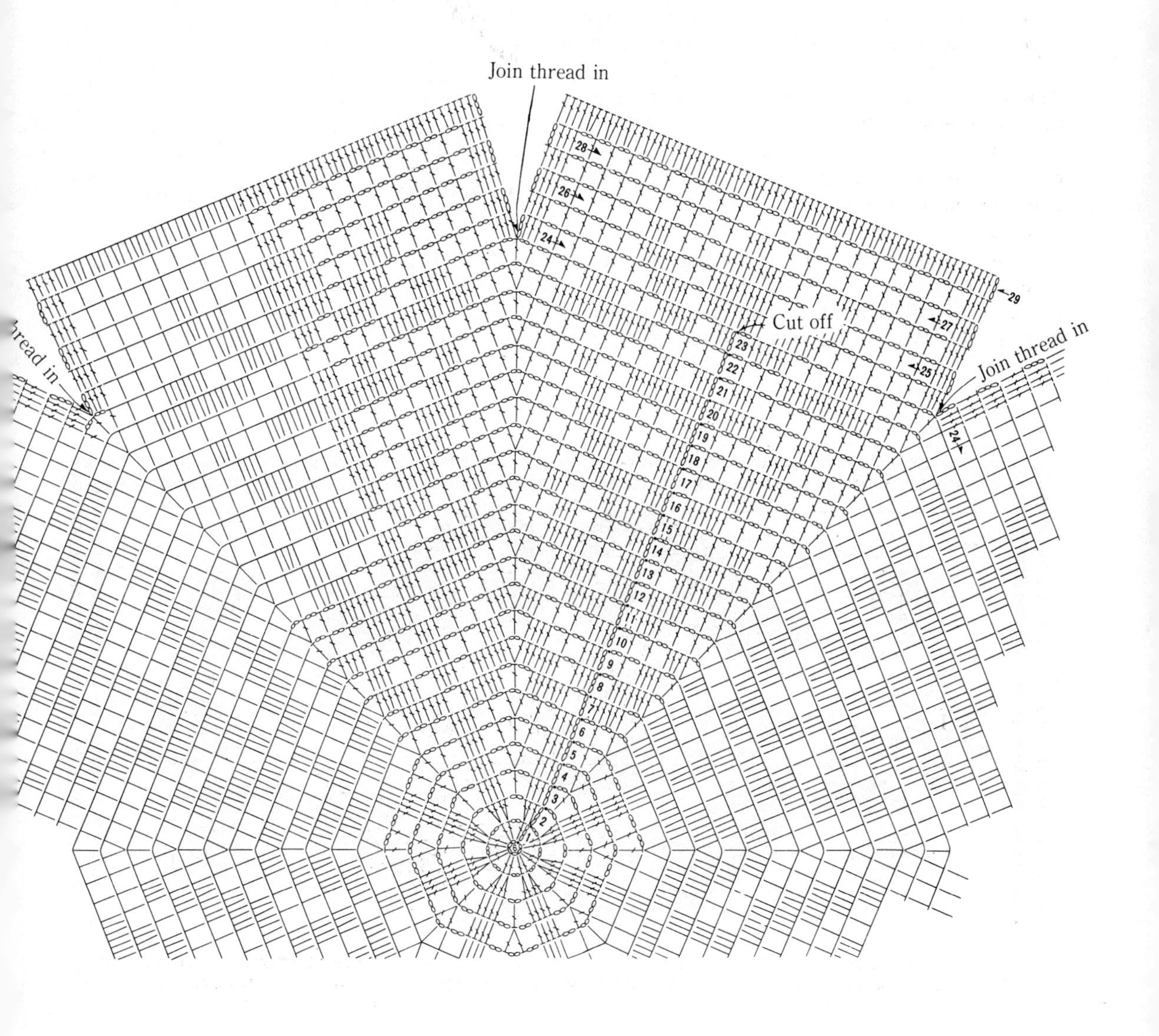

32 DRESSER MAT

YOU'LL NEED: Crochet cotton No. 20 3 20-gram balls White. Steel crochet hook size 0.90.
FINISHED SIZE: 48.5 cm by 23.5 cm
GAUGE: 10 cm of filet crochet=20 squares; 10 cm =23 rows.
MAKING INSTRUCTIONS:
Ch 280. **Row 1:** Ch 5, dc in 9th ch from hook, (ch 2, sk 2 ch, dc in dc) 92 times.
Row 2: Ch 5, dc in dc, (2 dc in 2 ch, dc in dc) 91 times, ch 2, sk 2 ch, dc in next ch.
Rows 3–9: Work as for row 2, referring to chart. Ch 2, sk 2 sts, dc in next st for each sp; dc in 3 sts for each bl.
Row 10: Work up to 39th square in same manner as for rows previous, ch 5, sk 5 sts, dc in dc. Work next 10 squares same as before, (ch 5, sk 5 sts, dc in dc) 2 times. Continue in same manner across.
Row 11: Work up to 38th square in same manner as for rows previous, ch 3, sc in the middle of 5 ch, ch 3, dc in dc. Work next 14 squares same as before, ch 3, sk 2 sts, sc in dc, ch 3, sk 2 sts, dc in dc. Continue in same manner across.
Row 12: Work up to 37 th square in same manner, ch 5, sk 2 3-ch lps, dc in dc. Work next 14 squares same as before, ch 5, sk 2 3-ch lps, dc in dc, ch 5, sk 5 sts, dc in dc. Continue in same manner across.
Rows 13–50: Work as for rows previous.

EDGING: Row 1: Join thread in where indicated, ch 1, sc in dc. 1 sc each in each st across. Where at corner sp, work 3 sc, ch 1, 3 sc. Work 5 sc each in each 2 rows length side. **Row 2:** Ch 1, sc in sc, ch 4, 3-ch p, (ch 1, tr in same sc as before, 3-ch p) 2 times, ch 1, tr in same sc as before, sc in corner ch. Ch 4, 3-ch p, (ch 1, tr in corner ch) 2 times, ch 1, tr in same ch, sk 6 sc, sc in next sc. Work in same manner around, sl st in 1st sc.

EDGING

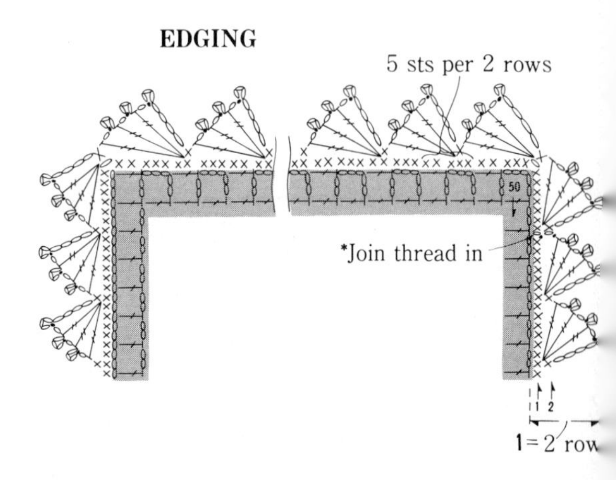

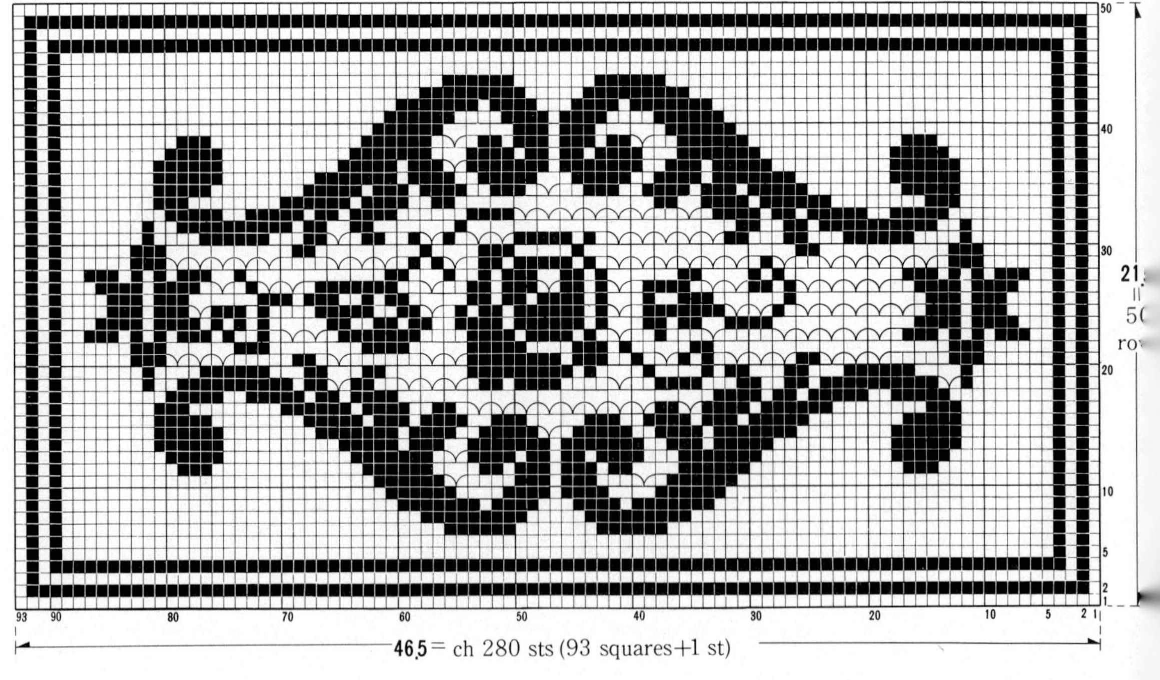

33 DRESSER MAT

YOU'LL NEED: Crochet cotton No. 20 1½ 20-gram balls White. Steel crochet hook size 0.90.
FINISHED SIZE: 30.5 cm by 23 cm
GAUGE: 10 cm of filet crochet= 19 squares; 10 cm = 15 rows.
MAKING INSTRUCTIONS:
Ch 157. **Row 1:** Ch 4, 1 tr each in 6 sts. Ch 2, sk 2 ch, 1 tr. 1 tr each in next 6 sts, (ch 2, sk 2 ch, tr in next ch) 3 times. 1 tr each in 9 sts. Ch 2, sk 2 ch, 1 tr. 1 tr each in 9 sts. Work in same manner across.
Row 2: Ch 3, 1 tr each in 6 sts, (ch 2, sk 2 sts, tr in tr) 2 times. 1 tr each in 6 sts. Continue in same manner across.
Row 3: Ch 6, sk 2 ch, tr in tr. Ch 2, sk 2 sts, tr in tr. 1 tr each in 6 sts. Work in same manner up to 25th square. Ch 4, tr in tr, 3-ch p, ch 4, sk 2 sts, tr in tr. Work following same as before.
Row 4: Work up to 25th square in same manner as for previous row, ch 5, sk 2 4-ch lps tr in tr. Continue in same manner.
Rows 5–30: Work as for rows 1–4, referring to chart. Ch 2, sk 2 sts, tr in tr for each sp; 3 tr for each bl.
EDGING: Row 1: Join thread in where indicated, ch 1, sc in tr. Ch 7, sk 5 sts, sc in corner st. Ch 7, 1 sc, skipping 2 rows each. Work in same manner around, ch 3, sk 5 sts, tr in 1st sc. **Row 2:** Ch 4, tr in cross side of tr, 3-ch p, tr in same tr. Ch 5, 2 tr in 7-ch lp, 3-ch p, tr in same lp. Ch 5, 2 tr in corner sc, 3-ch p, tr in same sc. Work in same manner around, sl st in 4th st of beg ch.

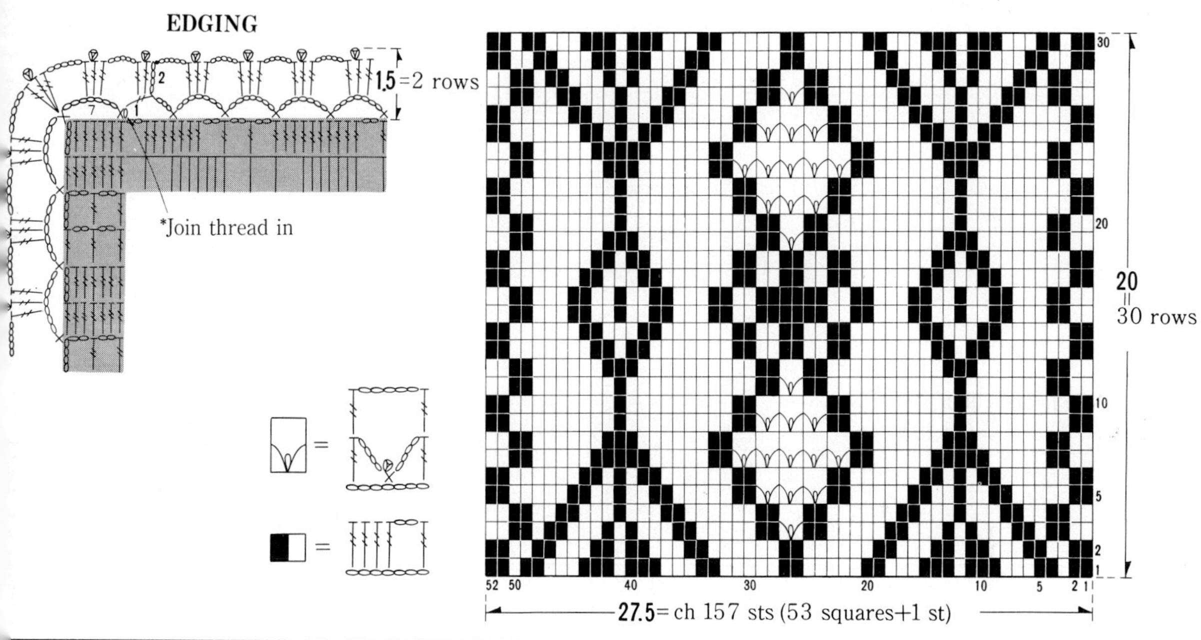

THE METHOD OF STARTING FROM ITS CENTER WORKING IN A RING

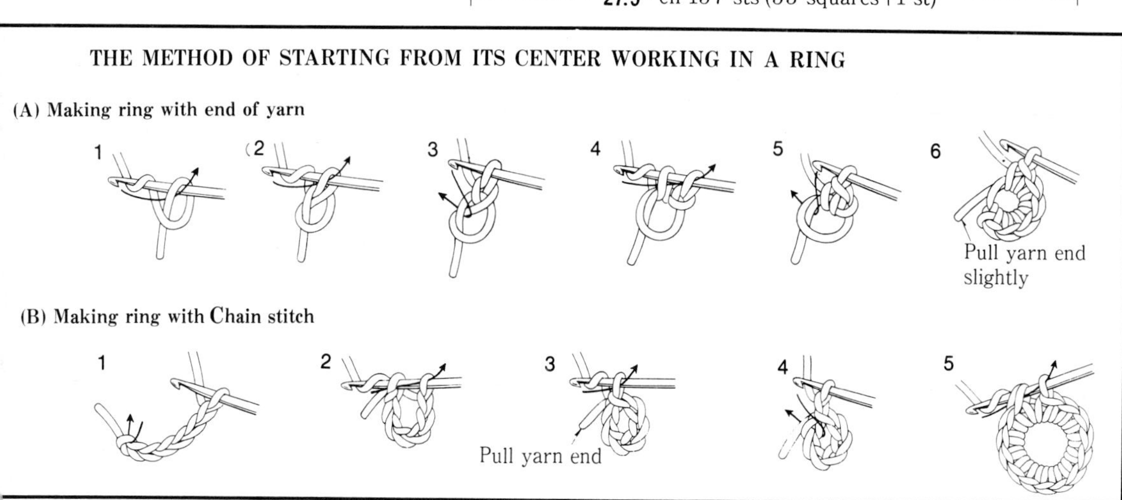

41 CENTERPIECE

YOU'LL NEED: Crochet cotton No. 20 12½ 20-gram balls White. Steel crochet hook size 0.90.
FINISHED SIZE: 99 cm in diameter (octagon, 33.5 cm each side).
GAUGE: 10 cm of filet crochet = 18.5 squares; 10 cm = 19.5 rows.

MAKING INSTRUCTIONS:
Make a loop at thread end. **Row 1:** Ch 5, 1 dc in lp, (ch 2, dc in lp) 6 times, ch 2, sl st in 3rd st of beg ch.
Row 2: Ch 5, dc in 2 ch. Ch 2, dc in dc. Ch 2, dc in 2 ch. Repeat in same manner around, sl st in 3rd st of beg ch.

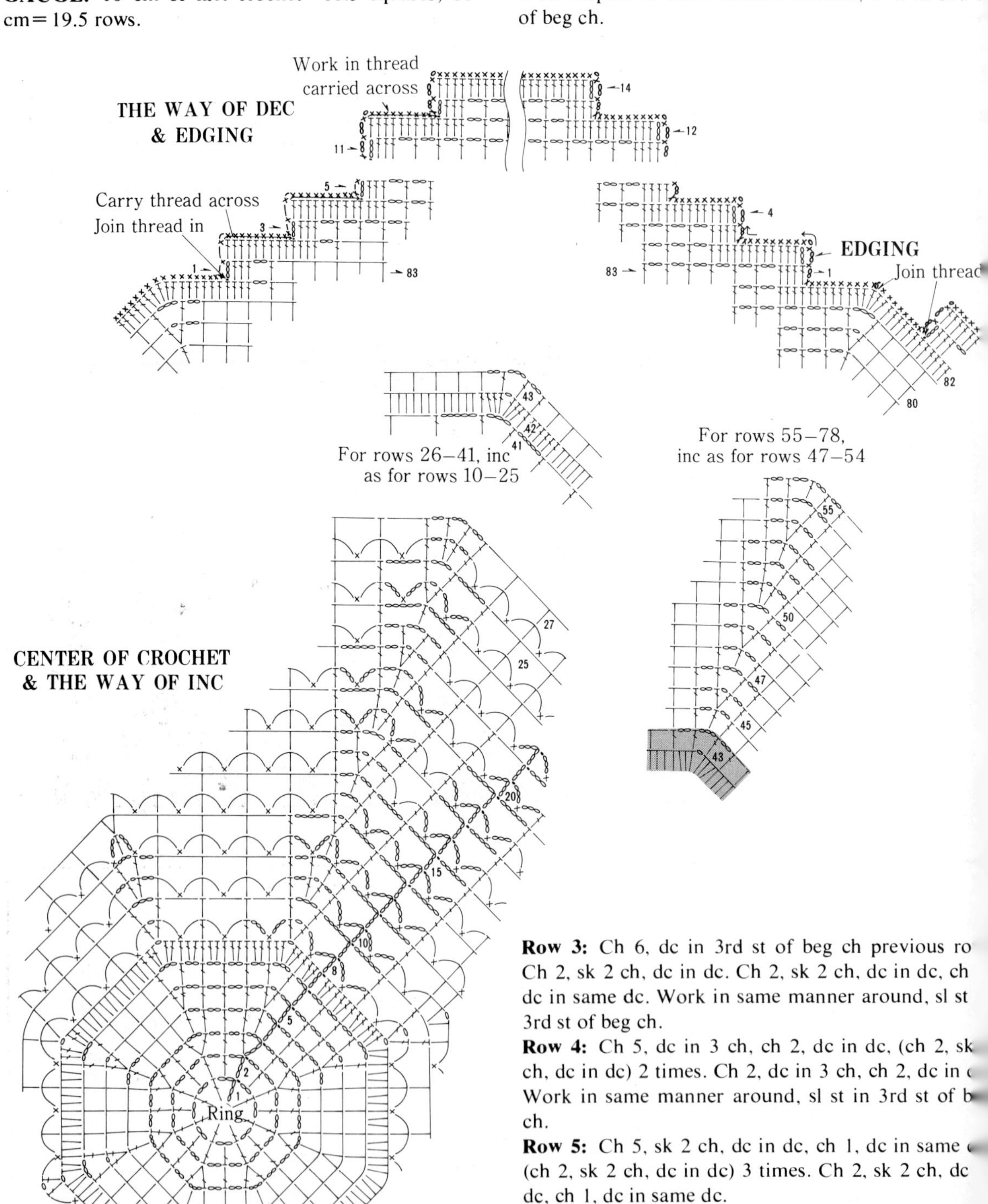

Row 3: Ch 6, dc in 3rd st of beg ch previous row. Ch 2, sk 2 ch, dc in dc. Ch 2, sk 2 ch, dc in dc, ch 3, dc in same dc. Work in same manner around, sl st in 3rd st of beg ch.
Row 4: Ch 5, dc in 3 ch, ch 2, dc in dc, (ch 2, sk 2 ch, dc in dc) 2 times. Ch 2, dc in 3 ch, ch 2, dc in dc. Work in same manner around, sl st in 3rd st of beg ch.
Row 5: Ch 5, sk 2 ch, dc in dc, ch 1, dc in same dc, (ch 2, sk 2 ch, dc in dc) 3 times. Ch 2, sk 2 ch, dc in dc, ch 1, dc in same dc.
Row 6: Ch 5, sk 2 ch, dc in dc, ch 3, sk 1 ch, dc in dc, (ch 2, sk 2 ch, dc in dc) 4 times. Continue in same manner around, sl st in 3rd st of beg ch.

Row 7: Ch 3, 2 dc in 2 ch, dc in dc. 2 dc in 3 ch, ch 1, 2 dc in same 3 ch. Dc in dc, (2 dc in 2 ch, dc in dc) 4 times. Repeat in same manner around, sl st in 3rd st of beg ch.

Row 8: Ch 6, sk 2 dc, sc in next dc. Ch 3, sk 2 dc, dc in ch, ch 1, dc in same ch. Ch 3, sk 2 dc, sc in dc. Ch 3, sk 2 dc, dc in dc. Repeat in same manner around.

Row 9: Ch 8, sk 2 3-ch lps, dc in dc. Ch 3, sk 1 ch, dc in dc. Ch 5, sk 2 3-ch lps, dc in dc. Continue in same manner.

Row 10: Ch 6, sc in the middle of 5-ch lp. Ch 3, dc in dc. Ch 2, dc in 3-ch lp, ch 1, dc in same lp. Ch 2, dc in dc. Ch 3, sc in the middle of 5-ch lp. Repeat around.

Row 11: Ch 8, sk 2 3-ch lps, dc in dc. Ch 2, sk 2 ch, dc in dc. Ch 3, sk 1 ch, dc in dc. Ch 2, sk 2 ch, dc in dc. Work in same manner around.

Rows 12–29: Work as for rows 10–11, increasing sts at 8 corners.

Rows 30–41: Work as for rows previous, increasing sts at 8 corners. Work 2 ch, sk 2 sts, 1 dc for each sp, 3 dc for each bl.

Rows 42–82: Work patterns in, increasing sts at 8 corners.

Rows 83–96: Join thread in where indicated, work each side straight across.

EDGING: Join thread in the corner of row 82. **Row 1:** Ch 1, 1 sc. Sc in dc 8 times. Sc in corner, ch 2, sc in between rows next. Ch 2, sc in corner, ch 1, sc in same corner. Continue in same manner around, sl st in 1st sc.

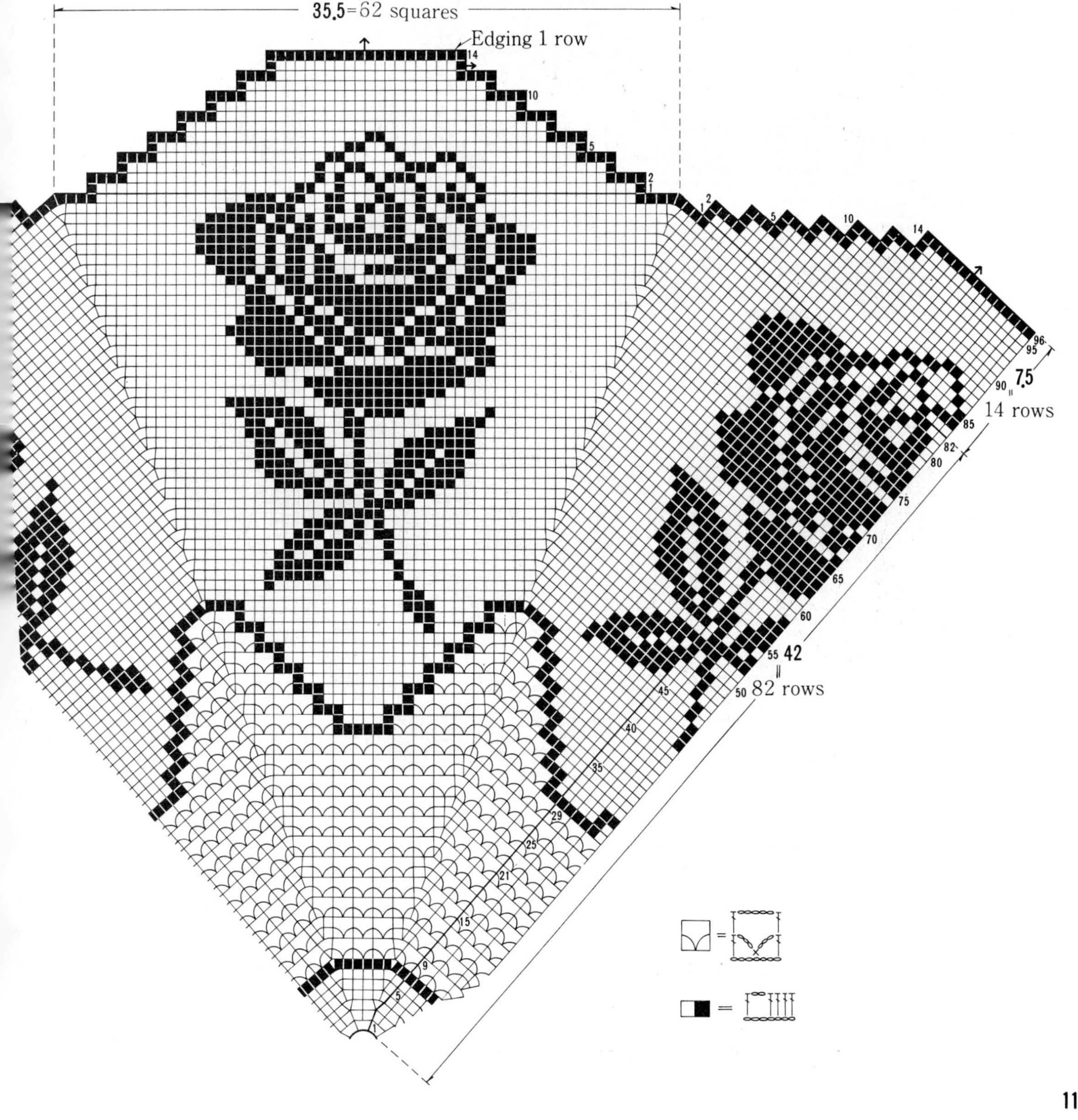

40 CUSHION

YOU'LL NEED (for each): Crochet cotton No. 20 7½ 20-gram balls White. Steel crochet hook size 0.90. Satin for inner case 50 cm by 96 cm. Kapok 450 gram.

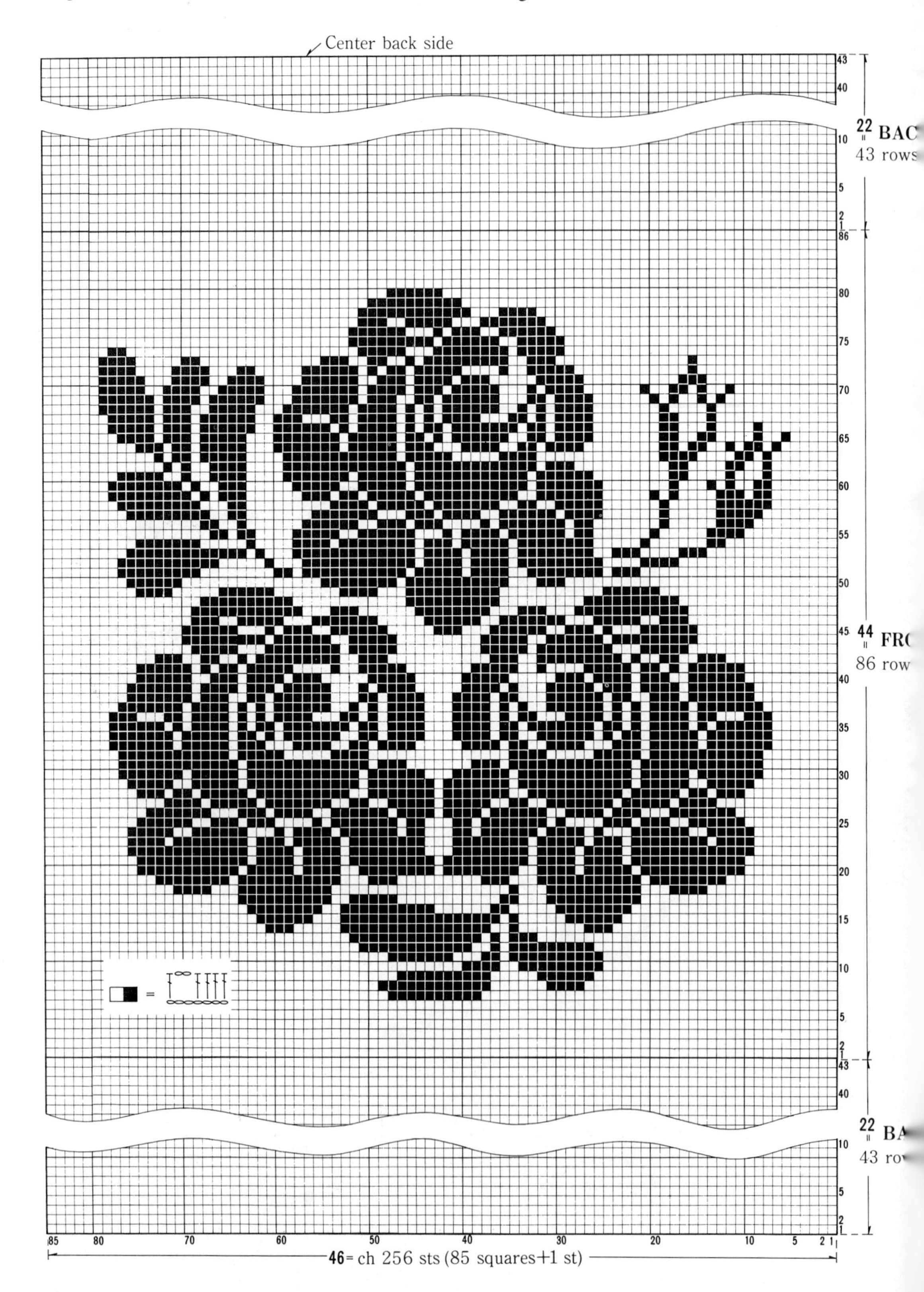

FINISHED SIZE: 46 cm by 44 cm
GAUGE: 10 cm of filet crochet = 18.5 squares; 10 cm = 19.5 rows.
MAKING INSTRUCTIONS:
Start from center back side, ch 256. **Row 1:** Ch 5, dc in 9th ch from hook, (ch 2, sk 2 ch, dc in next ch) 84 times.
Row 2: Ch 5, sk 2 ch, dc in dc. Work following as for row 1.
Rows 3–43 Rows 1–6: Work from back to front in same manner as for rows 1–2.
Row 7: Ch 5, sk 2 ch, dc in dc, (ch 2, sk 2 ch, dc in dc) 37 times, (2 dc in 2 ch, dc in dc) 10 times, *ch 2, sk 2 ch, dc in dc, repeat from *to the end.
Rows 8–80: Work as for row 7, referring to chart.
Rows 81–86 Rows 1–43: Work front to back in same manner as for rows up to 6th.
FINISHING: Put front and back right sides together, join both sides working sc along, put kapok cased in into, close the opening back side with whip stitch. Note: Make inner case 2 cm larger all around than outer case. (finish in the size of 48 cm by 46 cm).

43 TABLECLOTH

YOU'LL NEED: Crochet cotton No. 4 soft twist 15 50-gram balls White. Steel crochet hook size 1.50.
FINISHED SIZE: 123 cm by 118 cm
GAUGE: 10 cm of filet crochet = 13 squares; 10 cm = 14 rows.
SIZE OF MOTIF: 21 cm by 20 cm
MAKING INSTRUCTIONS:
MOTIF A: Ch 85. **Row 1:** Ch 3, dc in 5th ch from hook. Dc in each st following.
Row 2: Ch 3, dc in dc 3 times. Ch 2, sk 2 dc, dc in dc. Dc in dc 12 times, (ch 2, sk 2 dc, dc in dc) 16 times. Dc in dc 12 times. Ch 2, sk 2 dc, dc in dc. Dc in dc 3 times.
Rows 3–28: Work as for row 2. Make 13 pieces.
MOTIF B: Ch 85. **Rows 1–3:** Work as for motif A.
Row 4: Ch 3, 9 dc. Ch 3, sk 2 sts, sc in dc, ch 3, sk 2 sts, dc in dc, (2 dc in 2 ch, dc in dc) 2 times, (ch 2, sk 2 ch, dc in dc) 14 times, (2 dc in 2 ch, dc in dc) 2 times. Ch 3, sk 2 sts, sc in dc, ch 3, sk 2 sts, dc in dc, 9 dc.
Row 5: Ch 3, 9 dc. Ch 5, sk 2 3-ch lps, dc in dc. Ch 2, sk 2 sts, dc in dc. Work in same manner across.
Rows 6–28: Work as for rows previous. Make 12 pieces.
JOINING MOTIFS: Join A and B alternately with net crochet as shown. Join thread in motif A where indicated, work 1 sc. Ch 5, sc in between rows next, *ch 5, sc in between rows next, repeat from *to corner. Sc in corner st, ch 5, sc in same corner st, *ch 5, sk 2 sts, sc in next ch, repeat from *to next corner. Ch 5, sc in corner of motif B 28th row, *ch 2, sc in 5-ch lp of motif A, ch 2, sk 2 sts, sc in next dc, repeat from *to corner. Sc in corner st, ch 5, sc in same corner st, *ch 5, sc in between rows next, repeat from *to next corner. Having worked following sts up to next corner, ch 5, sc in corner of 28th row of A, work same as before. Thus outer motifs are joined in position. The motifs inward are joined with net st worked along 1 piece each. Join thread in the corner of A 28th row, ch 1, sc in corner, ch 2, work sl st pulling through 3 5-ch lps of 3 motifs at a time, ch 2, sc in same corner. Work following sts same as before.

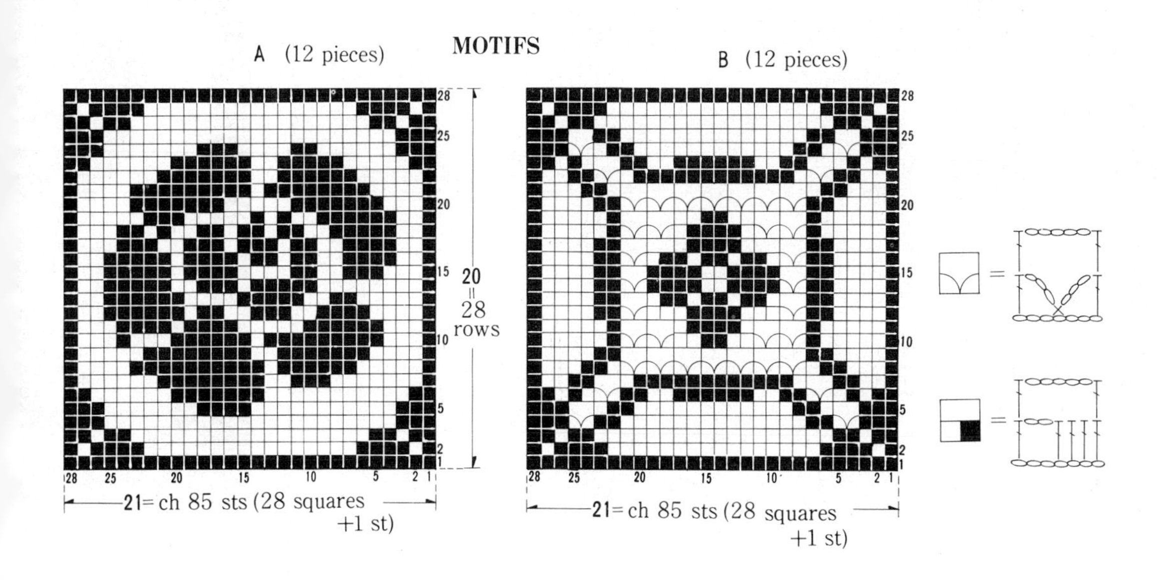

EDGING: Join thread in where indicated. **Row 1:** Ch 1, 1 sc, *ch 2, sc in between rows next, repeat from *to corner. 2 sc in corner, *ch 2, sk 2 dc, sc in next dc, repeat from *to corner. Where at the joint of motifs, sc in corner of motif, ch 2, sc in the middle of 5 ch, ch 2, sc in the corner of next motif. Work in same manner around, sl st in 1st sc. **Row 2:** Ch 3, 2 dc in 2 ch, ch 9, sk 2 2-ch lps, 3 dc in next 2-ch lp. Ch 7 at the corner, 3 dc in next 2-ch lp. Ch 9, sk 2 2-ch lps, 3 dc in next 2-ch lp. Work in same manner around, sl st in 3rd st of beg ch. **Row 3:** Ch 3, dc in dc 2 times. Ch 3, sc in the middle of 9-ch lp. Ch 3, dc in dc 3 times. Ch 3, sc in the middle of 7-ch corner lp. Ch 3, dc in dc 3 times. Work in same manner around. **Row 4:** Ch 3, dc in dc 2 times. Ch 4, sk 3 sts, sc in sc, ch 4, sk 3 ch, dc in dc 3 times. Ch 3, sc in the middle of 3 ch, ch 3, dc in corner sc. Ch 3, sc in the middle of 3 ch, ch 3, dc in dc 3 times. Ch 4, sk 3 ch, sc in sc, ch 4, sk 3 ch, dc in dc 3 times. Repeat in same manner around. **Row 5:** Ch 3, dc in dc 2 times. Ch 9, sk 2 4-ch lps, dc in dc 3 times. Ch 9, sk 2 3-ch lps, 3 dc in corner dc. Work in same manner around. **Row 6:** Work up to corner in same manner as for row 3. 3 dc in corner dc, ch 7, sk 1 dc, 3 dc in next dc. Work in same manner around. **Row 7:** Work up to corner in same manner as for row 4. Ch 3, sc in 7-ch corner lp, ch 3, dc in dc 3 times. Work in same manner around. **Row 8:** Work up to corner in same manner as for row 5. Ch 7, sc in corner sc, ch 7, dc in dc 3 times. Work in same manner around. **Row 9:** Ch 3, 2-dc pop in beg ch of previous row. Ch 1, 3-ch p, 3-dc pop in next dc. Ch 1, 3-ch p, 3-dc pop in next dc. Ch 1, 3-ch p, sc in the middle of 9-ch lp. Repeat in same manner up to corner, work 3 times of 3-dc pop, ch 1, 3-ch p in corner sc, sc in the middle of 7-ch lp. Continue in same manner around.

CHART ON MEASUREMENTS

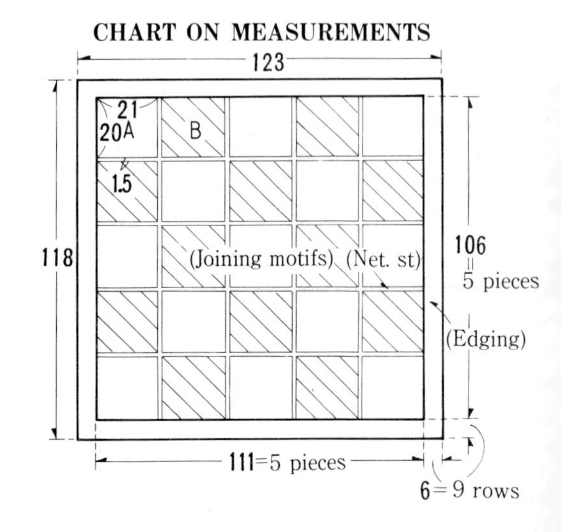

JOINING MOTIFS & EDGING

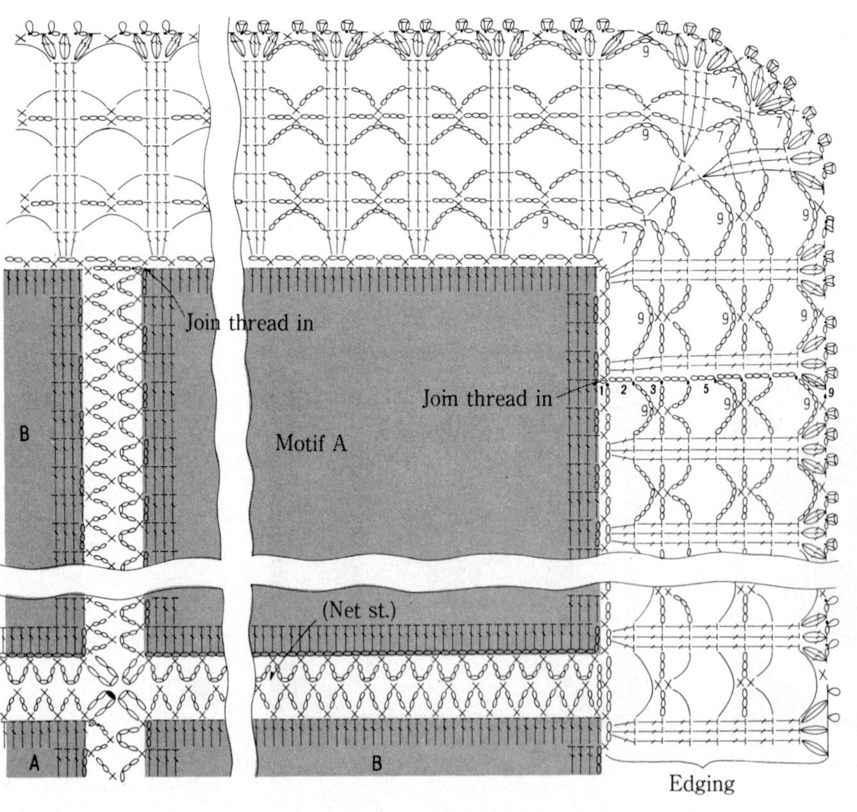

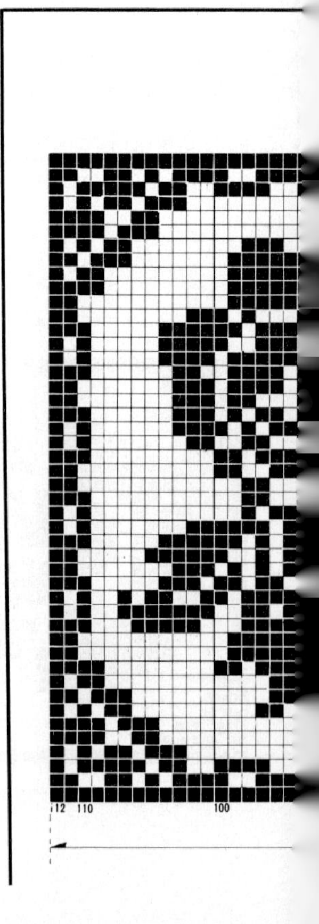

44 RUNNER

YOU'LL NEED: Crochet cotton No. 20 3½ 20-gram balls White. Steel crochet hook size 0.90.
FINISHED SIZE: 59 cm by 26 cm
GAUGE: 10 cm of filet crochet=22 squares; 10 cm =25.5 rows.
MAKING INSTRUCTIONS: Ch 337. **Row 1:** Ch 3, dc in 5th ch from hook, dc in each st to the end.
Row 2: Ch 3, 6 dc, (ch 2, sk 2 dc, dc in dc) 2 times. Dc in dc 6 times, ch 2, sk 2 dc, dc in dc. Repeat across.
Rows 3–46: Work as for rows previous, referring to chart. (1 sp = ch 2, sk 2 sts, dc in dc; bl = 3 dc).
EDGING: Join thread in where indicated. **Row 1:** Ch 6, sc in between rows next. Ch 3, dc in corner dc, ch 5, dc in same corner dc. Ch 3, sk 2 dc, sc in next dc. Ch 3, sk 2 dc, dc in next dc. Work in same manner around, sl st in 3rd st of beg ch. **Row 2:** Turn. Ch 8, sk 2 3-ch lps, dc in dc. *ch 5, sk 2 3-ch lps, dc in dc, repeat from *to corner. Ch 2, dc in 5-ch corner lp, ch 5, dc in same lp, ch 2, dc in dc. Repeat in same manner around, sl st in 3rd st of beg ch. **Rows 3–6:** Repeat 1st and 2nd row. **Row 7:** Ch 3, (5 dc in 5 ch, dc in dc) 3 times. 2 dc in 2 ch, dc in dc, 11 dc in 5-ch corner lp. 2 dc in 2 ch, dc in dc, (5 dc in 5 ch, dc in dc) 2 times. 4 dc in 5 ch, dc in dc, (5 dc in 5 ch, dc in dc) 4 times. 4 dc in 5 ch, dc in dc. Work 354 dc in same manner up to next corner. 11 dc in 5-ch corner lp, work 162 dc up to next corner. Continue in same manner around, sl st in 3rd st of beg ch. **Row 8:** Ch 3, 3 dc, *ch 2, sk 2 dc, 4 dc, repeat from *to corner. Where at 11-dc corner, work 2 dc, ch 2, sk 1 dc, work 2 dc, dc in middle dc, ch 5, dc in same dc, 2 dc, ch 2, sk 1 dc, work 4 dc. Continue in same manner around. **Row 9:** Sc in 2 ch, (ch 3, sk 4 dc, 3 dc in 2 ch, ch 3, 3 dc in same 2 ch. Ch 3, sk 4 dc, sc in 2 ch) 2 times. Ch 3, sk 3 dc, 3 dc in 5-ch corner lp, ch 5, 3 dc in same lp, ch 3, sk 3 dc, sc in 2 ch. Work in same manner around, sl st in 1st sc.

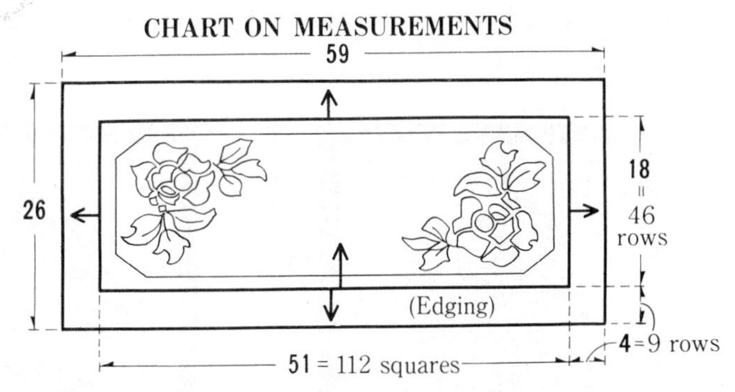

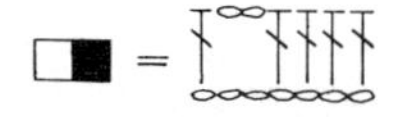

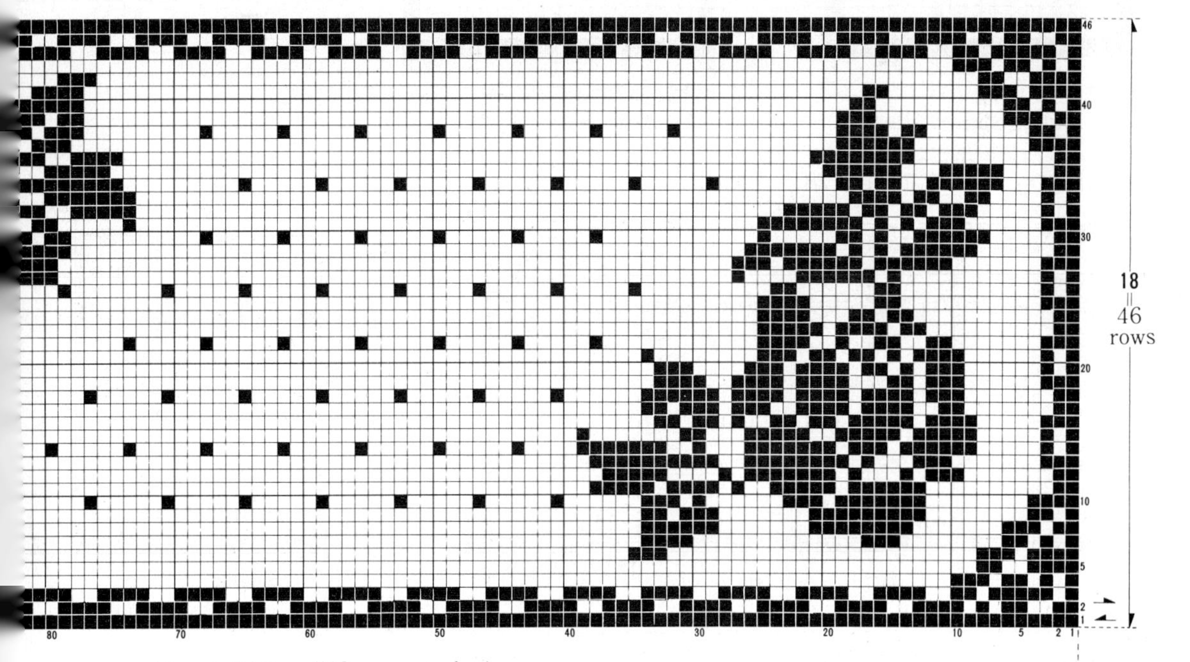

(EDGING CHART ON PAGE 126)

42 CHAIR BACK

YOU'LL NEED: Crochet cotton No. 4 soft twist White 12 50-gram balls for large, 3 50-gram balls for small. Steel crochet hook size 1.50.

FINISHED SIZE: Refer to chart.

GAUGE: 10 cm of filet crochet = 15.5 squares; 10 cm = 16 rows.

SIZE OF MOTIF: 13 cm by 12.5 cm

MAKING INSTRUCTIONS:

LARGE: Crochet A 30 pieces, use 15 pieces reversed, marked (a) on chart. Crochet B 25 pieces.

MOTIF A: Ch 61. **Row 1:** Ch 3, dc in 5th ch from hook. Dc in each st to end.

Row 2: Ch 3, 3 dc, (ch 2, sk 2 sts, dc in dc) 18 times, 3 dc.

Rows 3–20: Work as for rows previous referring to chart.

MOTIF B: Ch 61. Work as for A, following design B.

EDGING ①: Join thread in corner of motif, ch 1, sc in corner, ch 7, sc in same corner, *ch 7, sk 5 sts, sc in next st, repeat from *to corner. Sc in corner, ch 7, sc in same corner, *ch 7, sk 2 rows, sc in between rows next, repeat from *to next corner. Repeat in same manner around, sl st in 1st sc. From 2nd piece, work joining to previous motif as shown. Join thread in corner of motif, ch 1, sc in corner, ch 3, sl st in the middle of corner lp adjacent, ch 3, sc in same corner. Ch 3, sl st in the middle of lp adjacent, ch 3, sk 5 sts, sc in next ch. Join motifs in same manner.

EDGING ②: Join thread in where indicated. **Row 1:** Ch 1, 1 sc, *ch 7, sc in the middle of next 7-ch lp, repeat from *to the lp next to corner lp. Ch 4, dc in the middle of corner lp. **Row 2:** Turn the work reverse side up, ch 1, 1 sc, *ch 7, sc in the middle of next lp, repeat from *to last lp. **Row 3:** Turn right side up, ch 5, sc in the middle of next lp, ch 4, 3-tr pop in same lp, *ch 1, sc in the middle of next lp, ch 4, 3-tr pop in same lp, repeat from *to last lp. Ch 2, dc in sc, ch 7, sc in corner lp of edging (1). Ch 7 sc in the middle of next lp. Work in same manner around, sl st in 3rd st of beg ch.

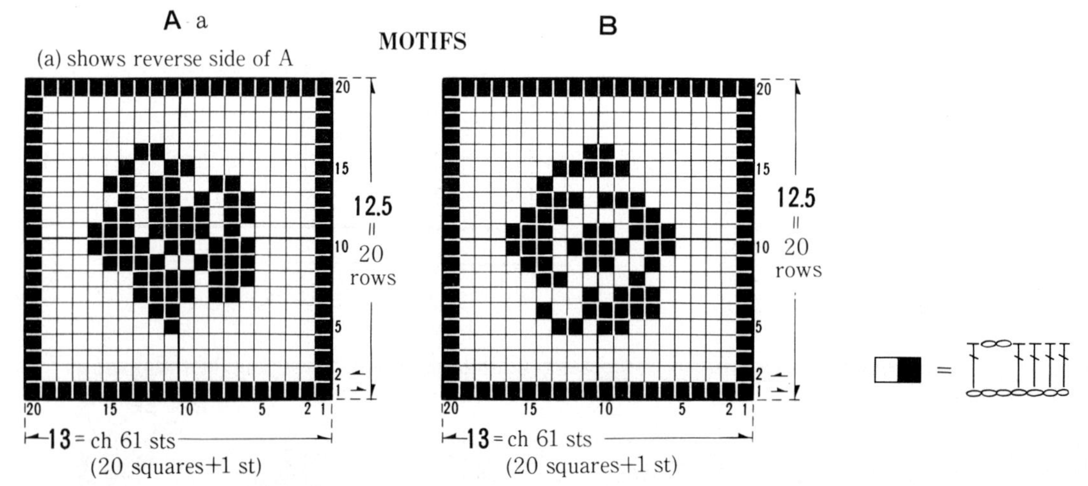

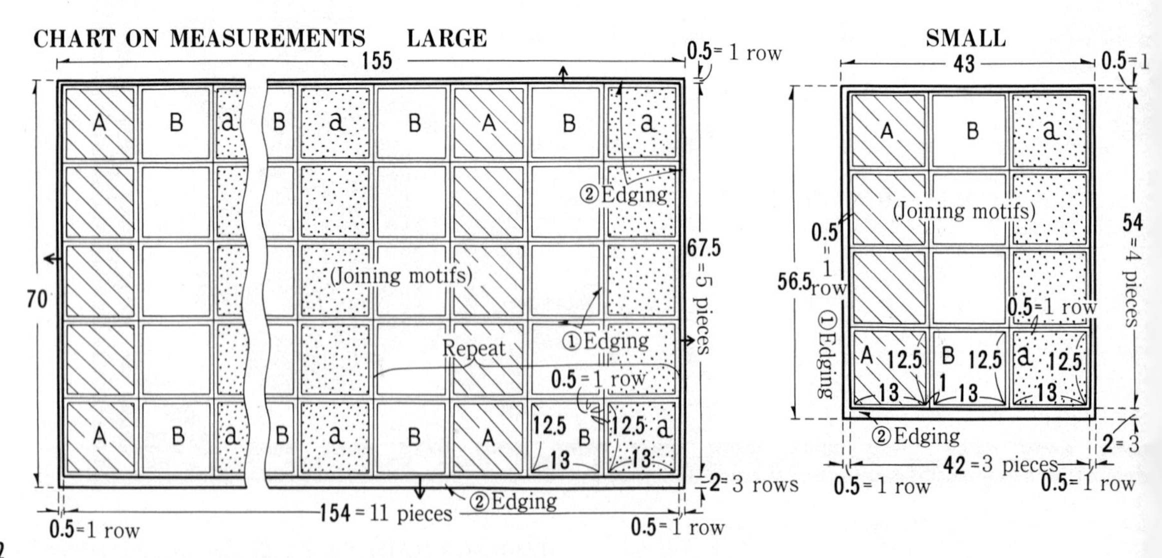

JOINING MOTIFS & EDGING

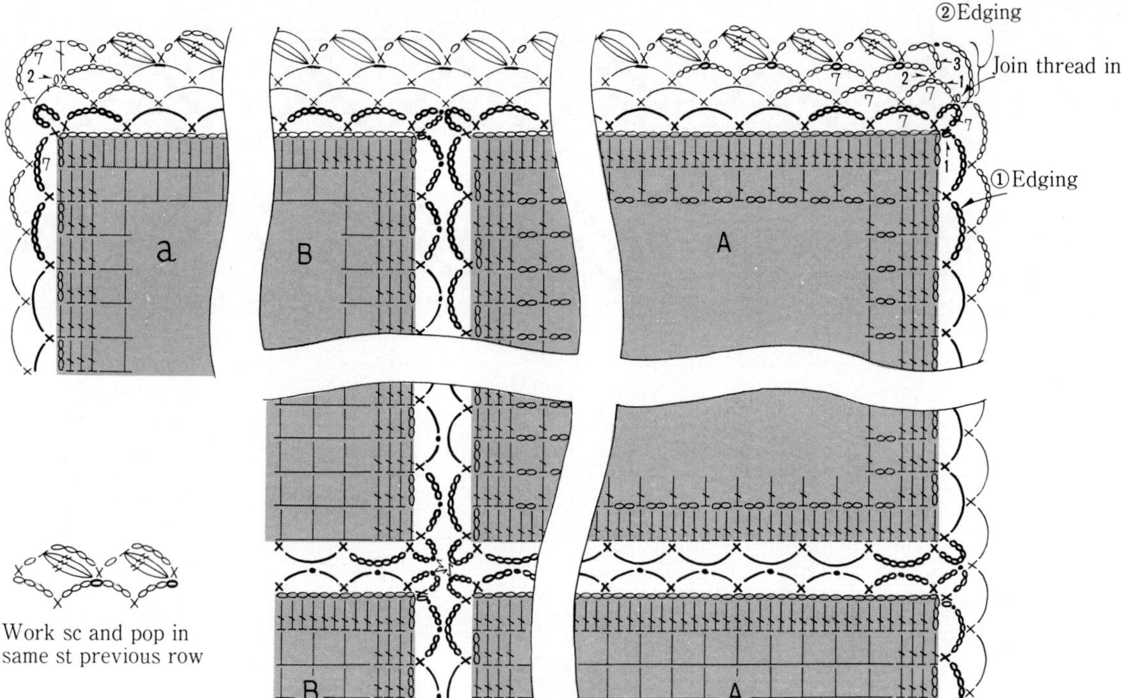

47 TABLECLOTH

YOU'LL NEED: Crochet cotton No. 20 27 20-gram alls White. Steel crochet hook size 1.00.
INISHED SIZE: 156 cm by 120 cm
AUGE: 10 cm of filet crochet = 18 squares; 10 cm = 18 rows.
AKING INSTRUCTIONS:
h 649. Crochet patterns top and bottom, right and eft finished in symmetry. **Row 1:** Ch 5, dc in 9th ch rom hook. *Ch 2, sk 2 ch, dc in next ch, repeat from to end.
Row 2: Ch 5, sk 2 ch, dc in dc, (ch 2, sk 2 ch, dc in c) 9 times. 2 dc in 2 ch, dc in dc, (ch 2, sk 2 ch, dc n dc) 12 times. Work in same manner to end.
Rows 3–281: Work referring to chart (1 sp = ch 2, 2 sts, 1 dc; 1 bl = 3 dc).
ATTERN A: The sts around A are worked as for ows previous.
Row 1: Dc in dc, ch 14, sk 2 dc, dc in next dc.
Row 2: Dc in dc, ch 6, sk 3 dc, 2 sc in 14-ch lp, ch , sk 3 dc, dc in next dc.
Row 3: Dc in dc, ch 6, sc in 6 ch, sc in each of 2 sc. c in next 6 ch, ch 6, sk 3 dc, dc in next dc.
ow 4: Dc in dc, ch 7, sk 3 dc, sc in 6 ch, sc in ach of 4 sc. Sc in next 6 ch, ch 7, sk 3 dc, dc in next dc.
Row 5: Dc in dc, ch 8, sk 3 dc, 2 dc in 7 ch, dc in each of 6 sc. 2 dc in 7 ch, ch 8, sk 3 dc, dc in next dc.
Row 6: Dc in dc, ch 9, sk 3 dc, 2 dc in 8 ch, dc in each of 10 dc. 2 dc in 8 ch, ch 9, sk 3 dc, dc in next dc.
Row 7: Dc in dc, 3 dc in 9 ch, ch 8, sk 2 dc, dc in each of 10 dc. Ch 8, sk 2 dc, 3 dc in 9 ch, dc in next dc.
Row 8: Dc in dc, 3 dc in 8 ch, ch 8, sk 2 dc, sc in each of 6 dc. Ch 8, sk 2 dc, 3 dc in 8 ch, dc in next dc.
Row 9: Dc in dc, 3 dc in 8 ch, ch 8, sk 1 sc, sc in each of 4 sc. Ch 8, sk 1 sc, 3 dc in 8 ch, dc in dc.
Row 10: Dc in dc, 3 dc in 8 ch, ch 9, sk 1 sc, sc in each of 2 sc, sk 1 sc, ch 9, 3 dc in 8 ch, dc in dc.
Row 11: Dc in dc, 3 dc in 9 ch, ch 2, sk 2 sc, 3 dc in 9 ch, dc in dc.
PATTERN B: Work as for A.
EDGING: Join thread in where indicated, ch 1, 1 sc. Work 3 sc in each row length side, 2 sc in corner st, 1 sc in each st cross side. Work in same manner around, end sl st in 1st sc.

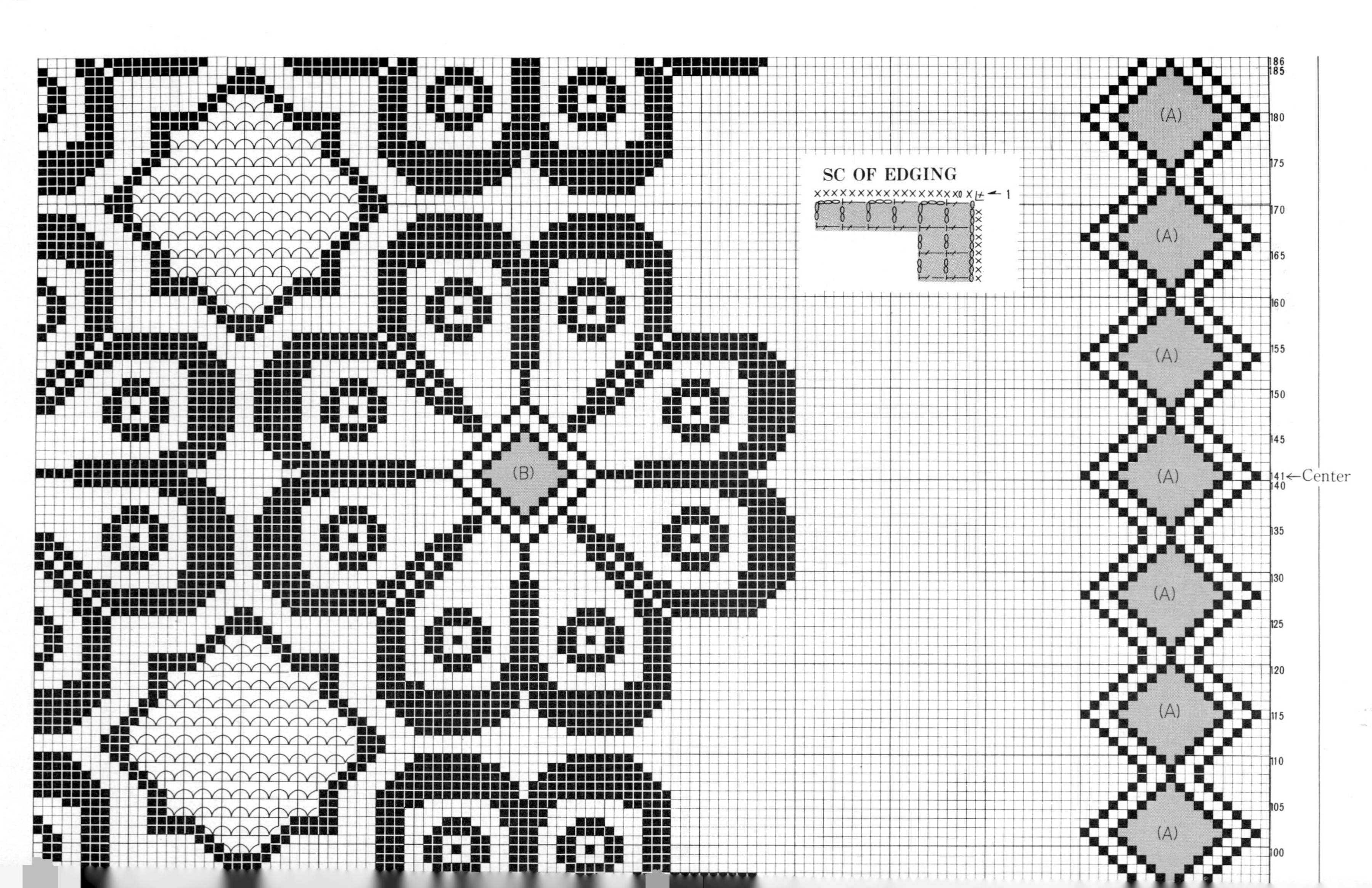

SC OF EDGING
1
(A)
(B)
186
185
180
175
170
165
160
155
150
145
141←Center
140
135
130
125
120
115
110
105
100

281 rows
(B)
(A)
120=ch 649 sts (216 squares+1 st)
Center

45 CENTERPIECE

YOU'LL NEED: Crochet cotton No. 20 12 20-gram balls White. Steel crochet hook size 0.90.

FINISHED SIZE: Refer to chart.

GAUGE: 2 rows of tr = 1.5 cm

MAKING INSTRUCTIONS:

Ch 6, sl st in 1st ch to form ring. **Row 1:** Ch 12, 1 tr tr in ring, (ch 5, tr tr in ring) 10 times, ch 2, dc in 7th st of beg ch.

Row 2: Ch 10, 1 dc in 5-ch lp, (ch 7, dc in 5-ch lp) 10 times, ch 3, tr in 3rd st of beg ch.

Row 3: Ch 11, 1 tr in 7-ch lp, *ch 15, tr in 7-ch lp, ch 7, tr in 7-ch lp, repeat from *around, end ch 12, dc in 4th st of beg ch.

Row 4: Ch 11, tr in the middle of 7 ch. Ch 7, tr in 15-ch corner lp, ch 5, sc in the middle of same lp, ch 5, tr in same corner lp. Ch 7, tr in the middle of 7 ch. Work in same manner around, end ch 2, dc in 4th st of beg ch.

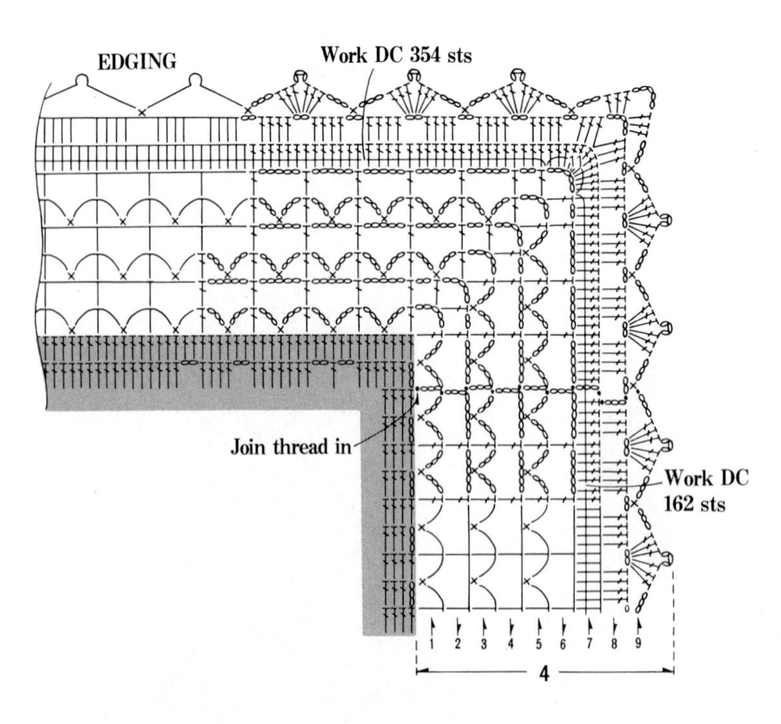

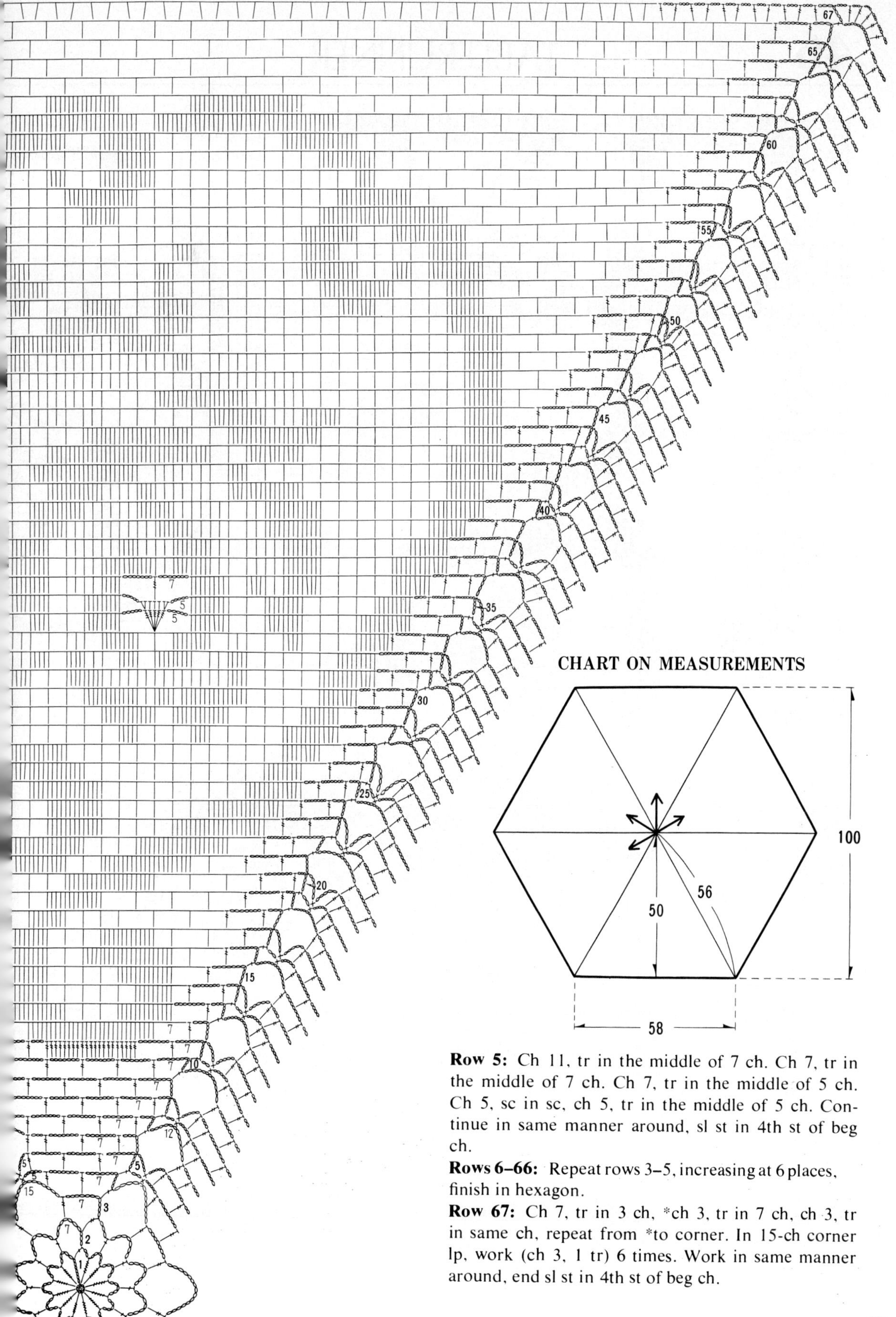

Row 5: Ch 11, tr in the middle of 7 ch. Ch 7, tr in the middle of 7 ch. Ch 7, tr in the middle of 5 ch. Ch 5, sc in sc, ch 5, tr in the middle of 5 ch. Continue in same manner around, sl st in 4th st of beg ch.

Rows 6–66: Repeat rows 3–5, increasing at 6 places, finish in hexagon.

Row 67: Ch 7, tr in 3 ch, *ch 3, tr in 7 ch, ch 3, tr in same ch, repeat from *to corner. In 15-ch corner lp, work (ch 3, 1 tr) 6 times. Work in same manner around, end sl st in 4th st of beg ch.

46 TABLERUNNER

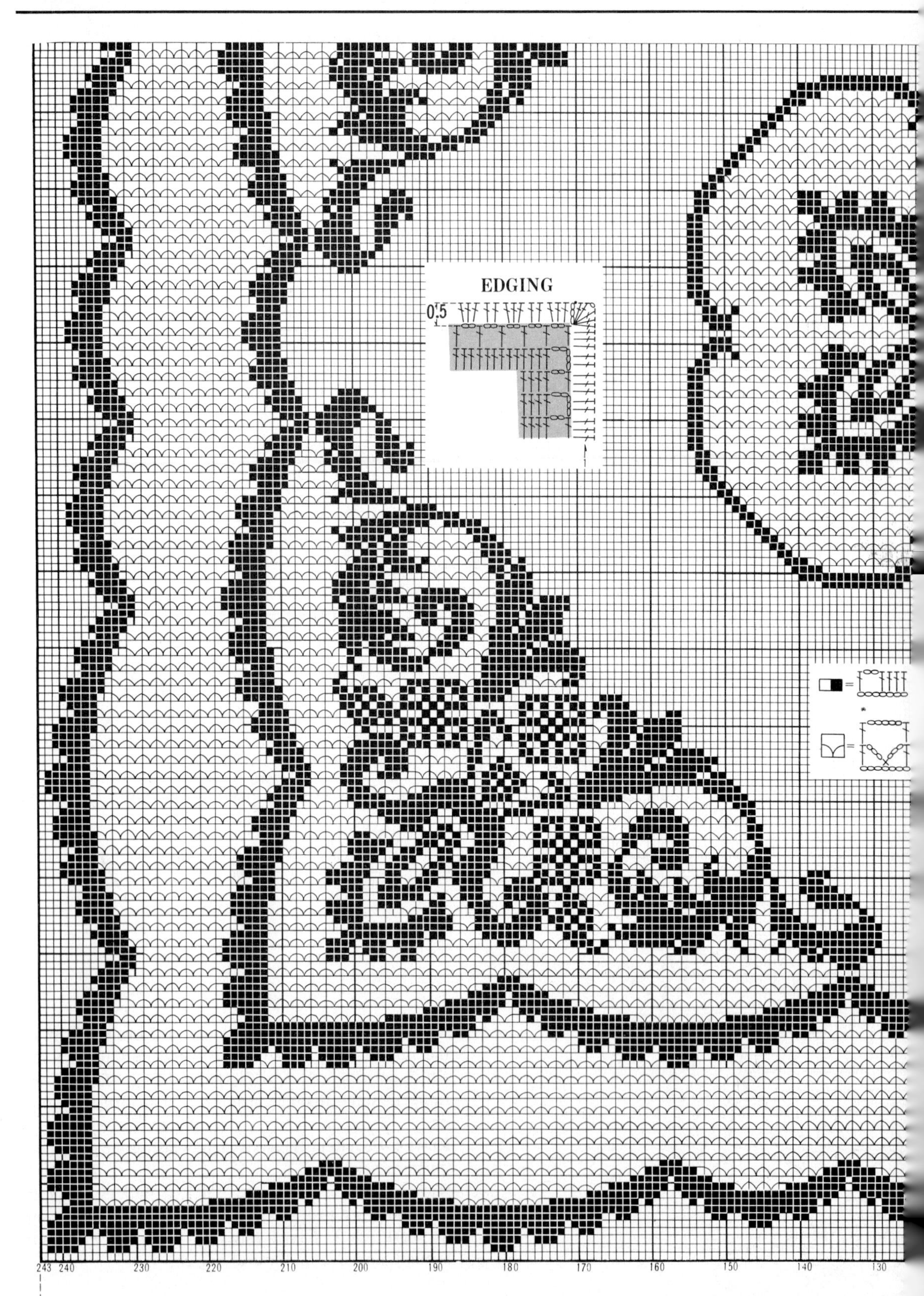

YOU'LL NEED: Crochet cotton No. 20 25 20-gram balls White. Steel crochet hook size 0.90.

FINISHED SIZE: 129 cm by 111 cm

GAUGE: 10 cm of filet crochet = 19 squares; 10 cm = 22 rows.

MAKING INSTRUCTIONS:

Ch 730. **Row 1:** Ch 5, dc in 9th ch from hook, *ch 2, sk 2 ch, dc in next ch, repeat from *to end.

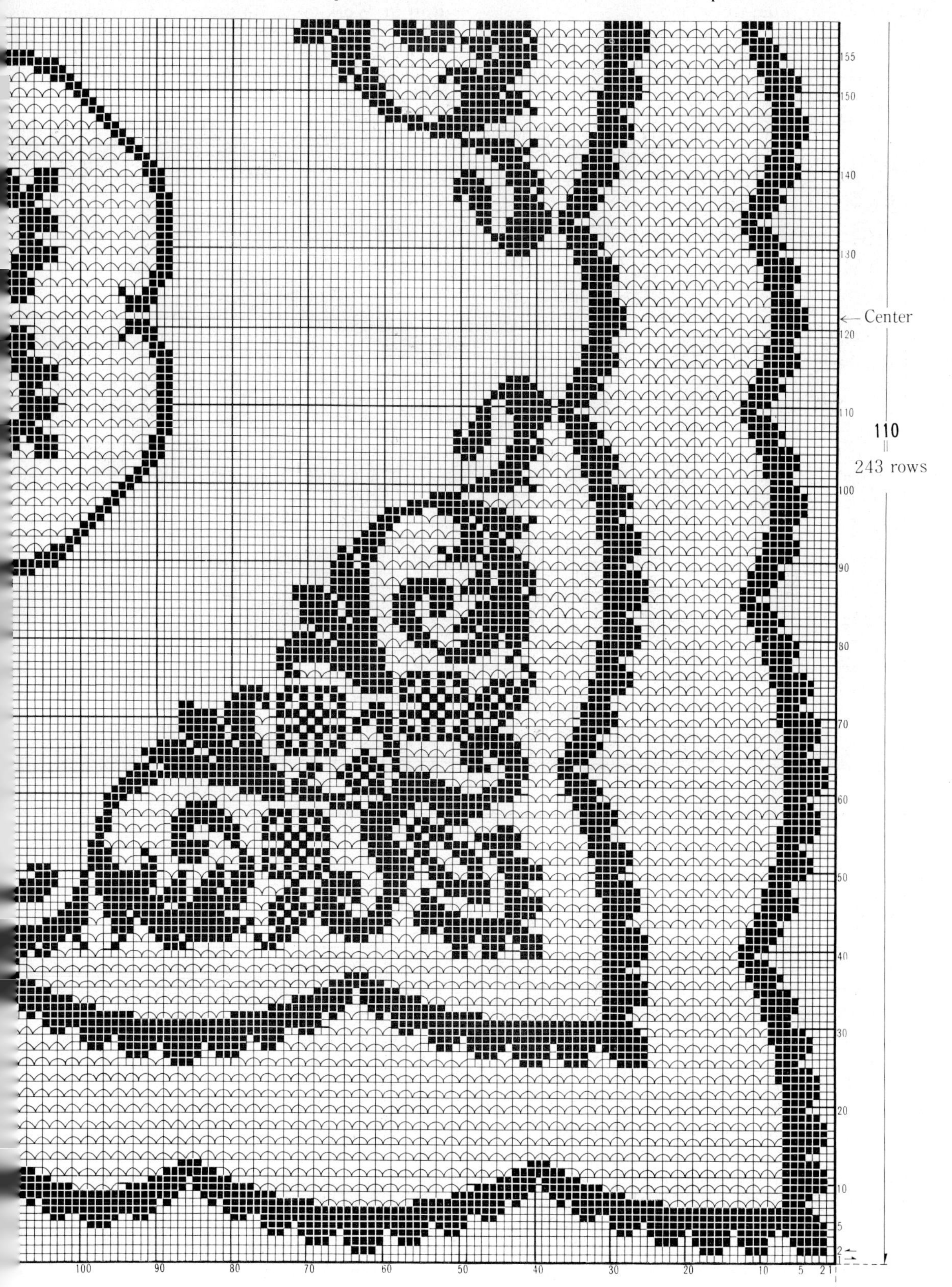

(CONTINUED ON NEXT PAGE)

Row 2: Ch 5, sk 2 ch, dc in dc, (2 dc in 2 ch, dc in dc) 4 times, (ch 2, sk 2 ch, dc in dc) 4 times. Work in same manner to end.

Rows 3–7: Work as for row 2, referring to chart (1 sp-ch 2, sk 2 sts, 1 dc; 1 bl –3 dc).

Row 8: Ch 5, sk 2 sts, 1 dc, (ch 2, sk 2 sts, dc in dc) 3 times, (2 dc in 2 ch, dc in dc) 3 times, (ch 3, sk 2 sts, sc in dc, ch 3, sk 2 sts, dc in dc) 8 times. Work in same manner to end.

Row 9: Work up to 7th square as for rows previous.

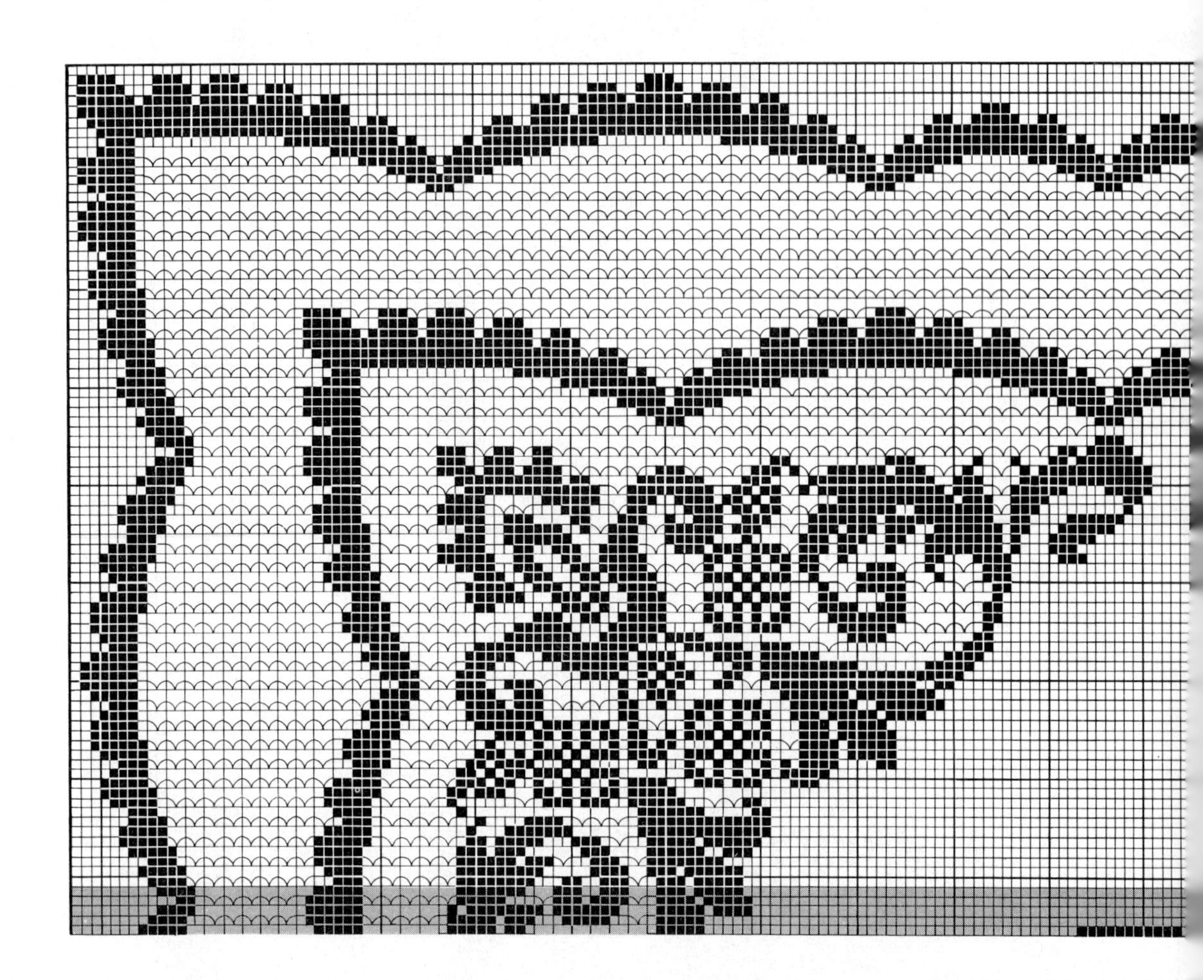

52 TABLECLOTH

YOU'LL NEED: Crochet cotton No. 20 30 20-gram balls White. Steel crochet hook size 0.90.

FINISHED SIZE: 128 cm by 110 cm

GAUGE: 10 cm of filet crochet=20 squares; 10 cm =23.5 rows.

MAKING INSTRUCTIONS:

Ch 727. Work filet crochet making design together with the length from center finish in symmetry.

Row 1: Ch 5, dc in 9th ch from hook, *ch 2, sk 2 ch, dc in next ch, repeat from *to end.

Row 2: Ch 5, sk 2 ch, dc in dc, (ch 2, sk 2 ch, dc in dc) 14 times, (2 dc in 2 ch, dc in dc) 5 times. Work in same manner to end.

Rows 3–4: Work as for row 2, referring to chart (1 sp=ch 2, sk 2 sts, 1 dc; 1 bl=3 dc).

Row 5: Work up to 40th square as for rows pr vious, (ch 3, sk 2 dc, sc in next dc, ch 3, sk 2 dc, in next dc) 4 times. Work in same manner across.

Row 6: Work up to 40th square as for rows previou (ch 5, sk 2 3-ch lps, dc in dc) 4 times. Work in sar manner across.

Rows 7–242: Work as for rows up to 6.

EDGING: Work changing crochet direction eve row. **Row 1:** Join thread in where indicated, ch 4. corner sp, work 1 tr, ch 2, 1 tr, ch 3, 1 tr, ch 2, 2 *Ch 4, tr in top of dc next row, tr in 1st ch next ro repeat from *to corner. 2 tr in corner sp, ch 2, tr same sp, ch 3, tr in same sp, ch 2, 2 tr in same Ch 4, tr in 2nd ch next sp, tr in next dc, *ch 4, sk sts, tr in ch, tr in dc, repeat from *to corner. Wc (ch 5, sk 2 3-ch lps, dc in dc) 8 times, (ch 5, sk 5 sts, dc in dc) 2 times. Work in same manner to end. **Rows 10–243:** Work as for rows up to 9. **EDGING:** Join thread in the edge of row 243. **Row 1:** Ch 3, 3 dc in 2 ch, *sk 1 dc, 2 dc in 2 ch, sk 1 dc, 3 dc in 2 ch, repeat from *to corner. 3 dc in corner st, ch 1, 3 dc in same corner st. Work 5 dc in every 2 rows length side. Work in same manner around, sl st in 3rd st of beg ch.

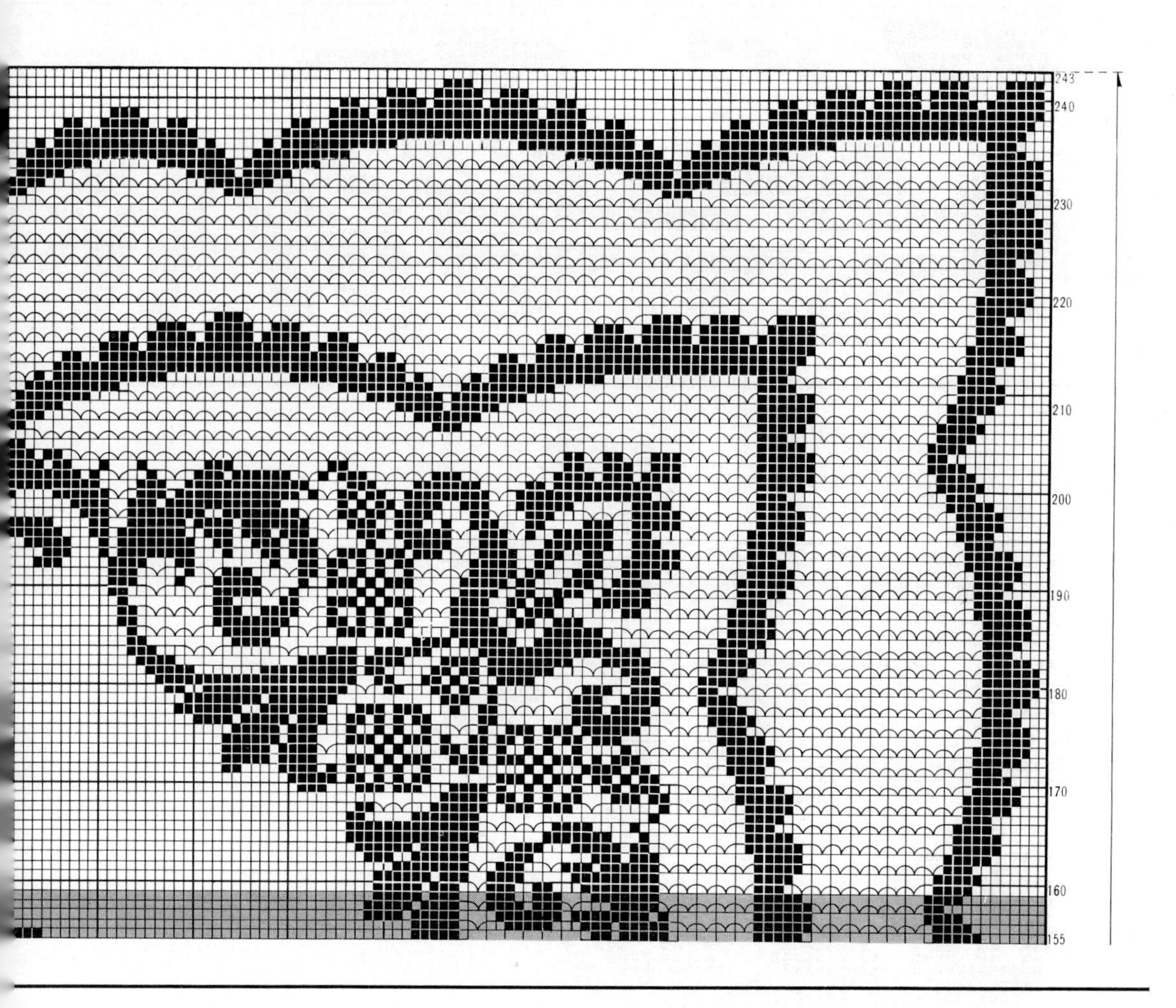

EDGING

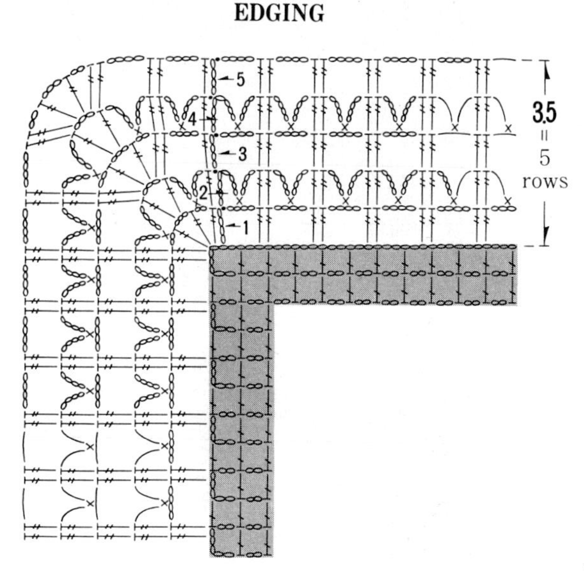

ı same manner around, sl st in 4th st of beg ch. **Row 2:** Ch 8, sc in the middle of 4 ch, ch 4, tr in each of 2 tr, *ch 4, sc in the middle of 4 ch, ch 4, tr in each of 2 tr, repeat from *to corner. Sc in 2 ch at the corner, ch 4, tr in 3 ch, ch 3, tr in same ch. Ch 4, sc in 2 ch. Work in same manner around, sl st in 4th st of beg ch. **Row 3:** Ch 4, tr in tr. Ch 4, sk 2 4-ch lps, tr in tr. In 3-ch corner lp, work 1 tr, ch 2, 1 tr, ch 3, 1 tr, ch 2, 1 tr. Tr in tr, *ch 4, sk 2 4-ch lps, tr in each of 2 tr, repeat from *to corner. Work in same manner around, sl st in 4th st of beg ch. **Rows 4–5:** Work as for rows 2–3.

Center
Center
Center
197
190
180
170
160
150
140
130
120
110
103
=
242
rows

Center
Center
121 = ch 727 sts (242 squares+1 st)
=
=

48 CENTERPIECE

YOU'LL NEED: Crochet cotton No. 20 3 20-gram balls White. Steel crochet hook size 0.90.
FINISHED SIZE: 52.5 cm by 30.5 cm in oval
GAUGE: 10 cm of filet crochet = 20 squares; 10 cm = 20 rows.
MAKING INSTRUCTIONS:
Ch 58. **Row 1:** Ch 3, dc in 5th ch from hook. Dc in each st to end.
Row 2: Ch 15, dc in 5th ch from hook. 11 dc, (ch 2, sk 2 dc, dc in next dc) 19 times. Inc 12 sts with tr.
Rows 3–37: Work as for row 2, increasing sts on both sides referring to chart. Work ch 2, sk 2 sts, 1 dc, for each sp; 3 dc for each bl.
Row 38: Work up to 29th square in same manner as for rows previous. Ch 5, sk 5 sts, dc in dc. Repeat in same manner to end.
Row 39: Work up to 26th square in same manner as before, (ch 3, sk 2 sts, sc in next st, ch 3, sk 2 sts, dc in dc) 4 times. Continue same as before.
Rows 40–70: Work as for rows previous.
Row 71: Work sl st from edge to 4th st, ch 3, 2 dc in 2 ch, dc in dc. Work in same manner up to 3 sts this side from edge, dec 1 bl.
Rows 72–105: Work decreasing sts on both sides, making design finish in symmetry at row 53.

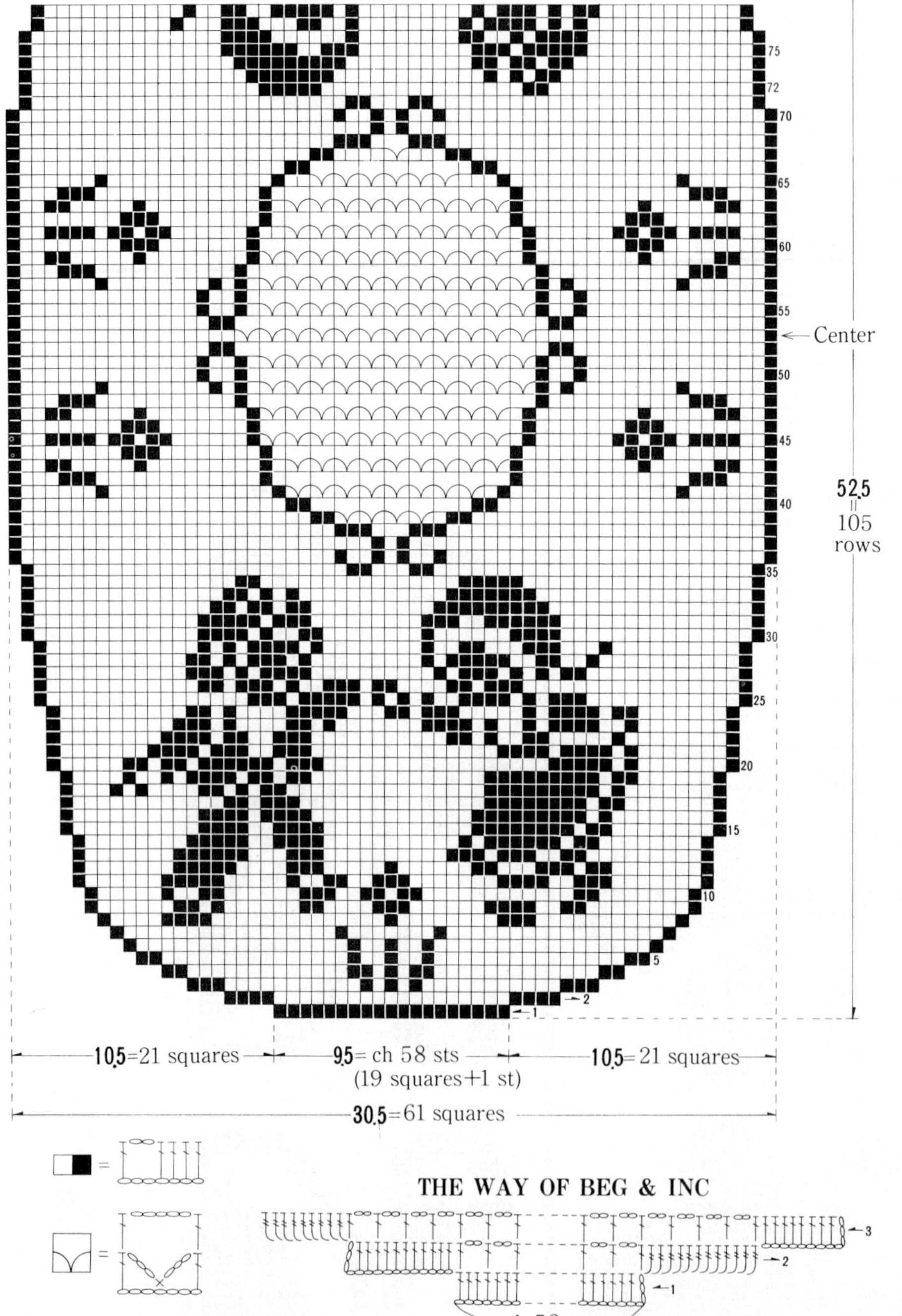

COVER DOILY

YOU'LL NEED: Crochet cotton No. 20 1½ 20-gram balls White. Steel crochet hook size 0.90.

FINISHED SIZE: 32 cm in diameter

GAUGE: 1 row of dc=0.5 cm

MAKING INSTRUCTIONS:

Ch 6, sl st in 1st st to form ring. **Row 1:** Ch 3, 2 dc in ring, ch 1, (3 dc, ch 1) 5 times, end with sl st in 3rd st of beg ch.

Row 2: Ch 3, 2 dc in next dc, dc in next dc, *ch 2, dc in 1 ch, ch 2, dc in dc, 2 dc in next dc, dc in next dc, repeat from *5 times, ch 2, 1 dc, ch 2, end with sl st in 3rd st of beg ch.

Row 3: Ch 3, 1 dc each in 3 dc, ch 2, dc in next dc, ch 2, dc in same dc, ch 2, *4 dc, ch 2, dc in next dc, ch 2, dc in same dc, ch 2, repeat from *5 times, end with sl st in 3rd st of beg ch.

Row 4: Work as for previous row, working dc in dc, ch 2, 1 dc in 2 ch, ch 2, dc in dc at every corner.

Rows 5–31: Work as for rows 3–4, increasing sts at 6 places. Work ch 2, 1 dc for each sp, 3 dc for each bl referring to chart.

Row 32: Join thread in where indicated, crochet one side each. Ch 3, 1 dc each in 69 sts.

Row 33: Turn the work reverse side facing to you, sl st in 22 sts, ch 3, 1 de each in 27 sts. Work remains in same manner and finish in hexagon.

EDGING: Join thread in where indicated, ch 1, 1 sc, *ch 3, sk 2 dc, 1 sc, repeat from *around.

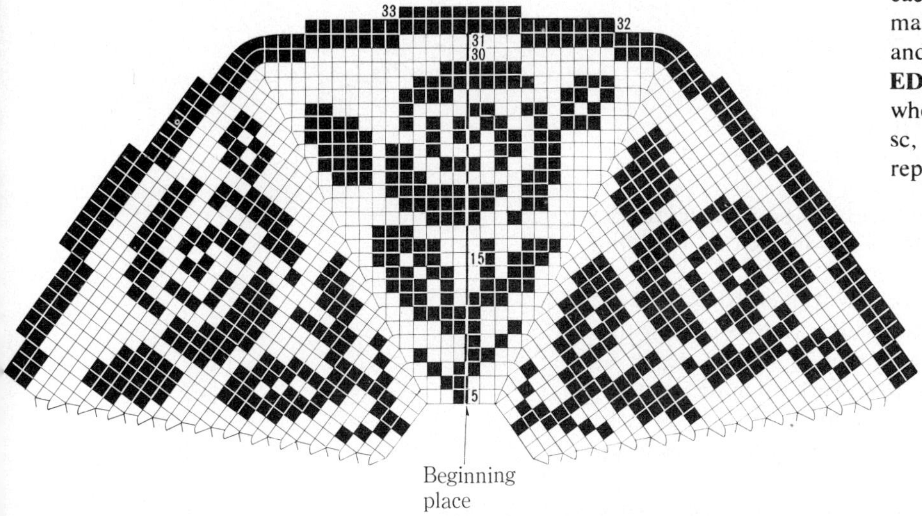

33

32

31

30

15

5

Beginning place

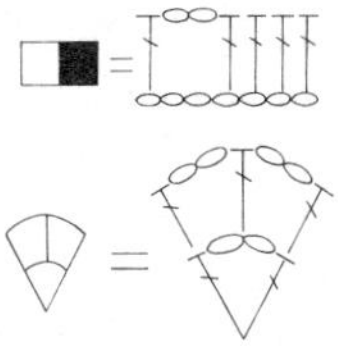

THE WAY OF DEC & EDGING

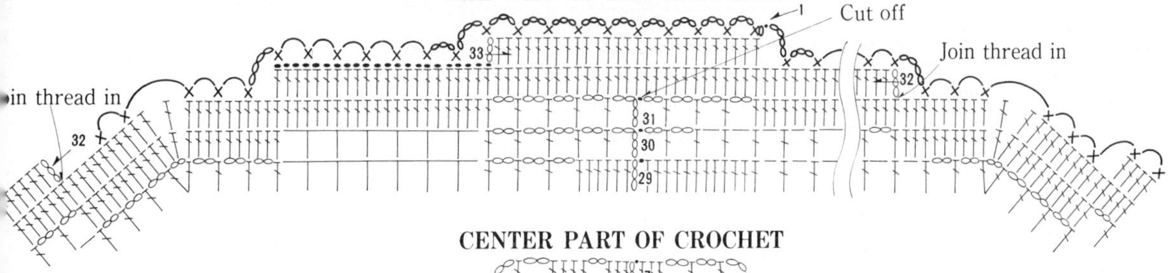

Cut off

Join thread in

Join thread in

33

32

31

30

29

32

CENTER PART OF CROCHET

7

6

5

4

3

2

1

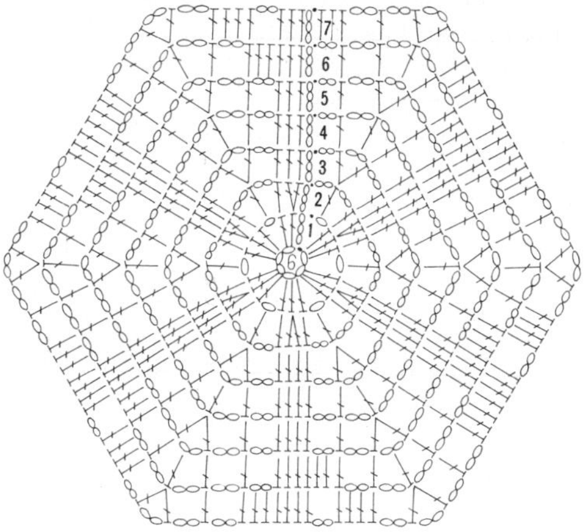

49 CENTERPIECE

YOU'LL NEED: Crochet cotton No. 20 3½ 20-gram balls White. Steel crochet hook size 0.90.
FINISHED SIZE: 61 cm by 29.5 cm in oval
GAUGE: 10 cm of filet crochet = 19 squares; 10 cm = 22 rows.

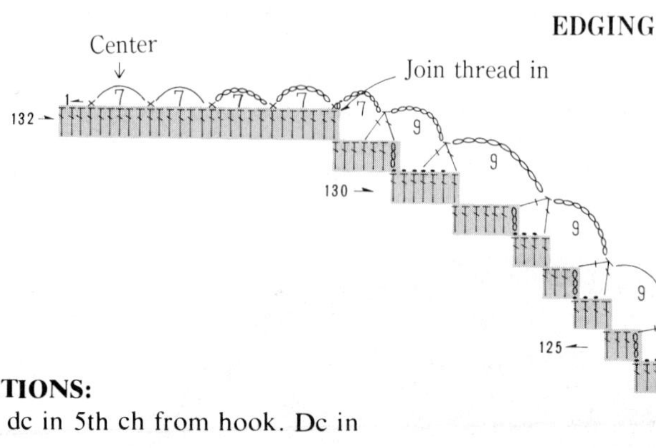

MAKING INSTRUCTIONS:
Ch 43. **Row 1:** Ch 3, dc in 5th ch from hook. Dc in each st across.
Row 2: Ch 9, dc in 5th ch from hook. 8 dc, (ch 2, sk 2 sts, dc in dc) 12 times. Dc in each of 3 sts, inc 6 sts with tr.
Rows 3–32: Work as for row 2, increasing sts both sides. (1 sp = ch 2, sk 2 sts, 1 dc; 1 bl = 3 dc) For the pattern crochet starting on row 28, work 1 dc, ch 5, sk 5 sts, 1 dc. On 29th row, work dc in dc, ch 3, sc in the middle of 5 ch, ch 3, dc in dc.
Rows 33–101: Work straight in same manner as for rows previous.
Row 102: Work sl st from edge to 4th st, ch 3, 3 dc. Work up to 3 sts this side of edge in same manner, dec 1 bl.
Rows 103–132: Work as for row 102, decreasing sts both sides.
EDGING: Join thread where indicated, ch 1, sc in dc, (ch 7, sk 5 dc, sc in dc) 7 times. Where at the place decreased, ch 7, work 2 dc at a time in 4th st from edge and edge st on the row next, (ch 9, 2 dc at a time in next 2 corners) 4 times, (ch 7, 2 dc at a time in top of next row and the corner next) 3 times, (ch 7, sk 2 rows, 2 dc at a time in top of next row and the following corner) 2 times, (ch 7, 2 dc at a time in top of next row and that of following) 2 times. Ch 7, sk 2 rows, 2 dc at a time in next row and the row next. Ch 7, sk 2 rows, sc in corner of next row. Where at the even side, work ch 7, sk 2 rows, sc in between rows next. Repeat along. Work in same manner all around, end sl st in 1st sc.

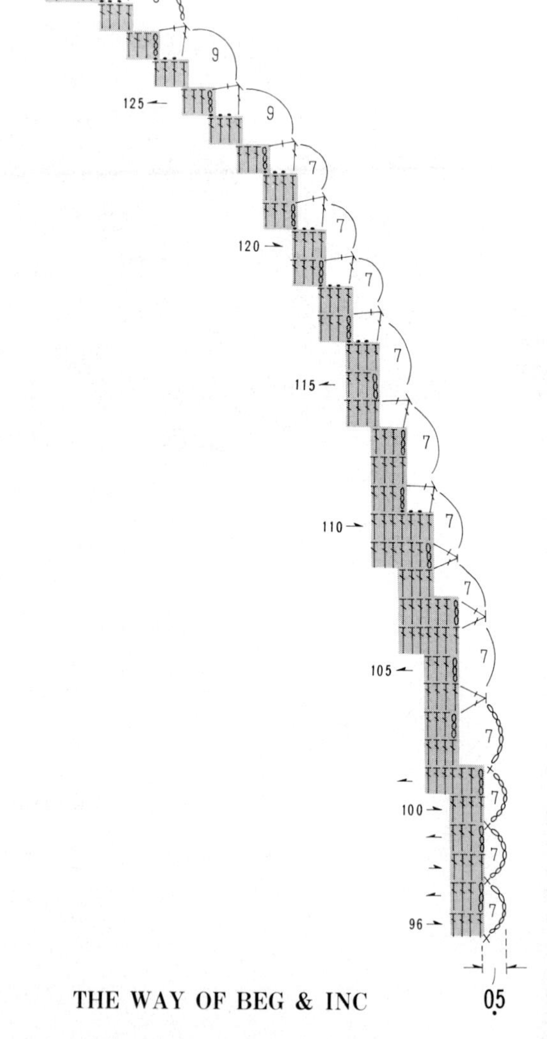

THE WAY OF BEG & INC

Ch 43 sts
(14 squares + 1 st)

28.5=54 squares
60
=
132 rows
10.5=20 squares
7.5=ch 43 sts
(14 squares+1 st)
10.5=20 squares

50 CENTERPIECE

YOU'LL NEED: Crochet cotton No. 20 8½ 20-gram balls White. Steel crochet hook size 0.90.
FINISHED SIZE: 96.5 cm by 51.5 cm
GAUGE: 10 cm of filet crochet = 18.5 squares; 10 cm = 18.5 rows.

MAKING INSTRUCTIONS:
Ch 286. **Row 1:** Ch 3, dc in 5th ch from hook. 1 dc in each of 5 sts, (ch 2, sk 2 ch, dc in next ch) 6 times, dc in each of 21 sts. Continue in same manner across. **Row 2:** Ch 3, dc in each of 6 dc, (ch 2, sk 2 ch, dc

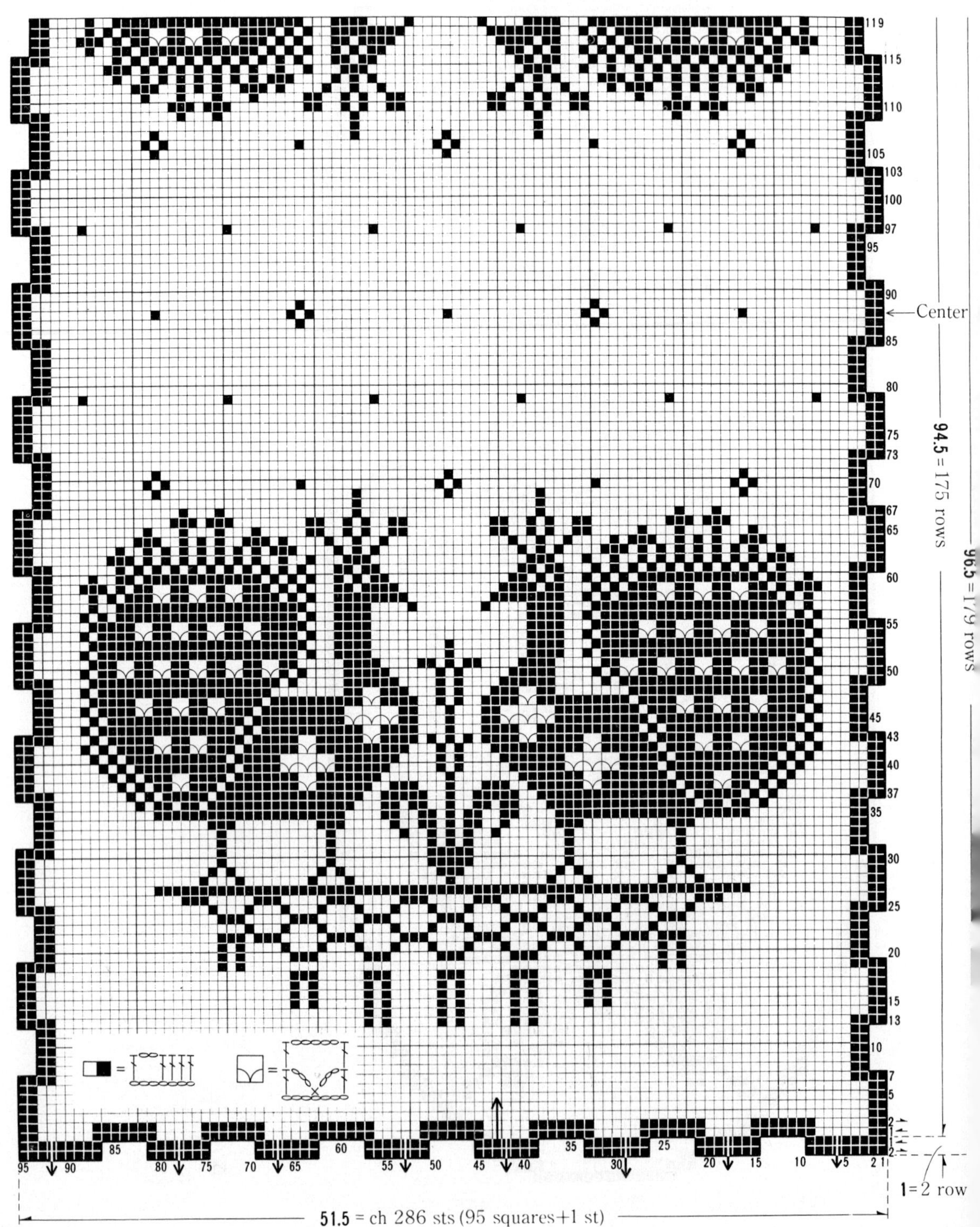

in dc) 6 times, dc in each of 21 sts. Continue in same manner to end.

Rows 3–7: Work as for row 2.

Row 8: Sl st from edge to 7th st, ch 3. 6 dc, ch 2, sk 2 ch, dc in dc. Continue in same manner up to 12 sts this side from edge, 6 dc, leave 6 sts.

Rows 9–37: Work as for rows up to 8th. Inc or dec following chart.

Row 38: Ch 3, 6 dc, work 15 squares same as before. Ch 3, sk 2 sts, sc in dc, ch 3, sk 2 sts, dc in dc. Work next 12 squares same as before, ch 3, sk 2 sts, sc in dc, ch 3, sk 2 sts, dc in dc. Work in same manner across.

Row 39: Ch 3, 6 dc, work 15 squares same as before. Ch 5, sk 2 3-ch lps, dc in dc. Work 12 squares same as before, ch 5, sk 2 3-ch lps, dc in dc. Work in same manner across.

Rows 40–175: Work as for rows up to 39th.

Rows 176–177 & Rows 1–2: Join thread in 8 places respectively, work 2 rows of dc.

EDGING: Sc in each st cross side. Sc in between rows, ch 2, sc in between rows next, continue along length side. Where at the corner, work sc in corner, ch 1, sc in same corner. Work in same manner all around.

THE WAY OF INC & DEC ON BOTH SIDES, EDGING

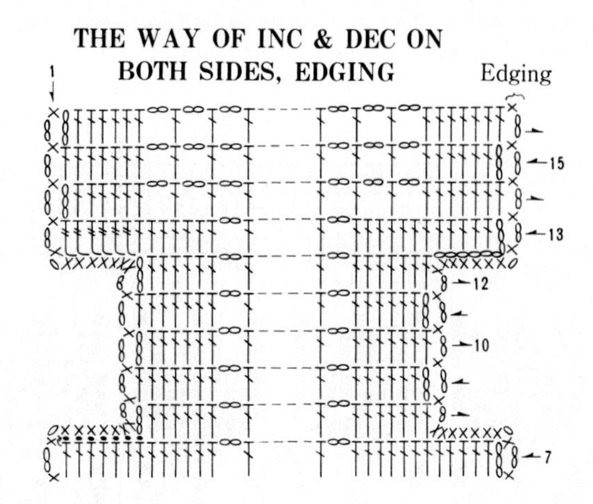

51 CENTERPIECE

YOU'LL NEED: Crochet cotton No. 20 7¼ 20-gram balls White. Steel crochet hook size 0.90.

FINISHED SIZE: 60.5 cm square

GAUGE: 10 cm of filet crochet = 19.5 squares; 10 cm = 19.5 rows.

MAKING INSTRUCTIONS: Ch 301. **Row 1:** Ch 5, dc in 9th ch from hook. *ch 2, sk 2 ch, dc in next ch, repeat from *across.

Row 2: Ch 5, sk 2 ch, dc in dc, *ch 2, sk 2 ch, dc in dc, repeat from *across.

Rows 3–10: Work as for row 2.

Row 11: Ch 5, sk 2 ch, dc in dc, (ch 2, sk 2 ch, dc in dc) 17 times. 2 dc in 2 ch, dc in dc, (ch 2, sk 2 ch, dc in dc) 3 times. 2 dc in 2 ch, dc in dc. Repeat in same manner to end.

Rows 12–33: Work as for row 11, referring to chart.

Row 34: Work up to 37th square as for rows previous, (ch 5, sk 5 sts, dc in dc) 2 times. 21 dc, ch 2, sk 2 sts, sc in dc. Ch 5, sk 5 sts, dc in dc. Repeat in same manner to end.

Row 35: Work up to 36th square as for rows previous. Ch 2, 2 sts (tr and dc) at a time in dc and the dc 2 sts skipped. Ch 3, sc in the middle of 5 ch, ch 3, dc in dc. Ch 3, sc in the middle of 5 ch, ch 3, 2 sts (dc and tr) at a time in dc and the dc 2 sts skipped. Continue in same manner to end.

Rows 36–63: Work as for rows up to 35.

Row 64: Work up to 33rd square as for rows previous. 2 dc in 3 ch, tr in sc, ch 2, sk 3-ch lp, dc in dc. Ch 5, sk 2 3-ch lps, dc in dc. Work in same manner to end.

Row 65: Work as for row 61.

Row 66: Work up to 35th square as for rows previous. 2 dc in 3-ch lp, tr in sc, ch 2, sk 3-ch lp, dc in dc, (ch 5, sk 2 3-ch lps, dc in dc) 2 times. Ch 2, sk

EDGING

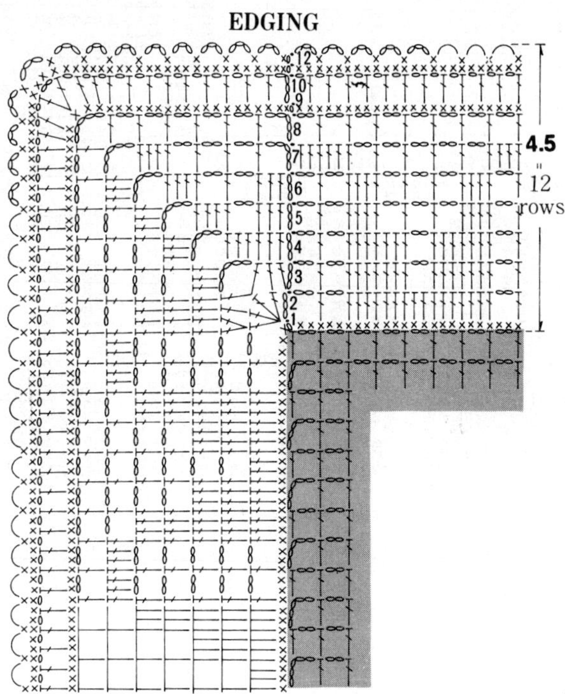

3-ch lp, tr in sc, 2 dc in 3-ch lp, dc in dc, (2 dc in 3-ch lp, tr in sc, 2 dc in 3-ch lp, dc in dc) 2 times. Work in same manner up to end.

Rows 67–100: Work as for rows previous.

EDGING: Join thread in corner dc of 100th row. **Row 1:** Ch 1, sc in dc. 3 sc in each row up to following corner. 2 sc in 2 ch, sc in dc along cross side. Work in same manner around, end sl st in 1st sc. **Row 2:** Ch 3, 4 dc in corner sc, *ch 2, sk 2 sc, dc in next sc, ch 2, sk 2 sc, dc in each of 16 sc, repeat from *to corner, 5 dc in corner sc. Work in same manner around, sl st in 3rd st of beg ch. **Row 3:** Ch 3, dc in 3rd st of beg ch previous row, dc in dc, dc in corner dc, ch 5, dc in same corner dc, dc in next dc, 2 dc in next dc, *ch 2, sk 2 ch, dc in dc, ch 2, sk 2 ch, dc in each of 7 dc, ch 2, sk 2 dc, dc in each of 7 dc, repeat from *to corner. 2 dc in 1st corner dc, dc in next dc, dc in center dc, ch 5, dc in same center dc, dc in next dc, 2 dc in last dc. Work in same manner around, sl st in 3rd st of beg ch. **Row 4:** Ch 3, dc in each of 3 dc. 3 dc in 5-ch lp, ch 5, 3 dc in same lp. Dc in each of 4 dc, *ch 2, sk 2 ch, dc in dc, ch 2, sk 2 ch, dc in each of 7 dc, ch 2, sk 2 ch, dc in each of 7 dc, repeat from *to corner. Work in same manner around, al st in 3rd st of beg ch. **Rows 5–8:** Work as for row 4. **Row 9:** Ch 1, sc in 3rd st of beg ch previous row. Sc in each st around, end sl st in 1st sc. **Row 10:** Ch 4 sk 1 sc, dc in next sc *ch 1, sk 1 sc, dc in next sc, repeat from *to corner. Dc in corner sc, ch 2, dc in same sc. Repeat in same manner around, sl st in 1st sc. **Row 11:** Ch 1, sc in 3rd st of beg ch previous row. Sc in each st around, sl st in 1st sc. **Row 12:** Ch 1, sc in sc *ch 3, sk 2 sc, sc in next sc, repeat from *around, sl st in 1st sc.

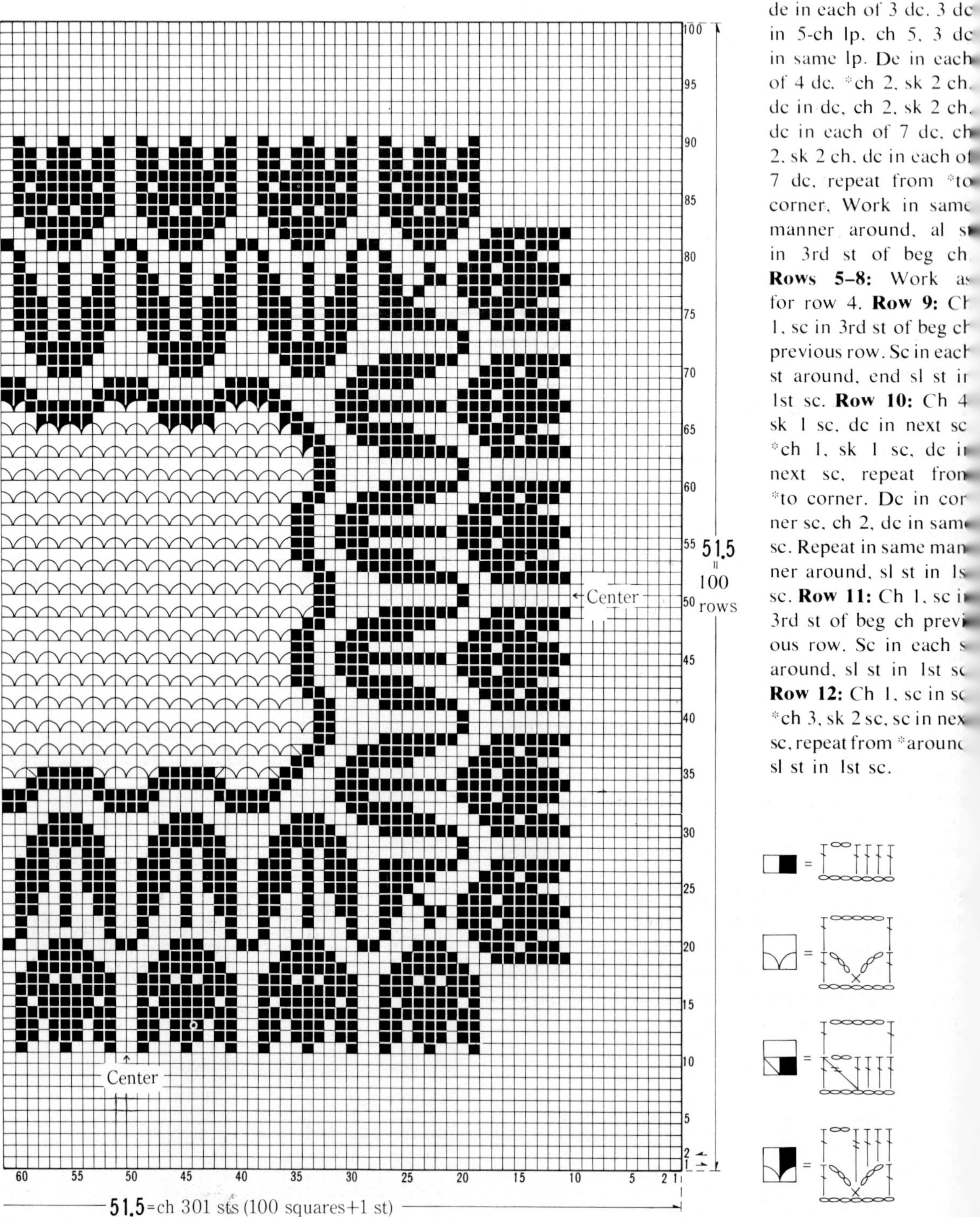

BASIC CROCHET LACE

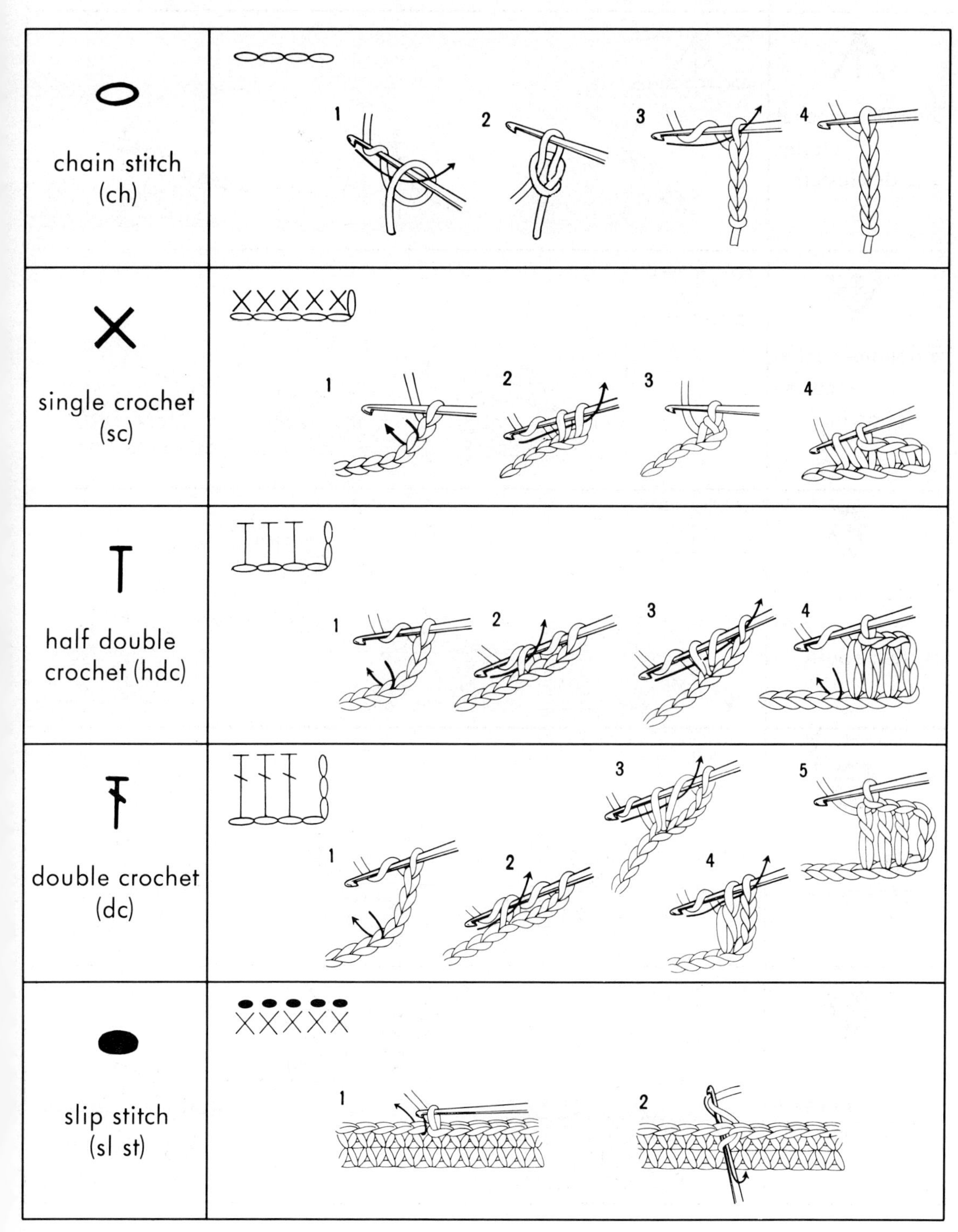

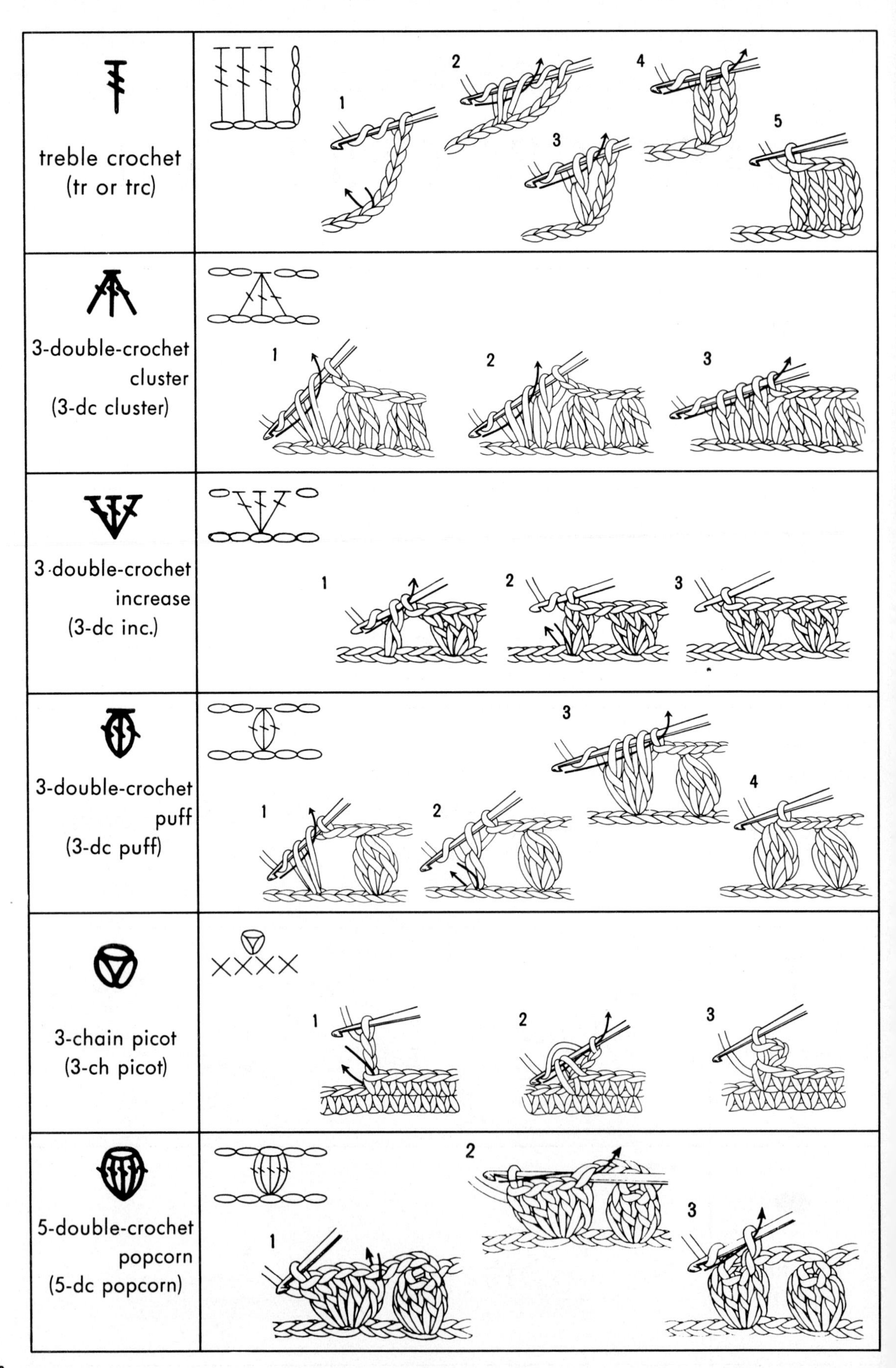
treble crochet
(tr or trc)
1
2
3
4
5
3-double-crochet cluster
(3-dc cluster)
1
2
3
3-double-crochet increase
(3-dc inc.)
1
2
3
3-double-crochet puff
(3-dc puff)
1
2
3
4
3-chain picot
(3-ch picot)
1
2
3
5-double-crochet popcorn
(5-dc popcorn)
1
2
3

HOW TO CROCHET MESH PATTERN

INCREASING:

***Increase at the beginning of row:**

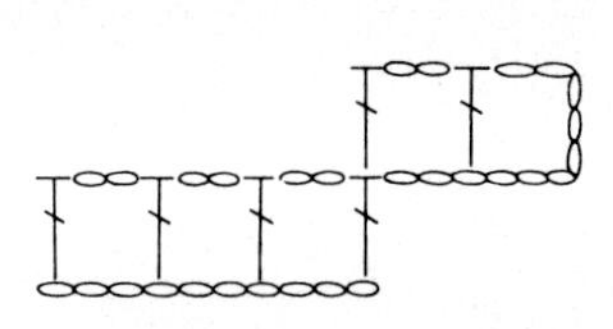
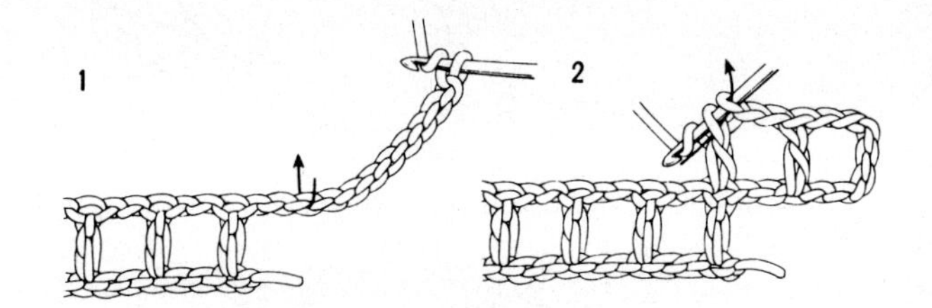

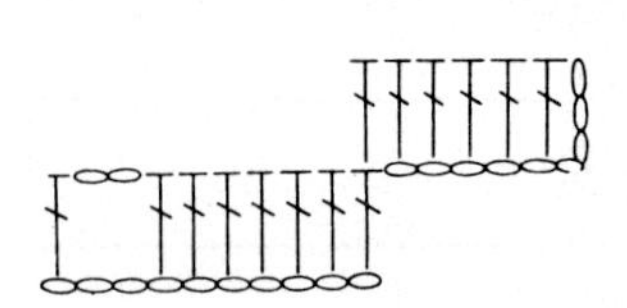
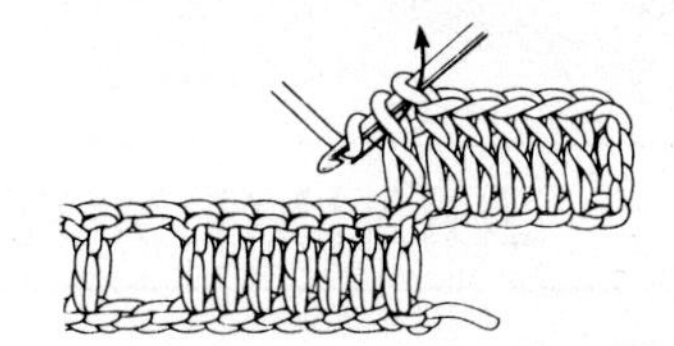

***Increase at the end of row:**

(a) Inc 1 sp with dtr

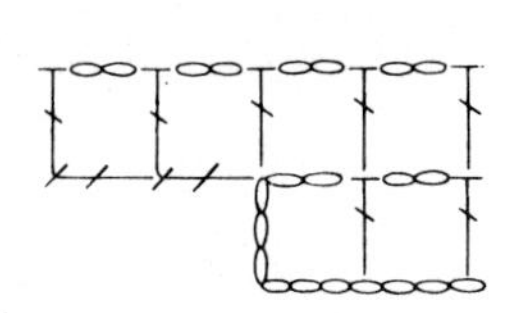
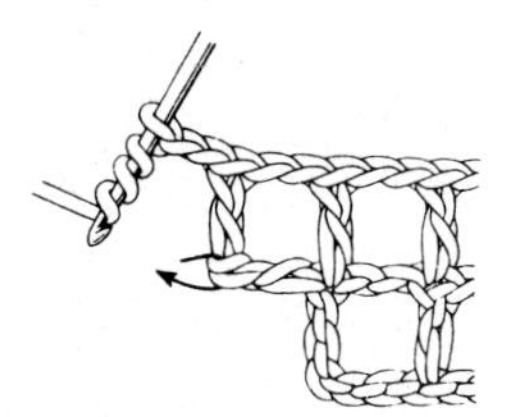

(b) Inc with ch sts added. Make a loop with new thread, insert hook in following to arrow, work foundation-ch (multiple of sps to inc).

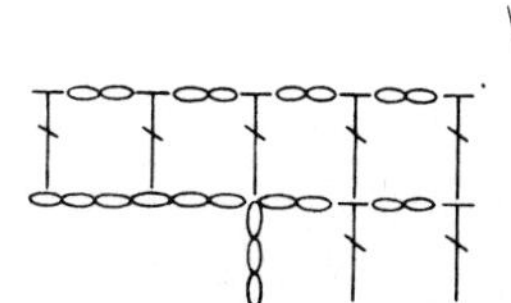
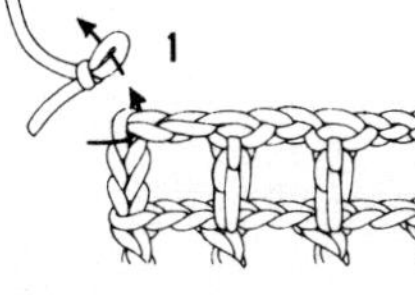
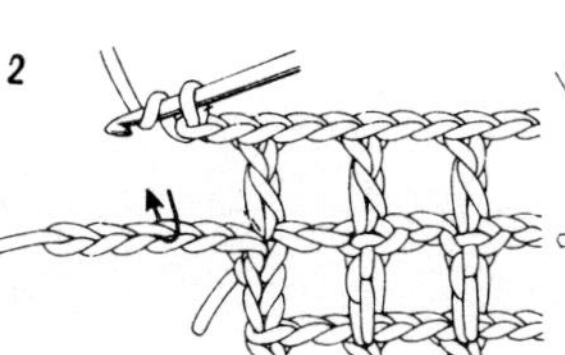
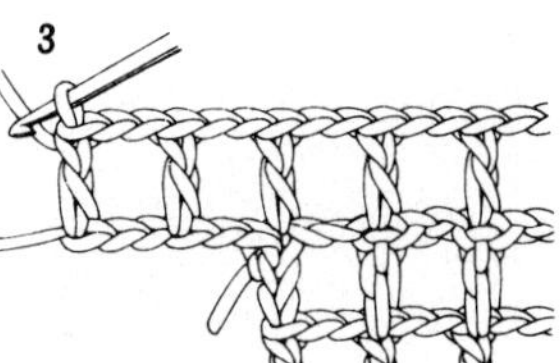

(c) Inc 1 st each with tr

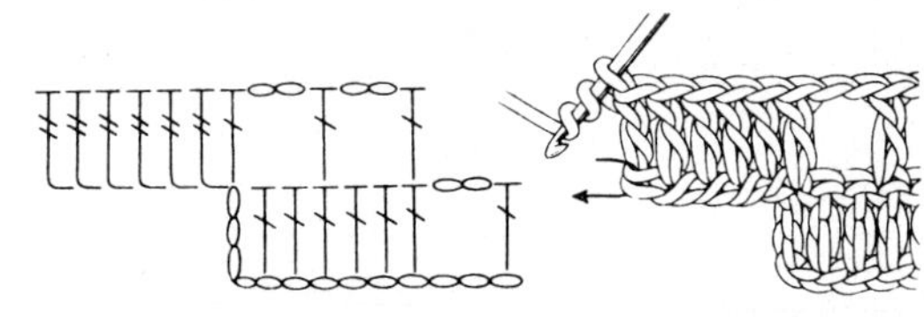

(d) Inc 1 st each with dc

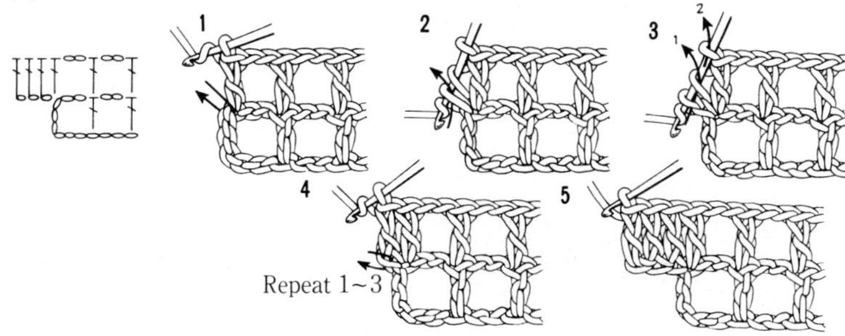

BEGINNING

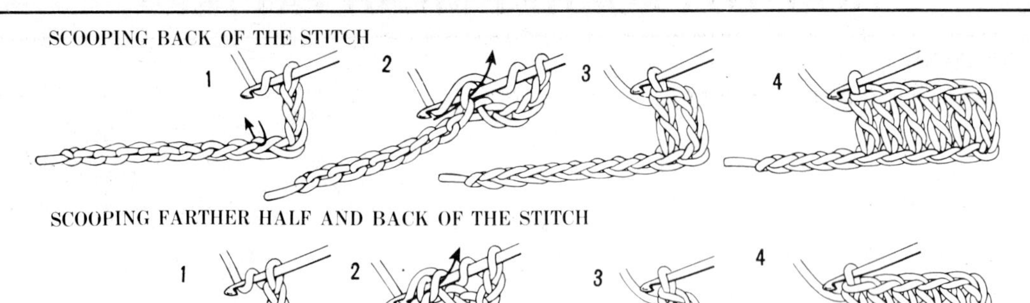

JOINING MOTIFS

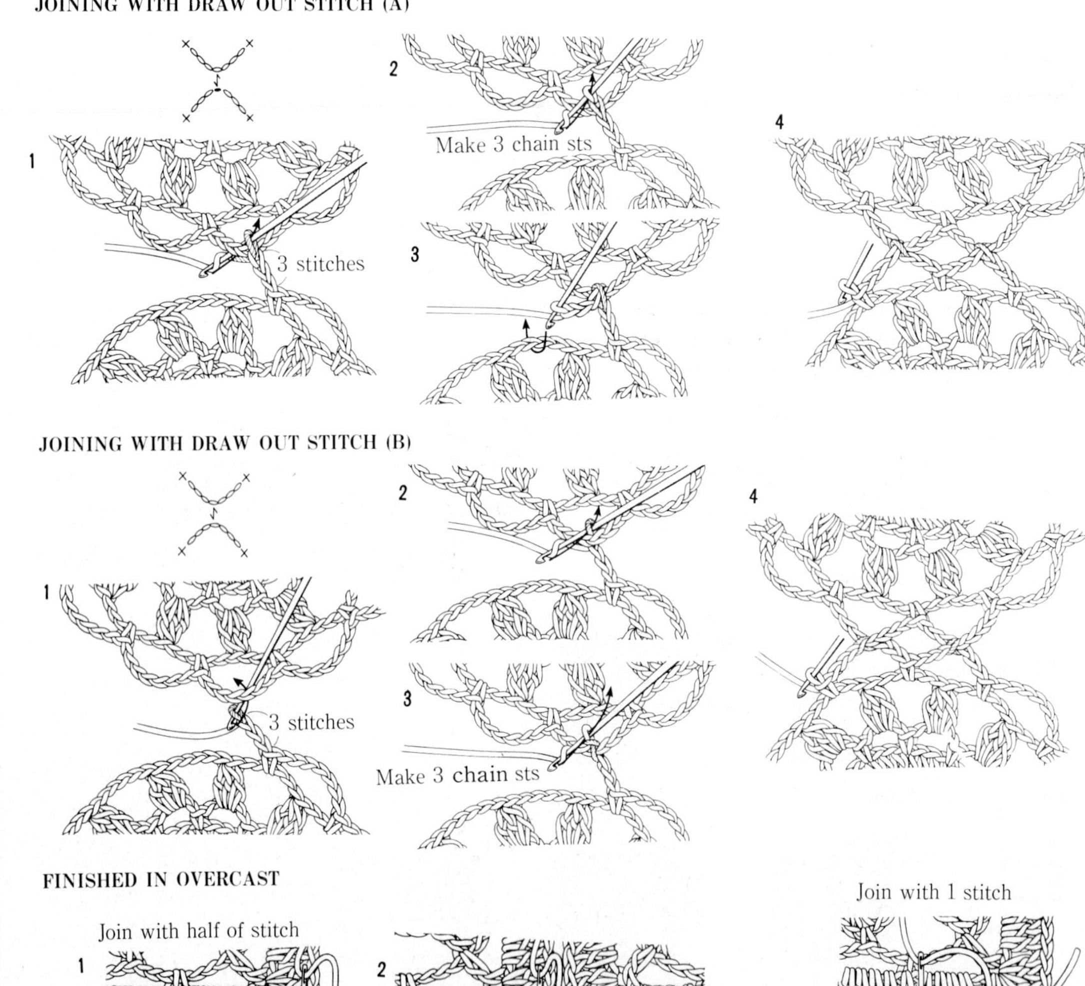

FINISHED IN OVERCAST

Join with half of stitch

1

2

Join with 1 stitch